Stages of Desire

Stages of Desire

Gay Theatre's Hidden History

Carl Miller

CASSELL

For a catalogue of related titles
in our Sexual Politics/Global Issues list
please write to us at the address below:

Cassell
Wellington House
125 Strand
London WC2R 0BB

127 West 24th Street
New York
NY 10011

First published 1996

British Library Cataloguing-in-Publication Data
A catalogue record for this book is available from the British Library.

ISBN 0-304-32815-4 (hardback)
    0-304-32817-0 (paperback)

Typeset by Ben Cracknell Studios
Printed and bound in Great Britain by
Biddles Ltd, Guildford and King's Lynn

Contents

Acknowledgements

I discovered lesbian and gay history while a pupil at Wanstead High School, to which I'm very grateful, even if it was extra-curricular. Afternoons hanging around quirky bookshops led me to discover works by Alan Bray, Lillian Faderman, Jeannette H. Foster, Barbara Grier and Rictor Norton which uncovered a past I had never imagined. They showed me that scholarship can be exciting and popular, and that from the richness and complexities of the past we can learn for the future. I hope this lives up to their examples.

As well as those role-models there are other people who have waited so long for me to finish writing this that I owe them huge thanks for their patience. They are not responsible for the book's failings, but it would never have existed at all without them. Steve Cook at Cassell, and Rod Hall, my agent, have put up with my procrastination nobly. My family and friends have provided love, support and welcome distractions: Barbara, Jeff, Russell, Jon and Jackie, Nick and Peter, Stephen, William, Wayne, Anya and Lucia. The staffs of the British Library, London Library, New York Public Library, New York Library of the Performing Arts and Theatre Museum Study Room have been consistently helpful. Elyse Dodgson and Dominic Tickell at the Royal Court Theatre have been employers between bouts of rewriting and friends throughout. David Benedict, Tony Fabian, Lyn Gardner, Andrew McLeod, John Padden and Alan Stewart lent me books and gave me advice. Paul Burston and Julian Grenier are inspirations, always.

Jonathan Sheldon is the man I hoped I would find when I was fifteen and playing truant in bookshops. This book is for him, and for Amy and Flora, who have a few years to go yet.

CARL MILLER
July 1996

1

A Queer Business

How Gay is 'Cats'?

This is the story of a romance. Theatre and homosexuality are inseparable companions, intimately involved for as long as anyone can tell.
They can tell us a lot about each other – not everything of course – but
each offers useful perspectives from which to look at the other. In
Britain during the five centuries covered by this book, they have been
both condemned and celebrated, their practitioners vilified and
venerated.

Even within these historical and geographical limits, the story of
homosexuality and the theatre includes a vast, sprawling mass of
material. Yet from this material, various themes emerge. As a
profession, the theatre has attracted, if not always welcomed, refugees
from erotic orthodoxy. Gender as performance was a fact of theatre
practice centuries before it became a subject for academic analysis. As a
communal experience, which also touches the intimacies of sexual and
emotional desire, the theatre has had, and occasionally used,
opportunities for subversion. For that reason, it has been the object of
suspicion and regulation by religious and secular authorities.

Carnival queens

There are no records of the earliest theatre in English. Some shreds
survive, the product of a heathen past older than the Christian church.
Sometimes the church would attempt to co-opt theatrical practice and
incorporate it into its rituals. At other times, particularly in its more
grimly fundamentalist manifestations, its response to theatre was
blanket repression and condemnation.

What did the church find so threatening? The theatre provided a rival common experience: a place and an occasion for people to come together. It was rooted in a different tradition, a persistent, unquenchable reminder of pagan alternatives. In those differences was also the possibility of erotic disruption. The first mentions of theatres imply that they are places of sexual assignation. The theatre brings together groups of people for secular excitement, its central mechanism being that its actors pretend to be someone they are not. The starkest example of that impersonation – the 'lie' at the heart of theatre – comes in cross-dressing, a persistent source of horror for anti-theatrical crusaders until women were allowed on stage in the seventeenth century.

Aside from the erotic alarm at the effects of male performers wearing women's clothes, one early twentieth-century scholar sees the practice as 'a last faint reminiscence of the once exclusive supremacy of women in the conduct of agricultural worship'. If male transvestite performance harks back to a time when women ran the world, it understandably disturbs a resolutely patriarchal religion. It is perhaps far-fetched to trace an unbroken line from Danny La Rue back to the primaeval earth mother, but the notion that gender can be played regardless of anatomical equipment is as old as theatre itself.

Nowt so queer as folk plays

In medieval English villages, a boy in women's clothing would reign over the spring festival as the May Queen. A similar ritual took place in church during December. This is the month of the Roman Saturnalia, a festival of misrule ultimately co-opted as Christmas. Its crowning of a mock king, dramatizing the temporary inversion of authority, becomes for the medieval church the Festival of the Boy Bishop: a choirboy being elected to reign as bishop from 6 to 28 December.

Such events both subvert and confirm the conventional distribution of authority which surrounds and licenses them. When the choirboys of Winchester visited a convent in 1441 to dance for the nuns, they dressed as girls, presumably an attempt to reduce rather than enhance the impiety of such an entertainment. The adoption of folk rituals and drama by the church, however, indicates their power and that they proved impossible safely to ignore. The misrule of the boy bishop would also travel back outside the church, influencing popular mischievous boy characters in early English drama like Garcio, Diccon and Merrygreek, discussed in chapter two.

Between the Boy Bishop and the May Queen comes the Bessey. She is another transvestite folk character, variously called Bessy, Betty, Besom Betty, Dirty Bet, Bridget, Madgy, Madgy Peg. Her appearances come in the early spring dramas celebrating the return of the Plough Boys, whom she accompanies to work at the start of the year. At Shrovetide, another festival of cross-dressing and even riot, she is the companion of a Tommy. Sometimes a sacrificial victim in the sword dance at the end of mummers plays, Bessey's role in these plays is romantic and sexual, as consort or object of desire. Men continued to take the role well after women took to the stage, confirming the ritual significance of the transvestite role. Indeed, where women are recorded performing similar rituals, these tend to be all-female presentations. Seasonal celebrations of agricultural renewal thus dramatically encourage fertility through a single-sex company. Even in Thomas Hardy's 1878 novel *The Return of the Native*, the folk play provides an excuse for sexual pursuit through transvestism, when Eustacia Vye disguises herself as the Turkish Knight in order to meet Clym Yeobright.

Some say the May Queen became Maid Marian, as the folk legend of Robin Hood inspired its own dramas of financial inversion: robbing the rich to feed the poor. Later plays written about Robin Hood would include cross-dressing to create sexual confusion. The 1595 play *George-a'-Green, Pinner of Wakefield* includes a sub-plot in which George-a'-Green's servant Wily dresses as maid to a seamstress. This allows him to give his own clothes to Bettris, who elopes with George. Meanwhile, however, Bettris' father Grimes falls for the cross-dressed Wily. They are due to marry, a wedding sanctioned by both George and the King, when Wily reveals the deception. Another gratuitous episode of cross-dressing involves Robin Hood himself, in the anonymous *Look About You*. Robin disguises himself as Lady Fauconbridge, using make-up, in order to embarrass Lord Fauconbridge, who is adulterously wooing another woman (who is actually Lady Fauconbridge herself in disguise). These plays reflect the theatrical conventions of their times, however, as much as the folk rituals and dramas on which they draw.

Under sanction of being fairies

The woman-man of folk drama would develop into characters such as these subversive transvestites, but she developed her role offstage as well. Revolutionary actors took the lessons of misrule and applied them outside the bounds prescribed. During the unrest which followed Jack Cade's unsuccessful rebellion against Henry VI, 'servants of the Queen of the Fairies' invaded and took deer from the park of the Duke of Buckingham. Natalie Zemon Davies gives many other examples of such revolutionary outbursts involving, and often headed by, transvestite figures:

> In 1641, in the dairy and grazing sections of Wiltshire, bands of men rioted and leveled fences against the king's enclosure of their forests. They were led by men dressed as women, who called themselves 'Lady Skimmington'. In May 1718, Cambridge students followed 'a virago, or man in woman's habit, crowned with laurel' to assault a Dissenting meeting house. Two years later labourers in Surrey rioted in women's clothes, and at mid-century country men disguised as women tore down the hated tollbooths and turnpike gates at the Gloucestershire border. In April 1812, 'General Ludd's wives,' two weavers dressed as women, led a crowd of hundreds to smash steam looms and burn a factory at Stockport. In Wales and Scotland, too, there were uprisings in female disguise. The *ceffyl pren* with its blackfaced transvestite males, gave way in the 1830's and 1840's to the Rebecca riots against the detested turnpike tolls and other sources of agrarian complaint. They were led by one 'Rebecca' and noisy men in women's clothes. And in 1736 in Edinburgh, the Porteous Riots, which were sparked by a hated English officer, oppressive customs laws, and resistance to the union of Scotland with England, were carried out by men dressed as women and with a leader known as Madge Wildfire.

Davies also describes a decade of revolutionary activity in Ireland during the 1760s, when the 'whiteboys' in long white frocks and blackened faces fought against land enclosure claiming to act under 'sanction of being fairies', and signing proclamations 'Ghostly Sally'. Dressing as women, like blacking up, enabled white men to break the law without being recognized. Fear of arrest led one woman to impersonate in the opposite direction, and disguise her identity as a male pedlar. She claimed as she died in April 1793 that her name was Fanny, but she had lived as a man to avoid discovery, following her role as a ringleader in earlier riots.

Transvestite rioting offered more than disguise, however. Its roots are in local pagan, seasonal festivals, part of a way of life which centralized authority sought to destroy. Although borrowed by the anti-dissenting Cambridge students, the most expressive transvestite riots were ones which rejected land enclosure and tolls, impositions on the common land. Like the Boy Bishop and the Saturnalian mock-king, they overturn the relations between ruler and ruled. Like Robin Hood, they seek to redistribute wealth. Like Bessey and the Queen of the May, they exist beyond male and female: supernatural fairies and ghostly Sallys. This is real radical drag: ferocious and uninhibited by social constraints.

Happy little bluebirds

The gender confusion of cross-dressed performance also offers forbidden sexual opportunities. The same licence which allows choirboys to become girls, and therefore safe entertainment at a convent, sanctions them as objects of male desire. Although forbidden to do so on stage and off, women who did take male disguise were able to marry other women, although some faced murderous penalties if discovered. The plays of the Elizabethan and Jacobean theatre would try every variation of desire possible within a transvestite theatre, while the masquerades of the eighteenth century commercialized the combination of entertainment and sexual opportunity originally provided by the folk ritual. The tradition of seasonal riotousness survives elsewhere in the world better than in Britain. Shrove Tuesday here is little more subversive than a pancake race, while Mardi Gras in Rio, Sydney or New Orleans is a festival which retains or revives the carnival of erotic possibility.

Modern gay liberation began with rioting men in women's clothing. The Stonewall riots, named after the New York bar raided by police in June 1969, have become a symbol of resistance, and the source of their own seasonal ritual. Martin Duberman's book and Nigel Finch's film *Stonewall* tell their versions of the events. The theatricality of the riots attracted the first dramatists of gay liberation theatre: the final scene of *As Time Goes By*, Noel Greig and Drew Griffiths' 1977 history play for Gay Sweatshop, leads up to the riot. Doric Wilson's 1982 play *Street*

Theater takes characters from the Broadway hit *The Boys in the Band*, premiered the year before the riots, pulling them off the stage and onto the streets. It contrasts the self-loathing of these figures from the legitimate theatre with the rebelliousness of those performing outside. Ironically, when the play was presented in London, twenty-five years after the riots, *Street Theater* was retitled *The Night Judy Garland Died* because otherwise, according to the director, people 'assumed it was going to be an actual piece of street theatre'.

Gay male icon Judy Garland was indeed buried on that hot Friday in June, making it possible to analyse the riots as their own folk ritual of death and renewal in an urban village. Guy Trebay describes an event during the twenty-fifth anniversary of Stonewall which makes the point with rather more glamour:

Saturday June 25, Radical Faerie Funeral for Judy Garland, Judson Memorial Church. Judy imitator Eugene Salandra sitting at edge of stage, dressed in black hostess pants, gold tunic, black pumps, sings 'If happy little bluebirds fly,' etc, to sound of Radical Faeries ululating, sobbing, drumming. Radical Faeries wearing glitter, hippy skirts, fairy wings, Pippi Longstocking braids, face paint, rope bras, *South Pacific* meets My Pretty Pony costumes, or nothing. Eugene/Judy rises, staggers across stage, gives fans a brittle wave, gulps handfuls of 'sleeping pills.' Faerie wearing button that says 'Wear a Dress/Throw a Brick' shouts, 'have a drink, dear.' Eugene/Judy lifts bottle of Rioja and drinks deep, then gently folds him/herself onto specially prepared funeral bier and dies. Several faeries place gladioli on body. One faerie rushes to stage and shouts, 'This is outrageous! I just heard that the cops have invaded Stonewall!' Faeries leap up, wild boys (and girls: several girl faeries) from Peter Pan, lift funeral bier, chant 'Ju-dy, Ju-dy' and carry dead idol into the middle of dyke gathering in Washington Square.

. . . 'Oh my God,' a woman is saying, 'it's not an AIDS funeral, is it?'

'No,' says Moon Morgan, Faerie name Sugar. 'It's a ritual for our mother, Judy Garland. It was on the night of her death that the Stonewall Inn was stormed.'

'Judy who?' the woman replies.

Greenwich Village is no ordinary village, and the Judson Memorial Church is one which has blessed and sustained the radical since the 1960s. The Stonewall riots are urban folk myth as much as political symbol. The history of what happened in June 1969 is fiercely disputed. If everyone who claims to have thrown stones during the disturbances was actually there, it is astonishing anything was left standing. Like pieces of the true cross, the number of genuine Stonewall rioters mushrooms beyond what is physically plausible. Both demand symbolic veneration nevertheless, their over-prevalence testifying to the power of the idea they represent.

As the celebrations of the Stonewall riots each June grow larger, so they are increasingly regimented and synthesized, inevitably meta-morphosing from a spontaneous outburst of anger and frustration. The original event is sentimentalized and simplified as it becomes part of myth. One of those who was there comments: 'If we had ever thought, when we were rioting at Stonewall, that it would become a keychain, we would have said, "What? This dive?"'

'They're destroying property?' asks a shocked Donald, one of the Boys in the Band, when he hears of the riot in *Street Theater*. Like the medieval festivals of misrule, arguments rage about the significance of this contemporary lesbian and gay folk ritual. Is the purpose political subversion or harmless fun? Can the two be combined? Even the twenty-fifth anniversary celebrations in New York spawned rival demonstrations as drag queens, AIDS activists and others accused the official events of selling out. Preppy alarm persists at the idea of destroying property as homosexuals are encouraged to pursue liberation through shopping instead. 'Our research tells us that these are affluent, well educated, brand-loyal customers who want high quality products' says telecommunications multinational AT&T. Nevertheless, radicals and conservatives coincide in finding a festival an occasion to dress up, get intoxicated and have sex.

Stick to your own kind

One of the more unpredictable variations on the Boy Bishop as an inversion of ecclesiastical norms is the Sisters of Perpetual Indulgence, a drag order first seen on 1970s Gay Pride Marches. Combining the traditional black and white garb of the convent with the trappings of

San Francisco clonedom, they gave birth, presumably immaculately, to an endearingly self-publicizing sorority active in Britain in the early 1990s. Well before all this, however, there was a real nun, or at least a member of a convent, whose contribution to the history of theatre is extraordinary. Hundreds of years separate her work from the Roman dramatists before and the next known European playwrights after her. She is a pioneer and an inspiration: there is little competition for her role as the first modern European dramatist. Comedies based on classical forms such as hers would not be written in Britain until five centuries after her death.

The little that is known about the life of Roswitha (or Hrotsvitha) comes from the introductions to her writing. She was born around the year 930 and entered the convent in Gandersheim Germany, where she was taught by a younger nun, Rikkards. She wrote secretly at first, but was later encouraged by the abbess Gerberga, of whose kindness she writes extravagantly. Her devotion to these other women is fulsomely expressed. There are fragmentary accounts of theatre in medieval convents, just as there are of lesbianism in medieval convents. Whether there was any of either in Gandersheim can only be speculated upon. By this century, however, there were lesbians making theatre, some of whom were crucial in rediscovering Roswitha's plays, but that comes later. What is clear from her writings, however, is that she understood the possibility of gay male sex.

Sometimes called the German Sappho, Roswitha's favourite subject is sex: specifically the horrors of threats to chastity. Drama is an ideal medium in which to represent anxieties about sexual licence, although it risks encouraging that which it condemns through such representation. Roswitha, writing inside a convent, manages to walk that tightrope with delicacy, in a way which would not be matched for years, thanks to the strictures of the church.

Her own choice to live among women set her apart from the predations of men, but she forced herself to imagine them in her works. She does this with determination, although pointing out the difficulty of doing so in her preface:

One thing has all the same embarrassed me and brought a blush to my cheek. It is that I have been compelled through the nature of this work to apply my mind and my pen to depicting the dreadful frenzy of those possessed by unlawful love, and the insidious sweetness of passion – things which should not even be named among us. Yet, if from modesty, I had refrained from treating these subjects, I should not have been able to attain my object – to glorify the innocent to the best of my ability.

The innocents whom she glorifies in her plays tend to be women in sexual danger. The exception comes in her poem telling of the martyrdom of her near-contemporary Saint Pelagius. He died in 925, just a few years before Roswitha was born, and it is the only work for which she claims authentic eye-witness evidence, stating 'The details of this were supplied to me by an inhabitant of the town where the Saint was put to death.' She continues, telling her readers the crucial fact about the saint, passed on by her informant: he was gorgeous. 'This truthful stranger assured me that he had not only seen Pelagius, whom he described as the most beautiful of men, face to face, but had been a witness of his end.'

Her poem tells how this end came. The beautiful youth Pelagius resists the advances of the caliph of Cordoba, a man 'corrupted by the vice of the Sodomites'. When the caliph attempts to kiss him, Pelagius, like a good chaste Christian, resists and says:

It is not right for a man washed in the baptism of Christ
To offer his pious neck for the embrace of a barbarian;
Nor should a Christian, anointed with holy oil,
Accept a kiss from a servant of the filthy demon.
Embrace with a clear conscience the stupid men
With whom you worship idiot clay gods.

As John Boswell points out, Pelagius' objection is not sexual but religious. As a Christian, he should not be embraced or kissed by a Moslem. The fact that they are both male is not commented upon, except in Pelagius' suggestion that men of the Caliph's own faith might be embraced by their ruler with a clear conscience. He does call them and their gods stupid, nevertheless, and there is an air of religious prejudice in this piece which depicts the resistance of a Christian youth to the advances of an Islamic ruler. It is hardly a trustworthy picture of tenth-century Islam and, despite Roswitha's assurances about her source, may well be an unreliable biography of Pelagius. What is clear, however, is the absence of disgust at the vice of the Sodomites itself.

Roswitha's purpose elsewhere in her work is to show chastity under threat, so she would be unlikely to underplay this moment. In addition, given that Pelagius abuses the Caliph's gods, he would hardly be holding back sexual revulsion to spare the ruler's feelings, if he felt any. Pelagius is reckless enough later: he hits the Caliph, for which he is executed. All this suggests that sex between men, although not approved by the poem, is no big deal in it, especially compared to the inappropriateness of cross-faith intercourse. This is always a dangerous business, but particularly in the middle of religious wars. As Anita tells Maria in *West Side Story*:

> A boy like that who'd kill your brother,
> Forget that boy and find another,
> One of your own kind!
> Stick to your own kind!
>
> A boy like that will give you sorrow,
> You'll meet another boy tomorrow,
> One of your own kind!
> Stick to your own kind!

Although Roswitha's story of Pelagius is hardly a progressive picture of well-adjusted gay sexuality, it is a remarkably calm account from a woman writing within a convent more than a thousand years ago. As a role model for feminist theatre pioneers, moreover, she is ideal. Ellen Terry, the legendary Victorian actress, played the Nun in Roswitha's play *Paphnutius* in its first modern revival at the Savoy Theatre in 1914. The play was directed by her daughter Edith Craig. Craig was advised by her lover Christabel Marshall, who as Christopher St John translated and edited the first edition of Roswitha's plays in English. Thus one woman, who lived in a convent but may never have worn a habit, makes rather more of a contribution to lesbian and gay history than a squealing youth in a wimple on rollerskates.

Gay designs of the limp-wrist set

Theatre is a politically senstive form, provoking censorship more than privately experienced art. Homosexuality was one of the issues which ultimately wore down Britain's theatre censor, the Lord Chamberlain. In 1948 he advised banning Leslie and Sewell Stokes' play *Oscar Wilde* on the grounds that 'It is undoubtedly a good play but . . . It is entirely about perverts'. Edward Bond's *Early Morning* was one of the last plays to be totally refused a licence in 1967, forcing the Royal Court Theatre to present it as a club performance, attended by the Vice Squad. It combined the persistently troublesome representation of perverts with the no less outlawed depiction of the royal family. Its suggestion that Queen Victoria and Florence Nightingale were lovers seems to have been more shocking to the censor than its analysis of Victoria's regime as corrupt, intrigue-ridden and contemptuous of human life. The same modest liberalization which partially decriminalized gay male sex in 1967 ended theatre censorship in the same year.

Whether there are more lesbians and gay men involved in the theatre than any other activity is impossible to judge. It offers the chance to dress up occasionally, but then so does the navy. It offers an environment detached from some social pressures, but then so does long-distance lorry-driving. Nevertheless, there is a common perception, inside and outside the theatre, that it is a sympathetic working environment. An entertaining evocation of that comes in Neil Bartlett and Nicolas Bloomfield's musical *Night After Night* which explores and celebrates the gay West End of the 1950s, with its chorus boys, Box Office, Cloakroom and Bar Queens, all providing a night of romance for a heterosexual couple.

In Los Angeles in 1950 an actor, Harry Hay, founded the first gay political organization in the United States, the Mattachine Society. Another gay liberation pioneer, Morris Kight, describes why he too worked in the theatre at that time: 'I was involved in theater for five years from 1950 to 1955. I just got into the theater because I felt that theater was a place where social consciousness could be inculcated, where there would be a chance to express onself and meet some very pleasant people.' As Kight's mention of social consciousness suggests, he, like many of the other early gay activists had radical political interests. Mattachine would purge communists and socialists within a few years, expelling its founders. This was in the middle of the witch-hunts against communists and homosexuals conducted by the United States government through Senator Joe McCarthy.

The theatre itself was a source of moral panic, according to scandal magazine *Tip-Off*, which in 1956 published a piece headlined: 'Why They Call Broadway the "GAY" White Way':

> Homosexuals have gained such a stranglehold over the theater, those in the know contend, that quite a few big stars in Hollywood have at one stage or another in their career, been forced to 'play the game' in order to get work. A young actor, currently considered 'the hottest thing in the theater,' looks like a genuine he-man, but is actually strictly for the boys and dates a notorious Lesbian actress merely as a front.
>
> 'Even the circus has been strongly infested with the limpwrist set from time to time in past years,' one well-known Broadway agent confided.

Loathing, envy and fear of lesbians and gay men in the theatre still surface in the gutter press. In September 1994 London's *Evening Standard* printed a diatribe by its superannuated former theatre critic Milton Shulman headlined 'Stop This Plague of Pink Plays'. His objections to there being a number of gay male works staged in London at the time were supported by *Daily Telegraph* critic Charles Spencer. Yet things are not as they were when *Tip-Off* exposed Broadway's 'lavender set'. Shulman's replacement at the *Standard* is the openly gay writer Nicholas de Jongh, and the pieces to which he was objecting were popular shows by mixed companies performing gay-themed work.

In a random week there will be shows produced, written, directed or designed by many openly gay men in many theatres in London yet few involving women who are openly lesbian. Some of those men run theatres themselves. Yet at the same time many young gay male actors argue that for their sexuality to be known will ruin their career, and no star actress or director has come out as lesbian, despite some of the biggest male names in their profession tumbling through closet doors. The issue is power. Men have more powerful roles than women in the theatre, as they do elsewhere. Performers fear that being openly gay will deny them access to heterosexual roles. Younger gay male actors point out that most of the celebrated openly gay stars are no longer at an age to be considered as Romeo, and that even if Ian McKellen did play it for the Royal Shakespeare Company at thirty-six, he was in the closet at the time.

Female roles, particularly in the classical repertoire, are even more likely to be defined by a sexual relationship to a male character. With no openly lesbian equivalents to gay male Artistic Directors like Neil Bartlett at the Lyric Hammersmith, Stephen Daldry at the Royal Court or Philip Hedley at the Theatre Royal Stratford, many women are reluctant to take what they fear to be a career-ending move, and come out in isolation. Given the defensive responses of critics like Milton Shulman or Charles Spencer, you can see their point. Thus a profession which attracts many for its relative freedom of expression is one which still leads its practitioners to the same heterosexual charades shockingly exposed by *Tip-Off* in 1956. Nominations for a 'young actor, currently considered "the hottest thing in the theater," [who] looks like a genuine he-man, but is actually strictly for the boys' on a postcard please.

Historical intercourse

Although many of the figures in this book have been persecuted or celebrated for their desires, the terms in which those are expressed do not easily correspond with the terms used to discuss love and sex today. The story of the love affair between theatre and homosexuality is not a simple one. Indeed, this investigation begins at a time before the words 'theatre' or 'homosexuality' existed.

As the evidence of a relationship begins to emerge, during the fourteenth century, so does 'theatre' itself, although it is another two hundred years before there is a theatre: the first building with that name and function. Today theatre is not just a place, but also an event. It is even a lifestyle: working in the theatre suggests in some minds a way of life easily overlapping with that of the homosexual, as Prince Edward discovered when he left the Royal Marines to do so.

Only by the late nineteenth century, the end of the period discussed here, is 'homosexual' coined to give pathological definition to a range of loving, sexual and romantic relations between men and between women. This book therefore uses the word as an occasional convenience, but always conscious that it, like 'heterosexual' and 'bisexual', reflects ideas about love and sex quite remote from many of the people mentioned in it.

Having rejected the pseudo-science of homo/hetero and bisexuality, however, the problem of which terms to use persists. 'Queer' has become modish as a term which can mean whatever its user wants to include as transgressive sexuality, but its slipperiness strikes me as too evasive. Throughout this period, there are in fact no easy alternative words, which is a useful reminder that this whole project is anachronistic, a reflection of a contemporary notion that sexuality is a subject appropriate for separate analysis. It risks making the book impossible to read, however, if there are no words in which to write it. This process of translation from the past is made no easier, indeed more difficult, by the fact that it is the same language. I have therefore used different words promiscuously, sometimes those like lesbian or gay, which have a clear contemporary context; at other points sodomite or sapphist have seemed more appropriate. The appropriate shades of meaning in all of these complex terms should emerge from their context.

All history is an act of intercourse with the past, but this concentration on theatre and homosexuality is perhaps a foolhardily exotic position for it. It therefore takes certain things for granted. Firstly, that love (or sex) between females (or between males) requires no particular justification. Secondly, that all these activities have been practised and imagined throughout the period covered by this book. These are by no means universally held positions, but taking them as read allows the book to move past the apologetics and get onto the interesting material.

Theatre studies is a young discipline, but lesbian and gay studies are even younger. This book is part of a diffuse greater project, inspired by gay liberation, which reclaims the history of love and sex between men and between women, providing a context for our contemporary loves and labours. It started well before 1969 however. Just as Christopher St John and Edith Craig were excited by Roswitha, Victorian antiquarians like Richard Heber and John Addington Symonds discovered in English Renaissance drama evidence that their passions were part of a greater history.

The process of unearthing a hidden past risks becoming either sentimental or apologetic. Gay history started with slim privately printed volumes on the lives of the Ancient Greeks, extended in later popular roll calls which proclaimed that great men (and the occasional woman) from Erasmus to E. M. Forster had been part of the lavender set. Chapter three discusses the dangers of that approach in drama. Increased civil liberties then led to a less apologetic tone, researching documents, particularly legal records, which pieced together the less glamorous facts of life, and often death, for homosexuals since antiquity. Medieval nunneries and Renaissance taverns were depicted like Ye Olde Lesbian and Gay Community Centres, where people like us had been gathering despite vicious oppression from the beginning of time.

It rapidly becomes apparent, however, as more material is dicovered and reassessed, that notions of sex and sexual preference vary spectacularly throughout history, just as they do between contemporary cultures. The consistent presence of those keen to love and lust after others of the same sex is not an argument that all other cultures through space and time would, if not constrained by homophobia, ideally resemble Old Compton Street. However comforting the conviction that we have recognizable foremothers and fathers throughout history, it quickly becomes clear that Erasmus would have felt out of place at Village Soho, probably almost as much as E. M. Forster.

Even with relatively easy areas of study, like modern United States history, methodological arguments about language, censorship, and accidental or deliberate misinterpretation of data have made questing in lesbian or gay history like tap-dancing in a minefield. Nevertheless that history, whatever it may turn out to be, is a vital resource, allowing us to learn from the past so that our present will not be rewritten.

This book represents my own interests and perspective as a playwright and theatre director, curious to interpret work which has been hidden or misrepresented by the relentless cultural promotion of heterosexuality. It does not seek to wrench simplistic parallels, but to relish the complexities and challenges thrown up by five hundred years of theatre history. It is a story of what happens on stage, rather than real life. The two may reflect each other, but through distorting mirrors. Imagine some future civilization reconstructing London in the 1990s as a city swarming with French urchins, singing railway trains and dancing cats. But then even *Cats* was produced by a gay man, starred a gay man, and has a hit song based on one of the poems T. S. Eliot dedicated to the love of a young man he met in the Luxembourg Gardens.

Like homosexuality, the theatre is sometimes disreputable, but just as often piss-elegant. Both spheres of activity offer the sublime and the tawdry. Are they dangerously subversive or impeccably respectable? Inevitably this is also a story of the culture which surrounds the theatre, and of the staging of heterosexuality. A sensibility which came up with the term 'straight-acting' senses that normality is a performance too.

Bum Boys

Arse Play in Early English Comedy

The earliest surviving examples of comic playwriting in English reveal a sexual obsession with bottoms which makes the average *Carry On* film look tame. In these plays, mostly written for schoolboy or male student casts, the entertainment to be squeezed out of anal intercourse seems inexhaustible. It is impossible to recreate the effect such material would have had on contemporary audiences, but we can assume that the intention was to amuse.

Laughing at the idea of sticking a penis or penis-substitute into the anus does not, of course, necessarily indicate a relaxed and open attitude to the activity. Indeed, it might be argued that the preponderance of such references in comedies created for all-male educational institutions is evidence for widespread anxiety about the practice. Certainly the acts depicted were illegal – one sixteenth-century playwright and teacher being famously prosecuted for buggery. What is clear, however, is that boy characters who flirted with the possibilities of anal intercourse were affectionately presented throughout the earliest English drama, the objects of fun rather than disgust.

Discussion of these plays has generally ignored the implications of sexual activity between males, but examination of the surviving texts, and the way in which they might work in performance, reveals arse play to be a major feature in early English comedy.

Cain's boy Garcio

The first plays in English of which written records still exist are over five hundred years old. These are cycles of short plays depicting biblical stories, called mystery or miracle plays. Their authors are unknown, and they were first performed by groups of amateur players, grouped around the professions practised by some or all of them: there are plays linked to dyers, fishmongers, shipbuilders, tanners and many other groups. Despite their religious basis, the plays are also important in the development of secular drama, providing a link between folk traditions and scripted theatre, as well as introducing themes which would directly inspire the popular playwrights of the sixteenth century.

One of the mystery cycles, called either the Wakefield plays, after the town where they originated, or the Towneley plays, after the family who owned the manuscript for two hundred years, contains a play whose explicit banter provides the first dramatic references to same-sex sexual activity in English drama. *The Killing of Abel* (*Mactacio Abel*) (c. 1400) is the second play in the sequence, and tells the story of the first murder in Biblical history: that of Abel by his brother Cain. It was probably first performed by the glovers of Wakefield and dates from around 1400 in the form it is written down, although it may well be a revision of an earlier work. Authorship of most of the plays in the Wakefield cycle is assigned to an unknown writer called The Wakefield Master. The extent of other people's contributions to *The Killing of Abel* and the rest of the plays in the group is much debated, however.

The performance opens with Garcio, a boy whom we soon discover is Cain's servant, talking to the audience, telling them to be quiet.

GARCIO

Bot who that ianglis any more	[But anyone that chatters again
He must blaw my blak hoill bore	He must blow my black (i.e. shitty) bore-hole
Both behynd and before	Both behind and in front
Till his tethe blede	Until his teeth bleed]

Garcio's origins as a character are not in the Bible, but in the cheeky servants of secular folk-plays. He is introduced here to get the attention of the audience, who would be watching the play performed on a cart in the open air. He tells them to be quiet, which is an entirely under-standable opening for a play, but backs this up with a threat that is distinctly obscene. The general meaning is clear enough – a variation on 'kiss my arse' – but the precise anatomical invitation is hard to decipher. I assume 'both behynd and before' is Garcio's reference to his cock as well as his arse, but he may mean his mouth, which is perhaps a little more respectable, if no less sexual in its implication. The suggestion that analingus makes your teeth bleed is unsupported by modern medical research – Garcio here conjures up the image of a particularly vigorous bout of rimming. This monstrousness may come from links between anality and the devil, which are extensive in art of the period.

Whilst far from an idyllic picture of sex between men, this passage has inspired direct censorship in virtually all editions of the play. Some remove it entirely, and even reputable works of scholarship ignore the interesting complexities in the image, ignoring or evading the problem passage. A different form of unease surfaces in two modern English versions of the piece. Tony Harrison's *The Nativity* (1980), the second of his three-part adaptation of plays from various medieval cycles for the National Theatre, includes parts of *The Killing of Abel* but misses out Garcio altogether. Adrian Henri's version of the Wakefield cycle, performed at Pontefract Castle in July 1988, does include Garcio – but makes him a girl.

> You've heard of Jack the Lad,
> Well I'm Jill the Lass!
> And if you don't like it
> You can kiss my ass!

Henri explains: 'We decided to make Garcio a girl, despite the name, for no good reason except to provide a good, comic female part. A male actor could do the part with suitable dialogue changes.' The original Eves and Marys of the cycles would almost always have been played by male performers, although women did occasionally take part in mystery plays: the *Assumption of the Virgin* play in the Chester cycle is supposed to have been played by 'the wives of the town'. There is therefore nothing inappropriate in casting medieval plays across gender boundaries. In making Garcio a female character, however, rather than a male character played by a woman, Henri eliminates the same-sex implications of the original.

Henri nevertheless does provide the unperformed text of his version for a male Garcio:

> Jack the Lad, game for a laugh,
> that's me. Now settle down,
> and pin back your lugholes:

and if you keep on chattering
You can kiss me arsehole!
(*He displays his bottom to the audience.*)

The stage direction included in this version confirms that in making Garcio female the character has been cleaned up. Henri's female Garcio is not scripted to expose herself: the boundaries of what is acceptable for a woman in this adaptation are narrowed, presumably by the same anxieties about the sexual implications of the original. A man can show his bum, but a woman can only talk dirty, before the event slips from bawdy fun to unacceptable crudity. Henri is a popular and far from conservative poet – an unlikely figure to be guilty of wilful censorship. In sanitizing *The Killing of Abel*, however, he joins a long line of scholars and adapters who have blocked this little homoerotic episode out of theatre history. If this is the first reference to oral-anal contact in English theatre, it takes about 568 years for American theatre to catch up, in Mart Crowley's *The Boys in the Band*:

HAROLD What happened to you?

EMORY (*groans*) Don't ask!

HAROLD Your lips are turning blue; you look like you been rimming a snowman.

EMORY That piss-elegant kooze hit me! (*Indicates Alan . . .*)

The Killing of Abel continues with the entrance of Garcio's master Cain, who scolds his boy for not properly feeding the animals who pull the plough. Garcio explains that he put the food at the arse-end of the creatures, presumably a deliberate sabotage of his master's work:

CAIN
Gog gif the sorrow, boy;   [God give you sorrow, boy;
  want of mete it gars   lack of food is the cause

GARCIO
Thare provand, sir, for thi,   Because, sir, I lay their fodder
  I lay behynd thare ars   behind their arses
And tyes them fast bi the nekis And tied them fast by the necks
With many stanys in thare hekis. With many stones in their food-
                                racks

CAIN
> That shall bi thi fals chekis.   That shall buy you false cheeks.]

Garcio's false cheeks are either his face or his buttocks, which Cain presumably slaps at this point, initiating a fight interrupted only by Abel's entrance. Verbal arse play is a feature of the entire piece, continued when Cain abuses his brother.

Com kys myn arse,	[Come kiss my arse,
me list not ban,	I don't want to be rude.
As welcom standis ther oute.	(You would be) as welcome anywhere else.
Thou shuld have bide	You should have waited
til thou were cald;	until you were called.
Com nar, and other drife or hald,	Come near and either drive or hold (the plough)
And kys the dwillis toute.	and kiss the devil's buttocks.
Go grese thi shepe under the toute	Go grease your sheep under the buttocks,
For that is the moste lefe.	For that is (what) you like best.]

Cain scorns Abel's gentle shepherding compared to his own vigorous ploughmanship. When he also suggests his brother would prefer to lubricate his flock for anal intercourse rather than help with the ploughing, it becomes too much for one editor, eliminating the lines with the note: 'Here, and in several places below, the language is too offensive to be reproduced.' Cain's liberal reference to the devil's arse continues through this short play, helping to confirm Cain as the villain of the piece, and drawing on the contemporary association already noted between the anus and the devil.

Garcio's moral status in the play is more complex than that of the characters taken directly from scripture. He is linked to his master's wickedness, but also undermines and fights Cain. He is a villain: apart from Garcio (meaning 'boy'), he is called Pike-harnes by Cain, suggesting he steals (picks) armour (harness) from soldiers killed in battle. He is, however, also popular: similar figures appear later in the cycle, notably Jack Garcio in the *First Shepherds' Play*. He may provoke the audience, but he also pleases them.

Whatever it provides in terms of discussion about attitudes to the anus as a sexual site, the prologue to *The Killing of Abel* hardly makes Garcio a heroic gay prototype. His lines may be the product of an anonymous dramatist, or an even more unknown young glover, who discovered that vulgarity was a good way to catch an audience's attention. His modern heirs include those men who might liberally say 'kiss my arse', but would not want you to take them up on the offer: sometimes even going so far as to expose their buttocks in an inadvertently revealing form of anti-gay abuse. Closer in spirit, however, are the performances of playfully vulgar comedians. Drag performer Julian Clary, who tames blatant obscenity with playfulness, appeals to audiences who delight in being shocked, opening his act with provocations like: 'I do like a warm hand on my entrance.'

Garcio's origins are not in the church, but in carnival, and its licensed outrage of public decencies. The material of mystery plays may be scriptural, but the theatrical form it takes is far freer than the Latin of the pulpit. In English theatre's first comedies Garcio's gay characteristics – a combination of mischief and male homosexuality – would have fuller scope. His brand of comic anality is handed on to the characters of Diccon in the anonymous *Gammer Gurton's Needle* and Merrygreek in Nicholas Udall's *Ralph Roister Doister*. Before these, however, comes an extraordinary episode in the earliest surviving English secular drama, *Fulgens and Lucrece*.

Joust between friends

Imagine having dinner with the Archbishop of Canterbury and being shown a racy avant-garde video as the night's entertainment. Henry Medwall, author of *Fulgens and Lucrece*, was chaplain to archbishop and Cardinal John Morton, a noted fifteenth-century builder of fen dykes. Medwall's play is the first English play known to have been published, and the earliest surviving play which is not on a Christian theme, having as its main plot the choice of a husband for Lucrece, daughter of the Roman senator Fulgens. Given the newness of the form, and the tension between sections of the church and the theatre, the first performance of his play, at Archbishop Morton's house as part of a banquet some time around 1497, must have been a remarkable enough event.

The play's subplot, which partly frames the Fulgens and Lucrece story as a play within the play, involves two unnamed Tudor youths, probably servants. They are rivals for Lucrece's maid, called Ancilla in the Roman story, Joan in the contemporary one. This parody of the main plot is of no consequence to the narrative, but does contain an outrageously bawdy fight sequence. As a way to decide which of them will succeed as lovers, youth B suggests:

But let us jest [joust] at fart prick in cule [buttocks].

The lads' hands are then bound by the woman over whom they are fighting, and they joust while carrying spears and riding staffs, presumably under their arms and between their legs respectively. The slapstick possibilities in staging this scene of phallic excess are extensive, its anal implications reinforced by the maid, who warns them while preparing for the fight:

But see ye hold fast behind
Lest ye trouble us in all.

Despite this warning, youth A indeed falls and shits himself in the mock joust, later claiming he has suffered a huge gash in his behind. From this, he claims, comes a great wind strong enough to blow out a candle: it is so large that you can get your nose in up to the eyes. This is presumably an exaggeration, but is a splendidly evocative image for a piece of dinner theatre at the archbishop's.

Similar wordplay to that in *Fulgens and Lucrece* survives in a record of an English folk play, part of a separate theatrical tradition. Ancilla/Joan rejects B, saying she is 'taken up before'. He replies:

Marry, I beshrew [curse] your heart therefore.
It should better content me
That ye had be taken up behind.

The pun is preserved in a version of the *Revesby Sword Play*, a record of a late eighteenth-century Morris play. In it, the old suitor Pickle Herring claims:

Nay, then, sweet Ciss, ne'er trust me more
For I never loved lass like thee before

and the Fool mocks:

No, nor behind neither.

The hilarity of anal intercourse between a man and a woman, enhanced by both roles being played by male performers, is a running joke in English comedy. It links the academic tradition of plays written by those accustomed to classical models, particularly Roman comedies, and the folk tradition. An almost unperformably bottom-fixated comedy from Cambridge University provides another link.

Of Dicks and Diccon

Gammer Gurton's Needle by 'Mr S.' was peformed at Christ's College Cambridge some time between 1561 and 1575. As the title suggests, it is the tale of Gammer Gurton, a woman who has mislaid her needle. Since she was using the implement to sew up the torn breeches of her servant Hodge, the loss causes both of them comic distress. You do not need to be Sigmund Freud to discern the play's phallic abundance. It bristles with spits, staffs, awls, and door bars, so that however lost the needle may be, its shape cannot leave our imagination. Given the surroundings, it is hardly surprising that Gammer Gurton has a boy servant called Cock. Since Cock also operates as a euphemism for God in the play, there is also much swearing by the penis substitute. By the end of the sixteenth century, the image of the needle itself had penetrated the language. In Thomas Dekker's scurrilous play *Satiromastix*, Tucca says to Mistress Miniver: 'for Gammer Gurton, I mean to be thy needle, I love thee'.

Hodge explains what has gone missing to the mischievous Diccon:

> HODGE . . . her nee'le [needle], her nee'le , her nee'le, man – 'tis
> neither flesh nor fish!
>   A little thing with an hole in the end, as bright as any siller
> [silver],
>   Small, long, sharp at the point, and straight as any pillar.
>
> DICCON I know not what a devil thou meanst!

Diccon deliberately misunderstands, forcing Hodge into inadvertent innuendo. Hodge is embarrassed that his trousers are ripped, exposing his bottom. That the breeches also seem to be muddy enhances the shameless anality of the comedy. He is desperate that his ripped breeches be repaired:

HODGE Chill [I'll] be thy bondman Diccon, ich [I] swear by sun
and moon,
And channot [I cannot] somewhat to stop this gap, cham [I
am] utterly undone!
(Pointing behind to his torn breeches)

DICCON Why, is there any special cause thou takest hereat such
sorrow?

HODGE Kirstian Clack, Tom Simson's maid, by the mass, comes
hither tomorrow. . . .

DICCON Shalt swear to be no blab, Hodge?

HODGE   Chill [I will], Diccon.

DICCON   Then go to.
Lay thine hand here; say after me as thou shalt hear me do.
Hast no book?

HODGE   Cha' [I've] no book, I!

DICCON   Then needs must force us both
Upon my breech to lay thine hand, and there to take thine
oath.

HODGE I, Hodge, breechless,
Swear to Diccon, rechless [recklessly],
By the cross that I shall kiss,
To keep his counsel close
And always me to dispose
To work that his pleasure is.
(Here he kisseth Diccon's breech)

Given Hodge's stage dialect, this episode may not immediately be clear.
Its humour centres on Hodge's sexual humiliation. He is anxious that
his trousers be repaired rapidly because there is a woman arriving the
next day, whom he presumably wishes to impress. Certainly the sight of
Hodge's bare muddy bottom is one he wants to spare Kirstian Clack.
Tricky Diccon takes advantage of this anxiety. He persuades Hodge to
place his hand on – and then kiss – Diccon's own breeches and swear to

do whatever Diccon asks of him in future. It is not clear from the text where exactly the hand and kiss are located. In rehearsal, experiment could be made to see how much Diccon enjoys ridiculing Hodge, and what pleasure he gains from the hand and kiss upon his breeches.

Diccon then gets Hodge to summon up the devil for their assistance in finding the needle. Hodge is so frightened at the thought he shits his pants, making the symbolic mud all over them all too real. Hodge rushes off, to change into his other trousers: the ones Gammer Gurton was mending when she lost her needle. Alongside its phallic obsession, therefore, the play has a plot of scatalogical frenzy.

Diccon's motiveless trouble-making is reminscent of Wakefield's mischievous Garcio. He deliberately creates more confusion by telling Dame Chat, the play's other householder, that Gammer Gurton suspects Chat of stealing from her. He says the item in question is not, however, the needle, but (no surprise here) her cock. This sets off yet more misunderstandings.

The men in the play are dominated by these two tough, independent women, who ludicrously come to blows over a missing item: whether needle or cock is irrelevant to its phallic implications. The women's fight is the comic centrepiece of the play. Hodge encourages Gammer Gurton from a doorway:

HODGE . . . Pull out her throat-boll!

DAME CHAT Comst behind me, thou withered witch!

There are entertainingly complex erotics in this wrestling match between two youths playing two women fighting, with a 'real man' on the sidelines, too frightened to get involved. Frantic violence offers another presentation of bodies out of control, one more palatable today than the earlier shitting jokes. Indeed, the farcical possibilities in extreme violence are a staple of modern film-making from Hammer to Tarantino. The script points up the gender-bending, drawing attention to the maleness of the actor playing Dame Chat with his Adam's Apple ('throat-boll'). Anal intercourse is another underlying image: Gammer wins by taking Dame Chat from behind.

The climax of the comedy comes when Diccon turns his trickery on Doctor Rat, a curate and therefore of doubtful manliness, also in search of the elusive pricker. Diccon asks Dame Chat:

Have you not about your house, behind your furnace [oven] or
　lead [large pot],
A hole where a crafty knave may creep in for need?

Dame Chat confirms that yes, she has a back passage. Once the curate is
sent to penetrate this entrance, he smells something (not a rat in this case).

Art thou sure, Diccon, the swill tub stands not hereabout?

Diccon reassures him until he pokes through and Dame Chat beats the
unfortunate Rat about the head. When this brings the authorities, in the
shape of Master Bailey, to sort out the dispute, Bailey is inclined to
blame the victim a little for his unorthodox mode of entrance:

To come in on the back side when ye might go about!
I know none such, unless they long to have their brains knocked
　out.

In pursuit of justice, Doctor Rat finds himself at the receiving end of
much of the most blatant double entendre in the play. There is relish in
the way sodomitical implications pile up on the clergyman. Dame Chat
denies hitting him, for she has been told by Diccon that her unseen
intruder was Hodge. She therefore assumes Rat got his injuries at the
other end of town, where he is said to have 'minions': androgynous
favourites. Rat contributes to the innuendo himself when he accuses
Diccon of setting him up:

. . . he said full certain, if I would follow his rede [advice],
Into your house a privy way he would me guide and lead,
And where ye had it [the needle] in your hands, sewing about a
　clout [cloth]
And set me in the black hole, thereby to find you out.

The humiliation of a curate takes place in the black hole – a playful spot
for Diccon as it was for his forebear Garcio. Diccon's disruptive
machinations are ultimately revealed, however. Dame Chat knows the
appropriate punishment: 'Come knave, it were a good deed to geld
[castrate] thee, by Cock's [God's] bones!' – not so much an eye for an
eye as a needle for a needle.

Master Bailey, as the representative of law and order, instructs Diccon to reverse the humiliation dealt out to Hodge:

> Then mark ye well: to recompense this thy former action,
> Because thou hast offended all, to make them satisfaction,
> Before their faces here kneel down, and as I shall thee teach,
> So thou shalt take an oath of Hodge's leather breech.

Diccon, as he does so, slaps Hodge, who cries out that 'He thrust me into the buttock.' This climactic event of perianal penetration reveals, as we expect, that the missing needle has been stuck all along into his trousers. This is the pair Gammer Gurton was mending when she lost the needle, which Hodge put on after his anal explosion in Act Two. It is a touching moment for the two as she examines his rear:

> HODGE Go near the light, Gammer. This – well, in faith, good luck!
>   Chwas [I was] almost undone, 'twas so far in my buttock!

> GAMMER GURTON 'Tis mine own dear ne'ele, Hodge, sickerly
>   [certainly] I wot!

> HODGE Cham I not a good son, Gammer, cham I not?

Order is restored: Gammer Gurton is thrilled at the rediscovery of her phallus; Hodge is deeply relieved that it did not penetrate his buttocks far enough to undo him. All are delighted and forgiving, and depart to drink and celebrate. Just before he follows the company offstage, however, Diccon turns to the audience as Epilogue, to make his last wordplays on behinds and endings.

> Soft sirs, take us with you – the company shall be the more;
> As proud comes behind, they say, as any goes before.
> But now my good masters, since we must be gone,
> And leave you behind us, here all alone,
> Since at our last ending, thus merry we be,
> For Gammer Gurton's needle's sake, let us have a plaudite
>   [applause]!

Though not a Cambridge boy, Joe Orton knew his classic theatre. Like the unknown Mr S., author of *Gammer Gurton's Needle*, he used the conventions of Greek and Roman comedy as a cue for contemporary comic outrage. The arch apotheosis of this homage to the ancients comes at the end of *What the Butler Saw*.

(Everyone embraces one another. The skylight opens, a rope ladder is lowered and, in a great blaze of glory, Sergeant Match, the leopard-skin dress torn from one shoulder and streaming with blood, descends.)

RANCE We're approaching what our racier novelists term 'the climax'.

(Reaching the floor Sergeant Match stares about him in bewilderment.)

MATCH Will someone produce or cause to be produced the missing parts of Sir Winston Churchill? . . .

(Geraldine picks up the box which she had upon entering the room. It has remained on the desk ever since. Sergeant Match opens the box, looks inside, and gives a sigh.)

MATCH The Great Man can once more take up his place in the High Street as an example to us all of the spirit that won the Battle of Britain.

(Sergeant Match takes from the box and holds up a section from a larger than life-sized bronze statue. Deep intakes of breath from everyone.)*

RANCE *(with admiration)* How much more inspiring if, in those dark days, we'd seen what we see now. Instead we had to be content with a cigar – the symbol falling far short, as we all realize, of the object itself.

(The dying sunlight from the garden and the blaze from above gild Sergeant Match as he holds high the nation's heritage.)*

[* Orton's original stage directions]

In the first production, which took place two years after Orton's death, the symbol fell short indeed, and the contents of the box were not seen. Not until the Royal Court Theatre's revival in 1975 was the supposed phallus of Winston Churchill, wartime Prime Minister and national hero, held aloft on a London stage. According to Stanley Baxter, the original Dr Prentice, Ralph Richardson, who played Rance, censored the moment:

Ralph got terribly, terribly depressed. He'd turned down the play a few times before finally accepting it, and he thought he'd made a terrible mistake taking part in what he came to regard as a dirty play.

Orton records himself in mischievous defence of the moment. His diaries with their carefully documented accounts of his own anal (and other) exploits reveal him as a self-styled heir to the pranksters of early English comedy.

'It's only a statue,' I said. . . . Oscar [Lewenstein, producer] said, 'and what about the laws of libel?' 'What am I saying about Churchill, though?' I said. 'You're saying he had a big prick,' Oscar said. 'That isn't libellous, surely?' I said. 'I wouldn't sue anybody for saying I had a big prick. No man would. In fact I might pay them to do that.'

Turning the Page

Sex between men and boys outrages contemporary morality more than any other sexual practice. Gay teachers in particular cause the tabloids to press the panic button. In some ways, times do not change: John Marston is disgusted in his 1599 *The Scourge of Villainy* that:

some pedant Tutor . . .
  in his bed
Should use my fry, like Phrygian Ganymede.

In other ways, attittudes could hardly be more different. If the Headmaster of Eton was publicly convicted of buggering his pupils today, he would hardly be likely later to be appointed Head of Westminster School. Yet that is what seems to have happened in the mid sixteenth century to Nicholas Udall, teacher, translator and friend of queens. More important here, Udall is also England's first comic dramatist.

Udall wrote comedies for his pupils to perform. He is thought to be the author of *Jack Juggler* which would therefore have first been acted by the boys of Eton around 1537. It is a farce of mistaken identity, based on a Roman comedy by Plautus. The mischievous Jack Juggler impersonates and persecutes another boy, Jenkin Careaway, the page of a Master Boungrace. His stated motivation is mixed, but includes envy at the indulgence of Careaway's master: 'against all other boys the said gentle man Maintaineth him all that he can' complains Juggler. It is also punishment for Careaway's vanity: Juggler describes him as 'Pricking, prancing and springing in his short coat.' Careaway's short coat exposes his bottom, with the pun on prick increasing the sexual innuendo in Juggler's disdain. Half a century later, in *Edward II*, a king's minion is abused in similar terms. In Christopher Marlowe's play, Mortimer derides Piers Gaveston for his favour with the king and the way in which he swishes about the court in fancy clothes, including that bottom-revealing short cloak:

> I have not seen a dapper Jack so brisk.
> He wears a short Italian hooded cloak,
> Larded with pearl, and in his Tuscan cap
> A jewel of more value than the crown.

The master's favourite is loathed for the indulgence he enjoys, his arrogance, and his sartorial excess. The two situations are parallel: king and subject, master and servant, and they inspire similar criticisms. We know that Gaveston is King Edward's lover, however. What do we make of the relationship between Master Boungrace and Jenkin Careaway? In Udall's play, sexual possibilities between master and page are part of the fun.

When Careaway realizes that Juggler has impersonated him, he describes him in a way which closely follows Udall's Latin source:

> He hath in every point my clothing and my gear,
> My head, my cape, my shirt and notted [cropped] hair;
> And of the same colour my eyes, nose and lips,
> My cheeks, chin, neck, feet, legs and hips;
> And of the same stature, and height, and age,
> And is in every point Master Boungrace' page –

At this point, Plautus makes a reference to scars on the impersonated slave's back. Udall rejects this as an identifying feature inappropriate to an English gentleman's pageboy. In place of this image, Careaway says of Juggler:

> That if he have a hole in his tail –
> He is even mine own self without any fail.

The mark of the whip is a sure sign of the slave's service. Here, however, the clinching evidence identifying Juggler as Master Boungrace's page would be 'a hole in his tail'. There is a perfectly wholesome explanation: tail can refer to the lower part of a coat, and Careaway may have a distinctive tear in that garment. We have been told quite clearly, however, that the page wears a short coat, without a tail. It is also a rather weak image with which to end this catalogue of similarities, unless, as in *Gammer Gurton's Needle*, references to torn clothing in the pelvic region have a lewder significance. In Udall's own translation of Erasmus, tail means 'bottom':

> He was forbidden to sit on his tail and charged to stand upon his
> feet.

Udall's contemporary John Bale also certainly has sodomy in mind when in his play *King John*, the character Sedition says he will be the Pope's ally as long as he has 'a hole within my breech'. Thus Careaway's speech plays on the fact that, on top of all the superficial resemblances, if Juggler has a hole in his arse, it would convince Careaway that the other boy had indeed become him. Like the slave's whip marks, it suggests a level of household service beyond a little light dusting.

It may be an allusion which many school plays would shy away from today, but the identification of pages as sixteenth-century houseboys is not unique to Udall. By the end of the century it was referred to as commonplace. Drayton's *The Moon Calf* (c. 1605) describes one such master and his boy:

> And when himself he of his home can free
> He to the City comes, where then if he
> And the familiar Butterfly his page
> Can pass the street, the ord'nary [tavern] and stage
> It is enough, and he himself thinks then,
> To be the only, absolut'st of men . . .
> Yet, more than this, naught doth him so delight
> As doth his smooth-chinned, plump-thighed catamite.

According to Thomas Middleton's *The Black Book* (1604), it is a mode of service particularly English:

this nest of Gallants . . . keep at every heel a man, besides a French Lackey, (a great Bay with a beard) and an English page, which fills up the place of an ingle

'ingle' being, in the charmingly authoritative definition of the Oxford English Dictionary:

A boy-favourite (in bad sense); a catamite.

The sexual duties of pages were not just the stuff of fiction, by the evidence of the following century. In 1621 Sir Simonds D'Ewes writes accusing Francis Bacon of:

keeping one Goodrick a very effeminate faced youth to be his catamite and bedfellow, although he had discharged the most of his other household servants

and according to Samuel Pepys in 1663

Sir J Mennes and Mr Batten both say that buggery is now almost grown as common among our gallants as in Italy, and that the very pages of the town begin to complain of their masters for it.

It is, however, a century after Udall before another dramatist, John Wilmot, Earl of Rochester, celebrates with some irony the pleasures of turning over the page, albeit in the privacy of a poem:

Love a woman! Y'are an ass!
   'Tis a most insipid passion
To choose out for your happiness
   The idlest part of God's creation

  . . .

Then give me health, wealth, mirth and wine,
   And if busy love entrenches
There's a sweet soft page of mine,
   Does the trick worth forty wenches.

Given this hundred-year catalogue of depravity in domestic service, Prince Hal's sight of Falstaff's precocious page in *Henry IV, Part Two* inspires understandable dismay at the likely state of the lad's morals. (Sodomy between Falstaff and Hal will be discussed in chapter eight.)

> And the boy that I gave Falstaff. A had him from me Christian, and
> look if the fat villain have not transformed him ape.

This all suggests that for a man to have sex with his page during this
period was, while hardly approved, not greeted with the universal
horror reserved for such acts today. The North American Man–Boy
Love Association would, however, be ill-advised to adopt *Jack Juggler*
as a manifesto for integenerational relationships. Rather than a healthy
flexibility on the age at which one can consent to sex, the attitudes
reflected are those of indifference to the rights of boys, particularly
servant boys. It is misguided to see a rallying call for sexual
libertarianism in the tacit acceptance that wealthy adult males could
and would fuck whoever they wanted. It nevertheless seems
extraordinary that at any time a headmaster would write a school play
which jests with the idea that some masters were thought to have sex
with their boys. Less comically, Udall would be prosecuted four years
after its first performance for doing that very thing with his pupils.

At the altar boys

It is a tricky and ultimately pointless business to guess at writers'
biographies from their works. *Ralph Roister Doister* is the only play
Nicholas Udall is indisputably agreed to have written. It has been used
to support various theories about his life, and his 1541 conviction in
particular. All this can only be conjecture, but the play certainly
continues the line of mischief-making anal pranksters in early English
comedy. The naughty but nice ambivalent Matthew Merrygreek is
cousin to Diccon in *Gammer Gurton's Needle* and Garcio in *The Killing
of Abel*. Like them, he opens the play by talking to the audience, and
leads us into the action of the play. He too is filthy minded and bottom-
obsessed:

> For exalt him and have him as ye lust, indeed,
> Yea, to hold his finger in a hole for a need

The anal humour also has antecedents in Roman comedy. Merrygreek is
reminiscent of Terence's Gnatho, whom Udall describes elsewhere as
following men 'at the tail'. His name, however, does not evoke images
of Rome, but the proverbial wantonness and effeminacy of the Greeks.

He may be one of the first camp characters on the English stage. When his friend, Ralph Roister Doister, claims to be admired by women, Merrygreek extravagantly encourages the delusion.

> Yea, Malkin, I warrant you, as much as they dare.
> And ye will not believe what they say in the street,
> Whan your ma'ship passes by, all such as I meet,
> That sometimes I can scarce find what answer to make.

'Malkin' is a word usually used of a vulgar woman; when used of a man it implies effeminacy. Imagine a contemporary adolescent boy addressing a male friend affectionately as 'slut' or 'slag' – it is a queen's idiom. Roister Doister is the straight man in this double-act, full of his own desire to be a lover. Merrygreek is the non-straight man: the wit with no apparent interest in women.

As in *Gammer Gurton's Needle* and traditional British pantomime, the main drag role in *Ralph Roister Doister* is that of a mature woman. The widow Christian Custance is the unimpressed object of Roister Doister's youthful passion. Like his contemporary John Bale, Udall makes drama out of unwanted sexual advances. In Bale's morality plays, however, these serve to support his Protestant propaganda, whereas Udall's play treats lewdness as nothing but comic. Oddly, both Udall's play and Bale's *Three Laws of Nature, Moses and Christ, Corrupted* include the same song: 'Pipe merry annot', which is also linked to the Protestant satire *A Poor Help*. Presumably political and religious sympathies between the two writers explain the coincidence that Dame Custance's nurse and maids, all played by boys, sing Sodomy's opening number in *Three Laws*.

Roister Doister's stab at heterosexual romance is deliberately foiled by Merrygreek, who compounds a series of disasters by wilfully misreading the punctuation of Ralph's love letter to Dame Custance and rendering it absurd. The inamorata storms out, and Merrygreek's textual inversion is followed by sexual inversion.

> ROISTER DOISTER Whough! She is gone forever! I shall no more her
> see!
> MERRYGREEK What weep? Fie, for shame! And blubber? For man-
> hood's sake,
> Never let your foe so much pleasure of you take!

Rather take the man's part, and do love refrain.
If she despise you, e'en despise her again.

Merrygreek calls on Roister Doister to be more manly, less like a woman. The most male response, he argues, is to despise his foe: the woman who has scorned him. The gullible Ralph is immediately convinced, and switches his loyalty to his friend, who goes into a camp combination of hyperbole and baby-talk.

ROISTER DOISTER By Gosse [God] and for thy sake, I defy her
    indeed!
MERRYGREEK Yea, and perchance that way ye shall much sooner
    speed.
For one mad property these women hath in fay [faith]:
Where ye will, they will not; will not ye, then will they.
Ah, foolish woman, ah, most unlucky Custance,
Ah, unfortunate woman, ah, peevish Custance,
Art thou to thine harms so obstinately bent,
That you canst not see where lieth thy high preferment?
Canst thou not lub dis [love this (childish)] man, which could
    lub dee [love thee] so well?
Art thou so much thine own foe?

ROISTER DOISTER Thou dost the truth tell.

The combination of inflated rhetoric and infantilized flirtation wins Roister Doister to Merrygreek immediately. With Ralph dependent on him, Matthew then pushes the scene yet further. His motivation is a matter for the actor. Does Merrygreek simply enjoy humiliating his friend, or does he also get pleasure from persuading him into ever deeper intimacy?

MERRYGREEK Well I lament.

ROISTER DOISTER   So do I.

MERRYGREEK   Wherefore?

ROISTER DOISTER   For this thing:
    Because she is gone.

MERRYGREEK   I mourn for another thing.

ROISTER DOISTER What is it, Merrygreek, wherefore dost thou grief take?

MERRYGREEK That I am not a woman myself for your sake.

Merrygreek goes on to woo Roister Doister with vigour. The comedy of the scene certainly comes from the inappropriateness of this seduction, given the boys' youth and gender. For an audience aware that boys can fall in love with each other, however, there is an additional layer of dramatic irony. Performed by a lesbian and gay youth group, for example, the scene would become an intriguing mixture of farce and sincerity.

MERRYGREEK I would have you myself, and a straw for yon Jill
And mock much of you, though it were against my will.
I would not, I warrant you, fall in such a rage
As to refuse such a goodly personage.

ROISTER DOISTER In faith, I heartily thank thee, Merrygreek.

MERRYGREEK And I were a woman –

ROISTER DOISTER   Thou wouldest to me seek.

Roister Doister has readily accepted all of Merrygreek's suggestions until this point. Now he has got the message, however, he seems to be resisting slightly. The sense of impropriety depends on a knowledge that romance between males is a possibility, albeit a prohibited one. Whether Merrygreek indeed has sexual or romantic interests in Roister Doister is a matter for the actor. That Ralph believes his friend's earnestness certainly provides an additional layer of comic tension. The text suggests that verbal advances may be backed up by physical ones at this point, enhancing the comedy born of embarrassment. The play requires an audience more knowing than Roister Doister. If he is aware that Merrygreek's physical flattery borders on impiety, it must be assumed that at least some of the original viewers would have thought so too.

MERRYGREEK For though I say it, a goodly person ye be.

ROISTER DOISTER No, no.

MERRYGREEK   Yes, a goodly man as e'er I did see.

ROISTER DOISTER No, I am a poor, homely man, as God made me.

MERRYGREEK By the faith that I owe to God sir, but ye be!

To aid his resistance, Roister Doister introduces God in an attempt to calm Merrygreek. Matthew asserts, however, that his love for him is not in defiance of faith, but inspired by it. Nevertheless, Merrygreek changes tack, switching to the more compelling argument of a dowry. Perhaps Ralph goes along with this because he knows that his friend will never be rich enough to make the match work. Or does wealth overcome Ralph's scruples: if Matthew were to have lots of money, why indeed should they not marry?

MERRYGREEK Would I might for your sake spend a thousand
   pound land.

ROISTER DOISTER I dare say thou wouldest have me to thy husband.

MERRYGREEK Yea, and I were the fairest lady in the shire,
   And knew you as I know you and see you now here –

Just at the point Roister Doister agrees, however, Merrygreek abruptly stops the game, to the relief of both:

MERRYGREEK Well, I say no more.

ROISTER DOISTER   Gramercies with all my heart.

MERRYGREEK But since that cannot be, will ye play a wise part?

That cannot be. Two school boys cannot get married, and that is the end of it.

Protestants and Perverts

Tony Higton, like Nicholas Udall, is an Essex Protestant clergyman:

The country is in a bad enough mess as it is, and any lowering of the homosexual age of consent is going to be yet another nail in the coffin for marriage and the family. The implication will inevitably be that homosexual relationships are on a par with marriage. I believe in human rights for every human being but I don't believe we have a right to behaviour which is contrary to nature, which is depraved, which is unnatural, whatever it may be. Homosexual behaviour fits into that category.

There are a lot of people in the church who seem to have very strange ideas and seem to want to go along with the current views in society.

In 1987 he proposed a motion to the General Synod that the Church of England should expel its gay clergy. Udall seems to have escaped the provisions of a similar ruling four centuries earlier. Higton's invective has more in common with the anti-sodomitical ravings of John Bale.

Although both Udall and John Bale were innovative playwrights and Protestant clergymen, Udall seems to have kept his balance rather better on the political and religious seesaw of mid sixteenth-century England. This is all the more remarkable since Udall seems to have been convicted of the crime against which Bale persistently and vehemently fulminates.

Born in 1505, Udall studied at Corpus Christi College, Oxford from the age of fifteen, but had his MA delayed following charges of Lutheranism. With the antiquary John Leland, also a friend of Bale, he wrote verses for a 1532 pageant celebrating the marriage of Anne Boleyn, the wedding for which Henry VIII split from Rome. Like Bale, Udall was paid for performances of his plays by Henry VIII's Chief Minister Thomas Cromwell, but he remained in his post as Headmaster of Eton when Cromwell fell from favour and was executed.

He was noted for his translations, particularly of Erasmus, the Dutch monk and writer who was a major influence on the English Reformation. Erasmus is also reported to have fallen in love with an English student, Thomas Grey, later Marquis of Dorset. A man-loving monk at the heart of this European religious and political movement is an unlikely figure to influence the rigorous certainities of John Bale's morally determined cosmos. He does, however, seem an appropriate intellectual bedfellow for Udall. Not that Erasmus's work is a hymn to buggery. Bale's monks may just want to toss off their cassocks, but Erasmus' passionate letters show a different level of devotion. He writes to a fellow monk, Servatius Roger, citing the devotion of mythical soulmates Orestes and Pylades, Theseus and Pirithous and Damon and Pythias:

> I place my hopes in you alone . . . I have become yours so completely that you have left me naught of myself . . . But since

lovers find nothing so distressing as not being able to meet one another . . . I long . . . to see you face to face as often as we please. That joy is denied us. I cannot think of it without tears . . . Farewell my soul, and if there is anything human in you, return the love of him who loves you.

Henry VIII's last wife, Catherine Parr, patronized Udall's translation of Erasmus' paraphrase of the book of St Luke. The favours continued under Henry's son Edward VI, during whose reign he was appointed canon of St George's Chapel Windsor, and before whom *Ralph Roister Doister* may have been performed. He managed, however, to keep from too close an identification with the Reformation. He was also commissioned by Henry's daughter, the Catholic Queen Mary, on whose accession John Bale fled to spend the reign in exile. Indeed Udall may have written the play *Respublica* to celebrate Mary becoming queen. He spent her reign as tutor to Edward Courteney in the Tower of London, employed in the household of the Bishop of Winchester and, from 1554 until he died in 1556, as Headmaster of Westminster School. This capacity to keep influential friends is either remarkable in the face of a conviction for buggery, or explains why it seems not to have been the end of him.

In 1541 Udall was Headmaster of Eton, a schoolmaster who had written a popular Latin textbook *Flowers for Latin Speaking* consisting of pieces from the Roman dramatist Terence, whose play *The Eunuch* influences *Ralph Roister Doister*. He was known as a playwright and had mounted school plays, although *Ralph Roister Doister* is almost certainly from a later period than his Eton years.

A crisis then occurred, according to the records of the Privy Council:

Nic. Uvedale [Udall], schoolmaster of Eton, being sent for as suspect to be of counsel of a robbery lately committed at Eton by Thomas Cheyney, John Hoorde, scholars of the said school and . . . Gregory, servant to the said schoolmaster, and having certain interrogatories ministered unto him, touching the said fact and other felonius trespasses, whereof he was suspected, did confess that he did commit buggery with the said Cheney, sundry times heretofore, and of late the 6th day of this present month in the present year at London, whereupon he was committed to the Marshalsea [prison].

What happened as a result of this hearing is unknown, but Udall later wrote a letter to an unidentified man, thanking this patron for help. He does say, however, that he has not been reinstated at Eton, and needs work. The tone is humble, and suggests he has been accused, and may have been guilty, of some great crime.

> Right worshipful and my singular good master . . . I trust ye shall find that this your correpcion [reproof] shall be a sufficient scourge to make me, during my life, more wise and more ware utterly for ever to eschew and avoid all kinds of all manner excesses and abuses that have been reputed to reign in me. . . . All vices of which I have been noted or to your mastership accused being oons by the roots extirped . . .

What did happen to Nicholas Udall? The truth is known only to men long dead. Collating the evidence from trial records inevitably misses crucial information. Imagine future historians studying fragmentary papers from the 1977 trial involving Liberal Party leader Jeremy Thorpe, accused of having plotted to murder Norman Scott, a man with whom he was alleged to have had a relationship. What would be clear, and would it be the truth? Across 450 years, the view is yet more blurred.

Did Udall ever spend time in the Marshalsea prison, as sentenced? If he did, how long? He was certainly free the next year, when he was paid the arrears on his Eton salary. Given the conviction, why should that money have been paid to him? Why was he not dismissed as vicar of Braintree, a post he retained despite the sodomy law clearly stating

> that no person offending in any such offence shall be admitted to his [Henry VIII's] clergy

and

> If any person shall commit the detestable sin of buggery with mankind or beast etc. it is felony . . . and he lose his clergy.

Far from losing favour, there would be a royal injunction to have his paraphrases of Erasmus in every church in the country; and the son of the king who enacted the sodomy law under which Udall was convicted, would make him canon of Windsor ten years later. How was it that a man who had confessed to buggery with a pupil was taken on as a tutor, and later made a headmaster again?

The least plausible argument to explain this unlikely sequence of events is that there has been a misprint: 'burglary' was misspelled 'buggery', and no one made any attempt to correct the records. It is a possibility: there is some confusion about the spelling of 'councail' in the same Privy Council record, which might mean either 'counsel' or 'council', two words with distinct meanings, although clearly not as much as the two possible versions of illegal entry. The spelling error theory is, however, a late development, introduced by twentieth-century scholars. One hundred and fifty years ago, a different technique for sanitizing the affair was used: an 1847 edition of *Ralph Roister Doister* deliberately misquotes the Privy Council records to have Udall confessing to 'a heinous offence'.

In those records, Udall appears to confess to buggery, rather than the robbery to which he was originally suspected of being an accomplice. It does indeed seem an odd additional piece of information to provide under questioning. Had Thomas Cheyney mentioned the sex when he was questioned, and was it connected with the conspiracy to rob his own school in which Udall is implicated? Who helped bring Udall back to favour after the trial and possible imprisonment – was it the unknown patron to whom he wrote? Was the whole affair hushed up, so that no one knew about it? Could this have included the king, who subsequently allowed Udall to collaborate with his queen and princess on the paraphrases of Erasmus? The people who paid Udall his back salary must certainly have been aware of the trial, in order not to have paid him it in the first place.

It is possible that the charges were not believed. Udall carefully avoids confessing in his letter to his patron, referring rather to 'excesses and abuses that have been reputed to reign in me' and 'vices of which I have been noted or to your mastership accused'. Did he maintain his innnocence despite the reported confession and conviction? If he did, why did people believe him? How was he questioned? Was there any connection between his trial and the earlier inquiries into his religious politics, or the fall of his patron Cromwell the previous year?

We cannot know if Udall ever confesssed to buggery and not burglary. We cannot know if he actually did have sex with Thomas Cheyney, 'sundry times' until 6 March 1541. It seems an odd thing to confess if he had not, unless he had something more to hide. We cannot know which of his influential friends knew of his supposed confession, and who among them believed it. He was not executed, however, and was able to go back to work. As a result, we do have one definite legacy from Nicholas Udall: *Ralph Roister Doister* and its account of the funny things boys can do together.

3

The Freaks' Roll Call

Sodomy Takes the Stage

Haig, Kitchener, Montgomery, Mountbatten . . . . The appeal to precedent is a popular weapon in the gay intellectual armoury. Campaigners against the armed forces' ban on lesbians and gay men draw attention to the homosexuality of famous military leaders. Lesbian teenagers reassure their anxious parents that even very respectable television presenters are sisters of Sappho. Some argue that the roster of gay celebrities through the ages is the tip of an ever present iceberg, demonstrating the existence of homosexual desire in all ages and cultures. It is a popular argument against persecution, having been around since the first stirrings of homosexual law reform. Horrified at the pogroms he saw against gay men, the eighteenth-century political theorist Jeremy Bentham wrote extensively on the monstrousness of the sodomy laws, in papers only brought to wider attention by Louis Crompton in 1978. This piece from 1774 uses arguments which would persist for two hundred years until the British government partially decriminalized sex between men:

> What would have become of Aristides, Solon, Themistocles, Harmodius and Aristogiton, Xenophon, Cato, Socrates, Titus – the delight of mankind – Cicero, Pliny, Trajan, Adrian, etc., etc. – these idols of their country and ornaments of human nature? They would have *perished on your gibbets*.

Although Bentham's private documents are the first systematic arguments for law reform, the listing of notable historical sodomites features in a series of dramatic works, dating back another two centuries before Bentham. These place love between men in a context which, depending on the character speaking, is more reassuring or more threatening.

In Christopher Marlowe's play *Edward II*, the list of notables is used by Mortimer the elder to calm his nephew's outrage at the king's indulgence of Piers Gaveston. By putting the argument into the mouth of an older, conservative figure in the play, Marlowe deftly gives it more weight than if Edward or Gaveston were to use the same argument themselves.

> Thou seest by nature he [Edward] is mild and calm;
> And, seeing his mind so dotes on Gaveston,
> Let him without controlment have his will.
> The mightiest kings have had their minions;
> Great Alexander lov'd Hephaestion,
> The conquering Hercules for Hylas wept,
> And for Patroclus stern Achilles droop'd.
> And not kings only, but the wisest men;
> The Roman Tully lov'd Octavius,
> Grave Socrates wild Alcibiades.

Mortimer is not necessarily arguing that it is good for the king to have a male lover, but he sees no harm in it, given the historical precedents. He also seems to accept that the love of another man is something which happens 'by nature', again an unexpectedly progressive notion. He has not read his Foucault, however: the construction of sexuality in the ancient world was very different from that of fourteenth-century England.

Elsewhere, sodomy was almost always defined as against nature, as in a play by the Bishop of Ossory, John Bale, the vituperatively anti-gay *Three Laws of Nature, Moses and Christ, Corrupted*. In that play, the roll-call of classical arse-bandits is presumably intended to alarm:

> We made Thalon and Sophocles,
> Thamiras, Nero, Agathocles,
> Tiberius and Aristoteles,
>   Themselves to use unnaturally.

The irony works here in the opposite direction to Marlowe's play. Bale puts the defence of sodomy in the mouth of a character he designs to be unappealing. In addition, the choice of names is different. A reputation for vicious excess still lingers over the Roman emperors Nero and Tiberius, and pederastic Greek poets like Sophocles and Thamyris are presumably less admirable role models than the roster of fighting men Marlowe chooses for Mortimer.

Whilst a fascination with the sexual habits of famous people is often merely the stuff of gossip, it has greater significance. As arguments about outing have shown, the public recognition of lesbian and gay behaviour fuels political discussion. It seems celebrity homosexuals boosted gay self-esteem even in the seventeenth century, if evidence reported in *An Account of the Proceedings Against Capt. Edward Rigby* at the Old Bailey in 1698 is truthful. William Minton told the court that Rigby, to persuade him to be fucked, argued from precedent: 'it's no more than was done in our forefathers' time', and cited elevated role models: 'the French king did it, and the Czar of Muscovy made Alexander, a carpenter, a prince for that purpose'. Rigby was unfortunately entrapped by Minton, who had the police waiting next door, so such arguments were wasted.

A more effective use of the laundry list approach to gay history is described by Charles McNulty, who claims 'I lost my virginity' while watching Larry Kramer's *The Normal Heart*. In that play, angry activist Ned Weeks calls the register:

> I belong to a culture that includes Proust, Henry James, Tchaikovsky, Cole Porter, Plato, Socrates, Aristotle, Alexander the Great, Michelangelo, Leonardo da Vinci, Christopher Marlowe, Walt Whitman, Herman Melville, Tennessee Williams, Byron, E. M. Forster, Lorca, Auden, Francis Bacon, James Baldwin, Harry Stack Sullivan, John Maynard Keynes, Dag Hammarskjöld . . . These were not invisible men.

For McNulty, hearing this list was precisely the boost to self-esteem Weeks claims it should be:

> Plunged into a world of possibilities, I slipped mentally into each of these names, and dreamily paraded them around (with sharp turns and lots of shoulder), each for a moment a perfect fit.

It is probably an over-libidinous response, since Weeks proposes the list to 'demand recognition of a culture that isn't just sexual'. Yet the speech, like the rest of the play, is better as sweeping rhetoric than as part of a coherent argument. Like Marlowe putting his roll call of homosexual warriors in the mouth of an old soldier, Kramer is out to prove a point.

One implication of the speeches in both *Edward II* and *Normal Heart* is that fags can still be tough. Indeed, Weeks omits Oscar Wilde, surely the most famously persecuted gay man his culture has ever known. Maybe it is because he is trying to convince a man who once wanted to be a soldier. Certainly he goes on to eulogize Alan Turing: 'an openly gay Englishman who was as responsible as any man for winning the Second World War'. In singling out Turing, who won the war and committed suicide, and omitting Wilde, who wrote plays and died of syphilis in a Paris hotel room, Weeks chooses a role model he can portray as socially responsible yet cruelly victimized. Turing is an extraordinary, complex figure worthy of admiration, but here he is praised for his contribution to a country which drove him to suicide. At least all Marlowe's soldiers had lovers.

Even theatre queens love men in uniform it seems. Michael Wilcox, editor of Methuen's *Gay Plays* series, has reprinted a number of out of print dramas from the pre-liberation era alongside modern work. The only one of these to have been taken up as a result of this wider circulation is a soldier play, J. R. Ackerley's *The Prisoners of War*. Although first performed in 1925, its 1993 London fringe revival had a topical frisson provided by the debate in Britain and the United States over the legality of their armed forces' ban on the employment of lesbians and gay men. As part of that campaign, activist group OutRage! posthumously outed the old soldiers listed at the start of this chapter, just as Marlowe's phlegmatic lord cites great soldiers and their same-sex lovers to calm his nephew's anxieties about the king's fondness for Gaveston.

The implications of such roll calls raise dilemmas, however, which the pragmatics of campaigning cannot address. Are military leaders really wholesome role models for impressionable young people? Like the priesthood, the armed forces have historically coped with being a haven for homosexuals by exaggeratedly blustering about how monstrous such a presence would be.

In *The Normal Heart*, Kramer via Weeks calls for gay fighters. For some gay men, the urge to prove we are not sissy can cause a disproportionate enthusiasm for the trappings of butch. As long as killing people is regarded as one of the most masculine activities possible, the fetishization of military paraphernalia is inevitable. Many, however, are content to get no closer to active service than dressing up: dancing on the deck in combat trousers. McNulty's frankly swishy response to Kramer's play suggests that audiences can read between the lines of the freaks' roll call. As in *Edward II*, it may be intended to say what great soldiers we are, but also functions as a general corrective to our invisibility. Role models are a risk, however: 'Unhappy the land that needs heroes', cries Andrea in Brecht's play *The Life of Galileo*.

The Laws of Bale

John Bale's play is a determinedly anti-heroic use of the historic homosexuals register. Ironically, his personification of unnatural sexual desire has new resonance with post-gay liberation theatre. In his play, *A Comedy Concerning Three Laws of Nature, Moses and Christ, Corrupted by the Sodomites, Pharisees and Papists Most Wicked*, the character of Sodomy prophesies:

In the first age I began
And so persevered with man
And still will if I can
    So long as he endure.

This was presumably written as a chilling warning in the 1530s, but seems like a statement of queer pride in the 1990s. It would even fit on a T-shirt.

As you might expect from the title, Bale's play tells how God's law is corrupted, through three set-piece confrontations. In successive acts, the laws of nature, Moses and Christ fall prey to sodomites, Pharisees and papists, all of these abstract conceptions being represented as characters in traditional morality style. As a sort of trailer, the Prologue tells us what is to happen, promising, for example, that we will see how:

The law of nature, his [Infidelity's] filthy disposition
Corrupteth with idols, and stinking Sodometry.

The combination of idolatry and sodomy as enemies of mankind is not unique to Bale. In a play of the same period, *Lusty Juventus*, the character of Hypocrisy tells his father, the devil, what he has been up to:

I set up great idolatry
With all kind of filthy sodometry
To give mankind a fall

Bale's theatrical innovation, however, is to make Sodomy a character. Thus, four and a half centuries ago, in a play not staged since the reign of Henry VIII and hardly known outside specialists of Tudor drama, a gay character takes the stage of British drama for the first time.

This is not entirely cause for celebration. *Three Laws* is a play concerned with Sodomy only as a threat to the law of God. The play is a great Christian journey, from the garden of Eden to the present, via the Old and New Testaments, using modern instances to illustrate Bale's theological arguments. In the first act, God the Father sends Law of Nature, Law of Moses and Law of Christ on a mission to instruct mankind. The action of the play will see each under attack from sexual, worldly and heretical foes. Law of Christ will be set upon by the Catholic, via False Doctrine and Hypocrisy; Law of Moses by the greed and ambition of Bale's Pharisees and Jews. The first great moral struggle, however, will be for Law of Nature, who is set upon by characters who bring with them all manner of sexual depravity: monks, witches, prostitutes, midwifes, and even Tudor members of the transgender community.

Act Two is titled 'The Law of Nature Corrupted'. Bale is always concerned that the message of the play is absolutely clear. He signposts the structure and teaching of the piece in a way which would cause great head-shaking amongst modern critics of politically engaged drama. Bale's plays are not closet dramas in any sense: he is writing not just for an intellectual elite, but for anyone he can get to listen. His theatre uses broad characterizations and immediate contemporary references to engage a large, popular audience, watching an open air performance by a touring company. He draws on and develops popular theatre forms, using any which help him get across his message. This creates contradictions, however, since the effect of any theatrical moment can never be entirely planned. Whatever Bale's intentions, there is no guarantee that his plays had the effect he desired in his audience. Indeed, at least one performance seems to have caused a riot against him, the power of theatre inadequate in the face of a hostile audience.

Just as Bale cannot guarantee to convince an audience of his plays, neither can he control responses to the popular theatrical devices he employs. He uses surprise and shock with tabloid enthusiasm, but that relish always has a tang of titillation. In using scandal to entertain, the risk is that you make it more, rather than less, attractive. Thus when Law of Nature meets Infidelity, who insults and teases him, Bale's intention must be to shock us with Infidelity's crude assault:

> Your mouth shall kiss my dock,
> Your tongue shall it unlock

This homoerotic banter is similar to that with which Garcio entertains his audience at the opening of the earlier mystery play *The Killing of Abel*. In the later *A Midsummer Night's Dream*, hole kissing is a great joke for the Athenian audience watching the Wall episode of *Pyramus and Thisbe*. In its use of these populist tricks, *Three Laws* becomes like a sixteenth-century Ed Wood movie, simultaneously condemning and celebrating its material. The staging of the following exchange is one example.

> INFIDELITY I will cause idolatry
> And most vile sodomy
> To work so ungraciously
> Ye shall of your purpose fail.
>
> . . .
>
> LAW OF NATURE God putteth now in my mind,
> To flee thy company.
>
> INFIDELITY You are so blessed a Saint,
> And your self so well can paint
> That I must me acquaint,
> With you, no remedy.
>
> LAW OF NATURE Avoid, thou cruel enemy,
> I will none of thee truly,
> But shurn [avoid] thy company,
> As I would the devil of hells. *[Exit]*

The most appropriate stage activity here is for Infidelity to make a determined pass at Law of Nature. How Bale expected his audience to react to such a presentation of sodomy in action is impossible to know, but the argument of the play condemns such activity. It might have been shocking to its original audience, or funny, or rather exciting – quite likely a mixture. Different audience members presumably reacted in different ways. Even today, right-wing evangelists in the United States use images of gay activity in their publicity, intending to shock; there is no guarantee that the same images do not amuse and arouse instead or as well.

It is unclear whether Infidelity's advances are in earnest, or simply to tease Law of Nature, who is understandably fearful of molestation whilst on his great cleansing mission. It clears the stage in any case, for Infidelity to invoke 'the devil's own kitchen slaves', Sodomy and Idolatry. He calls them with a spell, but Sodomy is already in the wings.

> SODOMY [*offstage*] Ambo is a name full clean,
>   Know ye not what I mean
>   And are so good a clerk.

> INFIDELITY By Tetragrammaton,
>   I charge ye, appear anon,
>   And come out of the dark.

Fittingly, perhaps, the meaning of the first word spoken by Sodomy on (in fact just off) the British stage is not clear. 'Ambo' may just mean 'both': that is, that he and Idolatry are coming, but that interpretation does not quite fit. He certainly seems to be making some innuendo: 'Know ye not what I mean?' A more likely explanation, given the context, is that it is an early abbreviation of 'ambosexous' meaning hermaphrodite. If so, it is an example of that usage more than a century earlier than the *Oxford English Dictionary* records. There is another play on sexual indeterminacy, however, which brings the word in that sense fifty years closer to Bale. In George Chapman's 1604 play *Bussy D'Ambois*, the boyish hero is subject to sodomitical interest from Monsieur, Duc D'Alençon, whose servant calls him 'Sir Ambo'.

Thus from his first utterance, Sodomy reinvents the language. His subsequent emergence is the first coming out in British Drama, and Bale writes his role with zest. Far from a gloomy figure, Sodomy delights in his role. According to the play he enters 'at a dash', singing – indeed almost swishing.

Have in then at a dash
With 'Swash, merry Annet, swash'.
Yet may I not be so rash
For my holy orders sake.

Bale, who lived in a Carmelite monastery from the ages of twelve to nineteen, is specific about Sodomy's costume: 'like a monk of all sects'. The choice presumably plays on popular notions of monkish depravity. The song of Sodomy seems to have been a popular one of the time, and is used in other Protestant propaganda as well as *Ralph Roister Doister*.

The all-singing, all-dancing monk Sodomy is accompanied by Idolatry, whom Bale wants 'decked like an old witch'. Again, the costuming must have been intended to evoke associations in the audience. Punishment by death for sodomy had been confirmed by the King in 1533, about the time of *Three Laws*, but witchcraft would not become a capital offence until 1542. Like the comic countryfolk in *Gammer Gurton's Needle*, she speaks a stage rustic dialect, which takes the edge off her threat.

Infidelity describes Idolatry, perhaps with irony, as 'a pretty minion'. The word is used for paramours of both sexes, and the old witch would have been played by a male performer. Bale gives his scheme for combining the parts, which is carefully planned for the practicalities of performance and the illustration of his themes, but makes no provision for a set of roles in the play specifically suitable for a boy. It seems likely therefore that Idolatry was played, like the other characters, by an adult male. She is therefore closer to the mature women in early English comedy and the Pantomime Dame than the young women played by boys in Elizabethan and Jacobean drama. These mature drag roles tend to be comic where the younger ones are romantic. Bale wants something grotesque, however, and shocks even his own lewd character with the revelation that Idolatry has had some sort of medieval sex-change.

INFIDELITY What, sometime thou wert an he?

IDOLATRY Yea, but now ich am a she,
    And a good midwife perdy.

Passing over the slur on midwifes, resented as independent women and often smeared as witches, here the first transsexual on the British stage emerges only seconds after the first sodomite. It seems that the organizers of modern Lesbian, Gay, Bisexual and Transgender events are with Bale in perceiving a common ground between sexual transgressors. Once again, *Three Laws* is inadvertently up to date in its attitudes.

The ensuing threesome is disgustingly bawdy. Bale writes vividly for these characters. The cloying flirtatiousness of Sodomy with Idolatry, full of obscene double meanings, seems to embarrass even Infidelity:

SODOMY The woman hath a wit,
  And by her gear [clothes, belongings, genitals] can sit.
    Though she be somewhat old
  It is mine own sweet bully
  My muskin [pretty face] and my mully [molly?],
  My gelover [gillyflower: wanton/old woman] and my cully
    [mate, testicle],
    Yea, mine own sweetheart of gold.

INFIDELITY I say, yet not too bold.

The flirtation may also indicate another unwelcome sexual advance, this time from Idolatry towards Infidelity. In any case, it sets Infidelity off on a condemnation of their unfettered sexual appetites. With its fecal and financial imagery, the exchange evokes images of both anal intercourse and prostitution.

IDOLATRY Peace fondling, tush a button.

INFIDELITY What wilt thou fall to mutton
  And play the hungry glutton
    Afore this company?
  Rank love is full of heat,
  Where hungry dogs lack meat
    They will dirty puddings [shit] eat,
  For want of beef and coney. [cock and cunt]

IDOLATRY Hie, minion for money,
  As good is draff [swill] as honey
  When the day is hot and sunny,
    By the blessed rod of Kent.

What follows is Sodomy's great set-piece, the morality play equivalent of a show-stopping number:

My self I so behave,
And am so vile a knave,
As nature doth deprave,
    And utterly abhor.
I am such a vice truly,
As God in his great fury,
Did punish most terribly
    In Sodom and in Gomorre.

In the flesh I am a fire,
And such a vile desire,
As bring men to the mire
    Of foul concupiscence.
We two together began,
To spring and to grow in man,
As Thomas of Aquine scanne [judged],
    In the first book of his 'Sentence'

I dwelt among the Sodomites,
The Benjamites and Madyanites,
And now the popish hypocrites,
    Embrace me everywhere.
I am now become all spiritual
For the clergy of Rome and over all,
For want of wives to me doth fall,
    To God they have no fear.

The children of God I did so move,
That they the daughters of men did love,
Working such ways as did not behove
    Till the flood them over went.
With Noah's son Ham I was half joined,
When he his drunked father scorned
In the Gomorrhites I also reigned,
    Till the hand of God them brent.

I was with Onan not unacquainted
When he on the ground his increase shed,
For me his brethren Joseph accused,

As Genesis doth tell.
David once warned all men of us two
Do not as mules and horses will do
Confounded be they that to images go
    Those are the ways to hell.

Both Esaye and Ezechiel
Both Hieremy and Daniel
Of us the abominations tell,
    With the prophets everyone.
For us two God strake with fyre and water
With battle, with plagues and fearful matter,
With painful exile, then at the latter
    Into Egypt and Babylon.

As Paul to the Romans testify,
The gentiles after Idolatry
Fell to such bestial sodomy,
    That God did them forsake.
Who followeth us as he confess
The kingdom of God shall never possess
And as the Apocalypse express
    Shall sink to the burning lake.

We made Thalon and Sophocles,
Thamiras, Nero, Agathocles,
Tiberius and Aristoteles,
    Themselves to use unnaturally.
I taught Aristo and Fulvius
Semiramis and Hortensius
Crathes, Hyliscus and Pontius
    Beasts to abuse most monstrously.

This is a striking change of mood after the knockabout grotesquery of
the exchanges with Infidelity. It is an extraordinary anti-sermon,
rhetorically and rhythmically rough and ready, but densely packed with
allusions to Biblical and classical history. The places and names are
piled on, one after the other: sometimes Sodomy claims to be working
with Idolatry, at other times alone. Far from making a confession, in
which he asks for all his other crimes to be taken into account, Sodomy
here relishes his outrages.

Bale knows his material. The speech is an encyclopaedic guide to Biblical prohibitions against sodomy and idolatry, with a few other more dubious claims for good measure. Part of the Reformation zeal was to preach the Bible in a language that people could understand. Bale's spirited exegesis here shows the influence of a fire and brimstone pulpit style. It is easy to see how he got the nickname 'bilious Bale'.

Judging from this speech alone, the horrors of Sodomy would seem an obsession. In fact they are a persistent theme throughout Bale's work, both in his theological and historical writings, and the plays *King John* and *Gods Promises*. This speech is his *tour de force*, however, the longest in the whole play, and Bale's comprehensive listing of all sexual crimes. It also allows two related Bale issues to be raised: the wickedness of Rome and its servants, and the unnaturalness of celibate priests. He was no armchair polemicist: not only did he tour the country with these plays, he was himself a married priest and Protestant convert.

Bale's Sodomy may be a robust and extraordinarily self-confident figure, but he is more complex than twentieth-century sexual categorization allows. Bale's conception of the sin of Sodom encompasses all forms of physical lust outside matrimony, including masturbation and bestiality. Unlike the great gay fighters speech Marlowe would write fifty years later, the focus here is not exclusively on sexual acts between males. As the scene continues, however, it is clear that these do particularly vex him, and are intimately bound up with his anti-Catholicism.

This torrent of historical and theological rhetoric is followed by more crudely topical satire at the expense of monks. Infidelity is understandably impressed by Sodomy's aria, and Idolatry full of praise for her partner. In case anyone had still missed the implications of Sodomy's costume, they have some fun with that, but he continues his tirade.

INFIDELITY Marry thou art the devil himself

IDOLATRY If ye knew how he could pelf [steal],
    Ye would say he were such an elf
      As none under heaven were else.

INFIDELITY The fellow is well decked
    Disguised and well necked

Both knave bald and pie-pecked [monkish]
　　He lacketh nothing but bells.

SODOMY In the first age I began
　　And so persevered with man
　　And still will if I can
　　　　So long as he endure.
　　If monkish sects renew
　　And popish priests continue
　　Which are of my retinue
　　　　To live I shall be sure.

　　Clean marriage they forbid
　　Yet can not their ways be hid
　　Men know what hath betid
　　　　When they have been in parel [apparel]
　　Oft have they buried quick [alive]
　　Such as were never sick,
　　Full many a proper trick
　　　　They have to help their quarrel.

　　In Rome to me they fall
　　Both Bishop and Cardinal,
　　Monk, friar, priest and all,
　　　　More rank they are than ants.
　　Example in Pope Julye
　　Which fought to have in his fury,
　　Two lads, and to use them beastly,
　　　　From the Cardinal of Nantes.

This last story, of Pope Julius acquiring two boys for sexual purposes, was a favourite of Bale's. It does not appear in other accounts of Julius' life but does feature in Bale's own book about Popes and also his *Mystery of Iniquity*, published in Geneva in 1545. In the Cambridge University Library copy of the latter, someone has underlined and marked in the margin the passage which refers to this episode. It also includes a similar charge against Cardinal Mendoza, which comes up in Act Four of *Three Laws*.

In King Ferdinand's time in Spain was a cardinal,
Petrus Mendoza was the very man that I mean.
Of lemans [sweethearts] he had great number besides the queen.
One of his bastards was earl, another was duke,
Whom also he abused and thought it no rebuke.

Sodomy's main activity, it seems, is provoking the leaders of the Roman Catholic church to sexual outrages. Buggery, or 'buggerage' is the subdivision of sodomitical activity which Bale most associates with the pope. Infidelity sends Sodomy off to

Study the popes decretals
And mix them with buggerage

and later in the play, Law of Christ confirms the link:

Whiles the pope's oiled swarm reign still in their old buggerage.

Although the scheme of the play passes away from sins against the Law of Nature after Act Two, the obsessive links Bale pursues between what he perceives as the religious heresy of the Roman Church and sexual perversion mean that the themes are reprised in Act Four. Infidelity accuses Law of Christ of both promiscuity and adultery, and appears to attempt the same unsolicited intimacies rejected by Law of Nature earlier in the play. Law of Christ is then offered Benedicte, a whore, for intercourse where he chooses: 'At her purse or arse?'

These are not isolated incidents, argues the play, but intrinsic to the structures of the Roman Church. Infidelity, the ringmaster for all of the attacks on God's three laws, clearly states the case:

Within the bounds of sodomy
Doth dwell the spiritual clergy
    Pope, cardinal and priest,
Nun, canon, monk and friar,
With so many else as do desire
    To reign under Antichrist.

Detesting matrimony
They live abominably
    And burn in carnal lust.

Shall I tell ye further news?
At Rome for prelates are stews [brothels]
Of both kinds. This is just [true].

Although Bale's mode of expression is particularly vehement, the Protestant association of sexual misconduct with Roman Catholicism continued. Christopher Marlowe uses the same costume codes as Bale for his slippery morality play *Doctor Faustus*. Faustus commands one devil:

I charge thee to return and change thy shape.
Thou art too ugly to attend on me.
Go, and return an old Franciscan friar:
That holy shape becomes a devil best.

A story from the time of Bale's youth about a young woman's membership of an order of nuns features in Andrew Marvell's 'Upon Appleton House', written over a century later. In the poem, the all-female Roman Catholic environment is viewed with erotic suspicion, just as Bale shudders at the sodomy of the monastery environment in which he grew up. As late as 1691, *The Fraud of Romish Monks and Priests* is still making identical allegations to Bale's:

I found at last, that they had secret Commerce with Women, or, what is worse, and that I would not willingly name viz. That they were addicted to the abominable sin of Sodomy.

The Homosexual addresses the audience

Bale could be dismissed as a crude, repetitive, single-minded zealot, the Ian Paisley of his day. He was, however, a great theatrical innovator. His *King John* created the new playwriting genre which would develop with Marlowe and Shakespeare's plays on the lives of English kings. As a playwright concerned to create effective political theatre, he can be seen as even further ahead of his times: a disgruntled godfather of agitprop. The style of performance which introduced Sodomy to the British stage in 1530 would be that adopted by the new gay theatre of the 1970s, exemplified by the work of Gay Sweatshop. In this context, Sodomy's great speech ranks first in a heritage of confrontational coming out addresses, which require performance with pride, whatever the purposes for which the pieces were written.

At the opening of Jill Posener's 1975 play *Any Woman Can*, Ginny enters and speaks out front:

You are looking at a screaming lesbian.
A raving dyke,
A pervert, deviant,
Queer fairy, fruitcake, freak,
Daughter, sister, niece, mother, cousin,
Mother in law,
Clippie, actress, bishop's wife, MP,
Machinist, typist, teacher, char,
I'm everywhere.
In your armies, in your schools,
peering out at you of passing trains,
sitting down next to you on the crowded bus
in seat D22, yes sir, right next to you.
I'm here to stay
to infiltrate
to convert.
Mary Mary if you're there, are you aware
that at your Festival of Blight, in your congregation of 20,000
19,000 of your little lambs were standing next to perverts
just like me?
Harrowing thought, isn't it?
Just think, at this precise moment there are lesbian nurses
    touching up
lovely women in hospitals, quite legally . . .
adjusting their dressings round their injured thighs,
washing, rubbing, massaging . . . oh stop it . . .

As with Bale, this is not just a speech of individual self-affirmation, but a contemporary political satire on modern-day sexual zealot Mary Whitehouse and the woeful Christian pressure group the Festival of Light, heirs of Bale's feverish sexual disgust but not his creative talents. Deliberately provocative allusions to sexual depravity in both plays can shock the homophobic but also delight, intellectually and even sexually.

This double reaction was obvious from Gay Sweatshop's first touring show, *Mister X*, a piece in the morality play tradition, in which the Everyman figure of the title encounters various symbolically named characters. Like Bale's group, Gay Sweatshop was a touring company as much concerned with spreading the word as entertaining the punters. One performance in Hendon was disrupted by local evangelists, who found the play's provocative manner and subject matter intolerable. Other hostilities included press outrage in Exeter and questions to Scotland's Procurator Fiscal about the possibility of prosecuting the show as a homosexual act, male homosexuality being still illegal in Scotland at the time.

Both Sweatshop and Bale see themselves as players in greater dramas than a single theatre performance. Bale styles himself 'compiler' rather than playwright on the printed version of *Three Laws*. Similarly, Drew Griffiths and Roger Baker place the writing of *Mister X* as part of a wider, nonfictional project. Both are revolutionary political movements, although gay liberation and the polemical project of *Three Laws* could not be more opposite.

Mr X was written during the summer of 1975 in response to a request from the Campaign for Homosexual Equality that the newly formed gay theatre group Gay Sweatshop, should produce an entertainment for their annual conference in Sheffield. We had all been reading, and had been deeply influenced by, the pamphlet *With Downcast Gays* by Andrew Hodges and David Hutter and this debt, in the composition of the play, must be acknowledged.

Modern gay theatre is often accused of preaching to the converted. This ignores the role drama can play in allowing a group of people to recognize and take strength in their own beliefs and ideas. This communal exhilaration is not ideologically based: what pre-1989 Romanian audience members felt watching coded anti-Communist productions can be the same as the sensation created by powerful Marxist-inspired dramas in Britain. It is a blunt and potentially dangerous instrument, however. When in the service of the beleaguered and disempowered, such work can be uplifting and inspiring; but the same techniques are available for all propagandists, including those who would encourage the strong against the weak.

The potential diversity of response in its audience is the weak link for all propagandist theatre. Some may simply not recognize the allusions, hence the tendency to heavy-handed symbolism: the top-hatted Capitalist, or the monk-habited Sodomy. Others may see what is presented as unsympathetic in a different light. The more convincing the characterization of the enemy, the more powerful the drama, but also the greater risk that our sympathies go in the wrong direction.

Bale did what he could to control the production process of his plays. He has left written instructions on suitable doubling of actors and their costuming. There are suggestions that he sometimes performed the prologues, and certainly used his own servants as actors on occasion. The audience did not always react as he wished, however: violent opposition to some performances is recorded. The cause of their dissension was presumably his religious stance: we will never know how the first steps of Sodomy on the British stage were greeted. Was it to disgust, embarrassed hilarity, shock or some combination of these? More intriguing, did Bale, in presenting this figure, unleash the possibility that this was something of which someone – even if only a character in a play – could feel no shame? The plays may be intended to further opposing causes, but there is not so much to choose between Bale's Sodomy and Gay Sweatshop's Mr X. Except that Mr X is not just a character: at the final speech of the play, Mr X, the play's Everyman figure, walks centre stage and faces the audience, coming out as both character and performer:

> MR X My name is Mr . . . My name is Alan Pope and I live at 10
> Marius Mansions, Marius Road, London SW17 and I'm gay.
> That means I like men . . . sexually, and I don't think I'll
> ever deny that again. And I don't think I'll wonder how I
> became gay ever again or wonder if I'm ill or who's to blame
> or 'somebody up there hates me'. I'm gay and I'm not
> pretending anymore.

It would be a mistake to say that *Any Woman Can* and *Mister X* were beyond John Bale's wildest dreams. On the evidence of *Three Laws*, the nightmares of the Bishop of Ossory were not so far from Gay Sweatshop.

The priest who married Dorothy

In a way, both Sweatshop and Bale relished their occasional theatrical martyrdoms as confirmation that their cause was brave and righteous. What we know of Bale's life story comes from his own autobiographical writings, which support his desire to present himself as a martyr for the English Protestant cause.

John Bale was born in Suffolk in 1495. When he was about twelve years old, his parents sent him to a Carmelite monastery in Norwich, where he remained for seven years. He attended Jesus College, Cambridge between 1514 and 1529, and also studied in Louvain and Toulouse during this time. Soon after he graduated as a Bachelor of Divinity, he left the Carmelite order and converted to Protestantism. All of his works are notable for the zeal of his dedication to his new faith, and the vigour with which he attacks the one in which he had been brought up, particularly the monks by whom he had been surrounded. How much of the depravity of which he accuses them is based on what he saw as a member of the order is impossible to measure, but the ferocity of his denunciations is unmistakeable.

Bale was actually a sexual radical. He married a woman called Dorothy soon after his conversion, and his attacks on the celibacy of the priesthood are in fact defiant of the established religious order of the 1530s. What part, if any, Dorothy played in his decision to convert, or her activities subsequent to their marriage are unknown, however. Although the bulk of the documentation of John Bale's life is his own, he seems not to have considered his wife's role in it worth mentioning.

In the following decade Bale combined two professions: priest and playwright. He had his own touring company of actors, which was at some time sponsored by Thomas Cromwell, King Henry VIII's Chief Minister and the architect of the Church of England's split from Roman Catholicism. At least one performance by the company was attended by Henry's Archbishop of Canterbury, Thomas Cranmer. These connections proved useful to Bale: Cromwell released him after charges of religious unorthodoxy: 'on account of comedies he hath written'. Cromwell was also politically sympathetic on other counts: one of the pieces of legislation he piloted through parliament for Henry was the Buggery Act, which still influences legal debate on gay rights over four centuries later.

With the religious changes taking place in England and Wales in the 1540s and 1550s, Bale came and went with each change of ruler. He left for Germany in 1540, when Cromwell fell from grace with the King and was executed. He returned in 1548 with the accession of Edward VI, who made him Bishop of Ossory in 1552. Arriving in Ireland at a time of heavy English settlement and fortification against the Gaelic people, Bale's determined religious stance proved controversial, and following

Queen Mary's arrival on the throne in 1553, he fled Ireland for the continent, coming back to England only on her death in 1558, later becoming canon of Canterbury Cathedral. He died in 1563.

Bale was part of the revolutionary political movement which would see the triumph of Protestantism in England. His plays are not dry tracts, however, *Three Laws* least of all. They are fired with luscious detail, describing at length the monstrosities he condemns. He is hardly an ally of the religious pamphleteers who would call for the theatre itself to be banned, or who would forbid the representation of Biblical characters on stage, a censorship which three hundred years later stopped Sarah Bernhardt performing Oscar Wilde's *Salome*.

His chief obsession is the wickedness of the Roman Catholic church, and the theatre is one mode of expression through which he can popularize his ideas. One can only speculate on what he saw of life with the Carmelite monks between the ages of twelve and thirty-three that led him to go so fervently to the other side. Since he is clear that Sodomy should be decked like a monk of all sects, there is no specific reference to that order. Posthumous psychoanalytical exploration seems hardly necessary given the openness of his desire to express the grossness and horror of sex between priests and boys – the main entry in his catalogue of revolting popish excesses.

Like the politically influential evangelists of the United States' Christian right, Bale's vehemence as a propagandist leads him to force people's attention on activities of which they might otherwise have continued unaware. The technology may have changed, but direct mail campaigns and television advertisements still seek to bring the same message about the horrors of sodomy to the public at large: broadcasting a video of men in leather dancing together; reprinting a photograph by Robert Mapplethorpe; or summarizing performance art pieces for political rhetoric:

'Jane Alexander [chairwoman of the United States' National Endowment for the Arts (NEA)] defends the slopping around of AIDS-infecting blood!' shouted Representative Robert Dornan of California on the House [of Representatives] floor on Thursday. . .

Mr. [Ron] Athey, who used at most $150 in NEA funds from the Walker Art Center in Minneapolis, did indeed cut a tattoo-like pattern into another man's back as part of a performance using ritual to dramatize his own struggle with suicide and healing. And he did blot the tiny amount of blood with paper towels. But the blood was HIV-negative, not positive, and no blood or towels had any contact with anyone on stage or in the tiny audience, as verified by the Minnesota health authorities.

Robert Dornan and Florida Republican Clifford Stearns were among those arguing for a reduced grant to the NEA as punishment for supporting such work. Grants to four artists, Karen Finley, John Fleck, Holly Hughes and Tim Miller, had already been stopped by former NEA chairman John E. Frohnmayer despite having been recommended, along with those to fourteen other performance artists, by the Endowment's assessment panel. All deal with sexuality; all except Finley are lesbian or gay: Dornan talks of 'porno jerk Tim Miller' and 'Karen jerk scum Finley'. An insistence by other Republicans, including Senator Jesse Helms – whose horror of sodomy makes John Bale look well-adjusted – that obscenity guidelines be attached to NEA grants has also led some organizations to refuse NEA money, including Joseph Papp's Public Theater in New York, where *The Normal Heart* was first produced.

In fact it is unfair to bracket Bale, an artist and theatrical innovator, with these cynical politicians. In the case of Ron Athey's piece, *Four Scenes in a Harsh Life*, neither Dornan nor Stearns had seen the show. Their outrage was based on a press report by someone who also had not seen it, details of which were subsequently contradicted by members of the audience. Ironically, Bale and Athey probably have more in common. Athey is HIV antibody positive, and explores issues of internal and external scarification, including heroin addiction, in his work. He too uses theatre to work out some of the lingering obsessions from a religious upbringing, in this case the sort of Californian Christian fundamentalism espoused by his enemies:

[Athey] says he can't feel judgemental about 'that Christian scene. I'm tolerant because I lived it. And I understand the way they think, so I know there's no dialogue to be had.'

All these years after John Bale preached there, Protestant activism in Ireland can boast Ian Paisley's unsuccessful campaign against homosexual law reform in the north, which sought to 'Save Ulster from Sodomy'. Bale's creative legacy lasts with his political opponents, however. Another English born playwright living in Ireland, John Arden, has written on the links between Bale and the politically engaged writing of the twentieth century including Brecht, and Arden's own work, whose politics are diametrically opposed to Paisley's. Arden's 1988 novel, *Books of Bale*, is a fictional account of John Bale's life which reveals a deep fascination with this contradictory figure.

There is a thin line between Bale's pride in his righteous cause and a zest for martyrdom. He escaped the worst penalties of his time's religious upheavals, but his desire to document the tribulations of himself and his fellow Protestants leads to self-dramatization elsewhere in his work. The desire to perform his own contentious plays in public to sometimes violently disapproving audiences adds to the suspicion that Bale was stimulated by the evidence of his persecution.

Just as Bale's spirited propaganda is not so distant from lesbian and gay pride, his concern to document suffering for a righteous cause is familiar from much lesbian and gay writing today. We love our unfairly persecuted heroines and heroes, like Ned Weeks' Alan Turing, or Larry Kramer's Ned Weeks. Misunderstood by our own times, theatre gives us the chance to be revered by posterity, just as we claim the sufferings of past martyrs as our own. It is a strong rhetorical device, but a dangerous one. Particularly at a time when it is fashionable to deny that real prejudice exists, we can cling to the evidence of our downtrodden state too enthusiastically. We scream slogans claiming we will not be victims, but act like them nevertheless. And the evidence from the ghettos is that we would not know what we would do if we weren't.

Boys R Us

Friendship for Beginners

What could be a more delightful way to spend an evening than watching adolescent boys swear undying love for each other? For the court of Queen Elizabeth, this was a regular highlight of the first half of her reign. Flattering, even fawning portraits of gods and rulers who preferred their chums to marriage provided charming and pathos-packed stories for boy-players to perform. These tales of inseparable chums eulogized non-marital relations, for a woman whose father had had far-reaching problems with the institution, and who would herself eschew it competely. Romantic love between male equals was celebrated and admired, not just in the drama but in other writings, and held up as more admirable than the tawdry materialism of wedlock. Although these idealized relationships bear more resemblance to contemporary gay partnerships than those between straight mates, they are carefully, if not always effectively, steered away from implications of sodomy.

Well-endowed friends

The legendary friendship of two young Greek men in the fourth century BCE inspired the court Christmas show in 1564, *The excellent comedy of two the most faithfullest friends, Damon and Pithias*, performed for Elizabeth by the Children of the Chapel Royal, the queen's choirboys.

Innovative Elizabethan schoolteachers encouraged drama as a way to teach moral lessons and remove inhibitions in their pupils. Richard Mulcaster, the first headmaster of the Merchant Taylors' School, was one enthusiast: a former pupil of Nicholas Udall at Eton, where his taste for the theatre presumably started. Much of the school dramatic repertoire seems to have been Latin drama, performed as an aid to comprehension and oratory. Some teachers, however, wrote their own plays for boys to perform, including Udall, Mulcaster, and Ralph Radcliffe of Hitchin. Sadly, Radcliffe's piece, *The Burning of Sodom and Gomorrah* , is lost – it must have been effective raw material with which to 'remove useless modesty' from the lads.

Choirboys had been performing since English theatre's first stirrings, and the Masters of the Chapel Royal singers are among its first playwrights. William Cornish wrote *Troilus and Pandar* for the boys as early as 1516. This is also lost, but is presumably a tale of sexual procurement: again fruity material, but appropriate as a means to instil what Mulcaster termed 'good behaviour and audacity'.

Richard Edwards, Master of the Chapel Children from 1561, wrote *Damon and Pithias* for his boys and the queen. His later play *Palamon and Arcite* is now lost, but was also based on a pair of legendary male friends, whose story would be dramatized again fifty years later in Fletcher and Shakespeare's *The Two Noble Kinsmen*. His subject matter is well suited to the boys' resources: the cast of *Damon and Pithias* is entirely male, avoiding the need for transvestite presentation. Female roles had been taken by other boys, but the spirited drag required for Gammer Gurton or Dame Custance was perhaps inappropriate to these command performances. The titles of plays performed by school and chapel groups suggest instead an enthusiasm for heroines in deadly, and often sex-related, crisis. These could be Biblical: Susannah wrongly accused of adultery, Judith risking all for the sake of her city; or Classical: queen Dido's suicidal despair was popular well before Marlowe wrote his boys' play about her. Pathos and virtuous suffering were part of the boy actors' repertoire: Edwards presumably used those talents to effect in his friendship plays, where young men are pushed to similar tear-jerking self-sacrifice.

Some idea of the proverbial adoration between the two young men comes from their happy servant, Stephano:

One Damon of Greece, a gentleman bought me.
To him I stand bound, yet serve I another,
Whom Damon my master loves, as his own brother.
A gentleman too, and Pithias he is named,
Fraught with virtue, whom vice never defamed.

What he describes is not Greek love, but a more contemporary notion. Oxford University, which Edwards attended, would became a hotbed of Euphuism in the next decade. Its name comes from the Greek word *euphyes*: variously translated as 'well-endowed', 'graceful' and 'goodly', and indicates a rather precious style of writing and argument which influenced many Elizabethan writers, among them Robert Greene – 'the Ape of Euphues' according to Gabriel Harvey in *Four Letters* (1592); Thomas Lodge – author of *Rosalynde*, the story on which *As You Like It* is based; and George Pettie. The key text was John Lyly's best-selling prose romance, *Euphues*, published more than ten years after *Damon and Pithias* was written.

Lyly would go on to write his own plays for the boys, but *Euphues* echoes *Damon and Pithias* in its ideal version of male bonding. Stephano describes the boys as:

All one in effect. All one in their going,
All one in their study, all one in their doing.
These gentlemen both, being of one condition,
Both alike of my service have all the fruition.
Pithias is joyful, if Damon be pleased.
If Pithias be served, then Damon is eased.
Serve one, serve both; so near, who would win them?
I think they have but one heart between them.

In Lyly's book, the friendship between Euphues and Philautus is described in similarly harmonious terms:

But after many embracings and protestations one to another they walked to dinner, where they wanted neither meat, neither music, neither any other pastime; and having banqueted, to digest their sweet confections they danced all that afternoon. They used not only one board but one bed, one book (if so be it they thought not one too many). Their friendship augmented every day, insomuch that the one could not refrain the company of the other one minute. All things went in common between them, which all men counted commendable.

A rift between these devoted friends occurs only when love for a woman intervenes, and Euphues replaces Philautus in the affections of Lucilla. Similar jealousies destroy the idealized friendship of Palamon and Arcite in *The Two Noble Kinsmen*, and presumably also in Edwards' lost play. Women are fickle in this male fantasy world, however, and Lucilla moves on to yet another lover, Curio. The two youths are left to reflect how friendship between men is stronger than love between men and women.

In his prose work, Lyly can get away with a minimal plot, as an excuse for extensive euphuistic correspondence. The drama of male friendship requires a little more action, however. Set in Syracuse, during the reign of the notorious tyrant King Dionysius, *Damon and Pithias* flirts with politics in its portrait of a ruler vulnerable to flattery and paranoia, which may glance at Elizabethan intrigues. Damon is unjustly arrested for spying, and sentenced to death, which leads Pithias to an outburst of grief. He calls for music to accompany his sorrow, and sings:

> Grip me you greedy griefs
>   And present pangs of death,
> You sisters three with cruel hands,
>   With speed now stop my breath.
> Shrine me in clay alive,
>   Some good man stop mine eye,
> Oh death come now, seeing I hear
>   Damon my friend must die.

Such alliteration, stock phrasing and emotional excess appear in Peter Quince's play *Pyramus and Thisbe*, performed for the court of Athens at the end of *A Midsummer Night's Dream*. The role of Thisbe, played by the boy actor Francis Flute, parodies the tear-jerking self-sacrifice of the early Chapel plays. Thirty years after Pithias makes his pathetic lament, Flute as Thisbe will despair over the dead Pyramus in similar terms:

> O Sisters Three
> Come come to me,
> With hands as pale as milk;
>   Lay them in gore,
>   Since you have shore
> With shears his thread of silk.

Damon is allowed home on bail, with Pithias offering to remain as surety. If Damon does not return, Pithias will be executed in his place. The offer of self-sacrifice by a devoted friend reappears, in a more sophisticated form, when Antonio pledges a pound of his flesh for Bassanio in *The Merchant of Venice*. To die for one's friend is the ultimate sacrifice, whose purity is emphasized by the reaction of the executioner, Gronno.

> GRONNO Here is a mad man I tell thee. I have a wife whom I love
> well, and if ich [I] would die for her, chould [would] ich were
> in Hell. Wilt thou do more for a man than I would for a
> woman?

> PITHIAS Yea, that I will.

Here the love of one man for another is explicitly demonstrated to be deeper than that of a man for his wife. In other works, the contrast between masculine love (friendship between men) and effeminate love (a man's lust for a woman) is enacted through the shifting loyalties of the same characters: Euphues and Philautus in Lyly's book, or Palamon and Arcite in *The Two Noble Kinsmen*. Here the contrast is different: Gronno is a working man, whose regional accent marks him out as a social inferior to Pithias and the elite audience of the play. Ideal friendship thus becomes an indication of a higher sensibility, confusing to the lower orders, unless, like the presumably unmarried Stephano, actually in the service of such a male couple. In placing wedlock and its concerns on a baser plane than that of pure feeling, Edwards may be aiming flattery at Elizabeth, at that time openly maintaining to parliament her own aversion to marriage.

When it looks like Damon has skipped bail and not returned, Pithias prepares to die, no less in love with his friend for being abandoned. His love will continue even after death:

> Oh my Damon farewell now for ever, a true friend to me most dear.
> Whiles life doth last, my mouth shall still talk of thee
> And when I am dead my simple ghost, true witness of amity,
> Shall hover about the place wheresoever thou be.

At the last moment, however, just as Pithias is about to be executed on his behalf, Damon rushes in. Each of them then pleads to be killed in place of the other:

> DAMON Oh my Pithias, now farewell for ever, let me kiss thee or I
> die,

> My soul shall honour thee, thy constant faith above the
> heavens shall fly

Such devotion on the scaffold would be hard to perform today without becoming cloying or faintly absurd. It is, however, sufficiently moving to the tyrant Dionysius for him to pardon them both, and ask if he can join their band of brothers.

Although all ends happily, there are fewer laughs in *Damon and Pithias* than in fruitier plays like *Ralph Roister Doister* or *Gammer Gurton's Needle*. It is impossible to judge whether Richard Edwards was simply a less smutty writer, or deliberately tailoring his material to what would be acceptable in front of the queen. Bawdy comic moments do occur, however, with Grimme the Collier. He passes comment on the underdevelopment of the sexual organs in two of the characters: perhaps played by the younger boys. Edwards is said to have been a 'great player of plays' and it has been suggested that he took the minor role of Grimme himself. Few teachers today would write a role requiring them to make humorous reference to their pre-pubescent pupils' genitalia, much less perform it in front of their employer and head of state. These were clearly very different times.

Damon and Pithias love each other to death, almost. Their mutual adoration brings admiration rather than scorn: it is the reason they survive. As role models for lifelong love between men, they are cited by Erasmus in one of his letters. Over three hundred years later, their story again inspired drama: John Banim wrote a version in 1821, revised and altered twenty years later by the Byron-influenced Richard Lalor Sheil. At one point, Edwin Forrest was performing in Banim and Sheil's *Damon and Pythias or the Tyrant of Syracuse*, while a one-act farce on the same subject by J. B. Buckstone was simultaneously running elsewhere in London.

Given their popularity during periods when sexual relations between men were condemned and actively prosecuted, the authors of the Damon and Pithias plays presumably do not intend the two youths to be interpreted as sodomites. Just as in Lyly's book 'all men counted commendable' the inseparable Euphues and Philautus, the love between Damon and Pithias is so pure that it serves a role model for a monarch in Edwards' play. Lyly comments elsewhere that a sodomite is 'a most dangerous and infectious beast'. These things are not always clear cut:

Christopher Marlowe, born in the year *Damon and Pithias* was performed, would tease a later Elizabethan audience to both loathing and admiration in his portraits of religious, political and sexual heretics. The moral flaws of Faustus, Barabas or the Duke of Guise are hardly discreet, however. If Damon and Pithias are closet sodomites, Edwards gives us no clue to it.

It does not take a depraved and ahistorical imagination, however, to suggest that this legendary love between two young men could go beyond hand-holding and the occasional manly hug. That the love of Damon and Pithias could have a sexual dimension is clear from the diatribe of the determinedly anti-sodomitical Captain Tucca in Thomas Dekker's scabrous satire *Satiromastix*. Tucca advises the poet Horace, a thinly disguised Ben Jonson, about his fellow poets Crispinus and Demetrius (John Marston and Dekker):

> they shall be thy Damons and thou thy Pithyasse

The wordplay on 'asse' is hardly accidental, in a play full of obscene speculation on the sexual activities of its characters. Although written forty years after Edwards' play, and part of a savage war between London's rival poets, *Satiromastix* is a play, also written for boys to perform, which is quite aware that classical friendship can be used as a metaphor for contemporary sodomy. Indeed, it seems to mock those who cannot see the connection. The absurd Tucca later invokes other Classical images of male bonding:

> lend me thy hand, thou and I hence forth will be Alexander and
> Lodwicke, the Gemini, sworne brothers: thou shall be Perithous
> and Tucca Theseus

Lodowick proved his loyalty for his identical friend Alexander when he married the Princess of Hungary in the other's name. He placed a naked sword between himself and his wife each night, in order to stop him having sex with his friend's rightful bride. The Princess's response to this intriguingly phallic manouvre has received less attention. Webster knew the story in 1613 or so, when he referred to it in his play *The Duchess of Malfi*. Shakespeare and John Fletcher's *The Two Noble Kinsmen*, written around the same time, describes the 'intertangled roots of love' belonging to Theseus and Pirithous. Tucca swears friendship, albeit deliberately feigned, using as role models men whose ability to put their pal before their wife has a distinctly sexual element. Dekker's putting the ass into Damon and Pithias may indicate Tucca's obtuseness: that he uses them as an example when he *does* have sodomy in mind may emphasize the absurdity of his accusation in their case. It is, of couse, possible to maintain contradictory positions. Many of those who profess a distaste for homosexuality as an abstract notion are nevertheless charming to their lesbian or gay dinner guests or family members. This is not simply hypocrisy, but a mechanism which allows reality to be perceived, albeit dimly.

Bedtime stories

Some still are determined to separate devoted friendship from the taint of homosexuality. Even in 1995, Ivy Compton-Burnett's biographer is vigorous in the insistence that two women's lifelong friendship need not (and the subtext is 'should not') imply lesbianism. What is significant here is not what Dame Ivy did in bed (or not) with Margaret Jourdain, but that it should still be necessary to police that particular boundary so heavily.

The legal boundaries between friendship and homosexuality were directly examined in one of the sorriest legal spectacles of 1995, the disastrous libel action taken by the Conservative MP David Ashby against *The Sunday Times*. Ashby argued that sharing 'not only one board but one bed' with another man was no evidence that he was homosexual. With his ex-wife in court giving evidence for the newspaper against him, Ashby faced a jury which, whether or not it thought his friendship commendable, concluded that it was probably also homosexual. The *Guardian*, bastion of liberal homophobia, found itself baffled: 'At what point . . . does male friendship develop into homosexuality?' it asked, a thin coating of irony hardly concealing its concern to determine the boundary:

> Does there have to be full sex? Does there have to be any sex at all? Though the two men admitted sharing a room in France, did that alone constitute a gay liaison? . . . Supposing Ashby and Kilduff cuddled but did not have sex, was that enough to declare gayness? . . . Is his heterosexuality – in evidence during much of his marriage – now compromised, even negated?

Physical contact is the key. If 'cuddles' were enough to discredit David Ashby, then the embracings of Euphues and Philautus would look ill to a contemporary jury. Their documented rivalry over Lucilla would not protect them, any more than Ashby's heterosexual record, which the *Guardian* gallantly defends.

The *Guardian* is unhelpful on what it considers 'full sex' for lesbians. Bewilderment about the practicalities of sex without a penis may account for the rather higher level of discussion about the definitions of female friendship and lesbianism. Lesbian history has grappled with the dilemma extensively: do historical romantic friends 'count' as lesbians in the absence of evidence of sexual activity? Would a forty-year marriage be considered valid purely for the sexual activity of its participants? The devotion of Elizabethan male friends, particularly in its rejection of marriage, surely parallels many more contemporary gay male partnerships than it does the bonding of heterosexual men.

There is, however, an alternative argument: that sex itself is our heritage, and that we risk ignoring the possibility of sexual expression – particularly between women – by concentrating on romantic friends and rejecting any investigation of the potential sexual components of relationships. It is a position which is broader in its definition of sexual possibility, with no need to become obsessed about emission. Just as one Jacobean judge requires:

> Note, Sodomy is with mankind, and is Felony, and to make that Offence, *Oportet rem penetrare et semen naturae emittere et effundere*; for the Indictment is, *Contra ordinationem creatoris et naturae ordinem rem habiut veneream dictung; puerium canaliter cognovit*; and so it was held in the Case of Stafford, *Paederastes amator puerorum.*

Alan Bray has written interestingly on the symmetry between the (admired) masculine friend and the (despised) sodomite in Elizabethan England. Such determined separation of the two categories in Edwards' world helps to explain why Damon and Pithias were suitable entertainment for an unmarried queen. Fifty years later, with James I on the English throne, playwrights were less innocent in their treatment of male friendship, now a subject of major political importance. The purity, selflessness and non-sexual nature of masculine friendship were now in question. Damon and Pithias become examples of not just a naive and old-fashioned model of friendship, but also a sentimentalizing and now outmoded drama. The boy companies were now acting sexual and political satire so ruthless that it risked imprisonment for its authors, a long way from Edwards' careful flattery of his queen.

By dramatizing male devotion Edwards, and other writers of plays depicting friendship, would increase the dilemma of its representation, and the risk of confusion with the love against God's and the natural order. The business of audience-pleasing introduces a certain crudeness and comic sexual reference even in *Damon and Pithias*, but these are little willy jokes, and do not bear directly on the title characters. The theatre was inherently more risky than prose, however. Alan Bray concludes of sodomy that:

> its shadow was never far from the flower-strewn world of Elizabethan friendship and it could never wholly be distinguished from it.

On the pages of Lyly's *Euphues* books, the moral tone is carefully controlled. In their prose, the possibilities of sodomy can be buried beneath the flowers of friendship, to be unearthed only by determined textual excavations of a later age. On the stage, however, the necessity of conjuring images for an audience is fraught with danger. Imagine a stage version, in which are presented Euphues and Philautus' inability to remain apart, their 'many embracings and protestations one to another' and use of 'one board . . . one bed, one book'. The physical staging of Euphues and Philautus entwined would provide images, for some in the audience at least, of love expressed through more than simply dancing together all afternoon after a good lunch.

This, certainly, was the view of those who assaulted the English theatre in the late sixteenth century. Most agreed that plays made people think about sex, which was a bad thing. They were vexed by the spectacle of transvestite performance, yet equally opposed to the sight of women on stage. Although some exempted academic and other dramas whose moral credentials could be assured, the public stage causes shudders of disgust in every pamphlet. If the theatre was by its very nature immoral and a stimulant to lustful thoughts, stage presentations of male friendship could hardly hope to keep their pure distance from the shadow of sodomy.

One irony emphasizes the sodomitical potential of the theatre, compared to the greater respectability of prose. Euphuism, the literary style to which Lyly's prose work gave its name, was encouraged among Oxford students in the 1580s by the popular lecturer John Rainolds. This man, who would influence not just Lyly, but other future playwrights, including Robert Greene, would also write some of the most vehement attacks on the theatre to which his former students were contributing, collected as *Th' Overthrow of Stage-Playes* in 1599. A lecturer who could inspire a literary movement exemplified by a prose work of love between men, and whose main exponents would be dramatists, was a fierce opponent of the presentation of anything at all – let alone human feelings – on any stage.

I love, Hephestion, I love

A love between men from antiquity even better known than that of Damon and Pythias is that between Alexander the Great and Hephaestion. It lasted from their boyhood until Hephaestion's early death, just a year before that of Alexander. Both were military commanders, Alexander the greatest of his time. Their devotion was so great that Alexander, who had conquered virtually every country he knew existed, broke down on his lover's death, wailing and refusing to eat, clutching the decaying corpse to him. The combination of mighty warrior and tearful lover has captured the imagination of writers from Plutarch to Mary Renault, and has become a useful reference point for those wanting to argue for the noble, manly possibilities of same-sex love. The two lead a catalogue of comparisons to Edward II and Piers Gaveston made in Marlowe's play.

Social inequalities are inevitable in relationships with a monarch, but Hephaestion was a Macedonian noble, not a stable-boy or slave. In addition, he and Alexander are almost exact contemporaries. Their love resembles the easy fraternity of equals with which Damon and Pithias seduce another king, Dionysus. Edward and Gaveston were also more evenly matched than their opponents claim: hostile accounts falsify the latter's status, age and nationality.

John Lyly chose the legendary friendship between Alexander and Hephaestion as the backdrop for his own play, *Campaspe* (1581), about the emperor's unsuccessful love for a woman. Called the 'vicemaster of

Paul's', Lyly was the great playwright of Elizabethan same-sex friendship, both male and female. He knew his Plutarch, for it was in paraphrasing the Greek that he made his comment that a sodomite was 'a most dangerous and infectious beast'. Whatever it is that keeps sex offstage in his pictures of same-gender love, it is not ignorance of its possibility. In *Campaspe*, which may be his first play, the choice to subdue the relationship between Alexander and Hephaestion to the main plot of love for a woman is hardly accidental. Later works would flirt with other male relationships – Ganymede accompanies Jupiter silently in *The Woman in the Moon* – although his portraits of female characters in love have had the most lasting influence.

Campaspe is one of those whom Alexander has captured during his conquest of Thebes. He confides his love of her to Hephaestion, who advises him that such love for a woman is dangerous to his role as a military leader. In a huge speech of persuasion, Hephaestion's passion for Alexander is translated into loyal advice: 'man hast a camp to govern, not a chamber'. There is no sense of direct competition for Alexander's love, but Campaspe represents 'the maidenly skirmishes of love' rather than 'the fiery assaults of war' and Hephaestion clearly wants Alexander safely back in the man's world. This removal of personal motivation from Hephaestion is part of his moral elevation as a character. He still loves Alexander, but selflessly, as no woman can do.

Like *Antony and Cleopatra*, *Campaspe* dramatizes the catastrophic effects of heterosexual surfeiting. In a twist on the gays in the military debate, two Macedonian officers Clitus and Parmenio report that effeminacy – love for women – is ruining Alexander's army, hitherto famous for its effective all-male training, bonding and loyalty. This might seem a misogynist view for a piece to be performed by boys to a queen, but Elizabeth is ruler before she is a woman: Alexander not Campaspe. She is flattered in the portrait of a great general, herself having reigned for over twenty years of peace, with the Armada yet to come.

Lyly's avoidance of sodomite implications between Alexander and Hephaestion is not the only way in which he sexually sanitizes the source material. He also omits the Rape of Timoclea as inappropriate for his purposes. Only in his sub-plot, featuring the cynic philosopher Diogenes, does Lyly indulge in unsavoury sexual matters. Like

Campaspe, Diogenes challenges Alexander's status, but where hers is the passive effect of her beauty, his is through a deliberate snub. When the king calls for him, the philosopher refuses, preferring to sit in his tub reading Greek to a young boy.

Alexander is tempted by Campaspe, Diogenes by the courtesan Lais. When Diogenes finally does advise Alexander, his misogyny is even more extreme than Hephaestion's:

ALEXANDER What dost thou dislike chiefly in a woman?

DIOGENES One thing.

ALEXANDER What?

DIOGENES That she is a woman.

Unlike Hephaestion, however, Diogenes is implicated in sodomy. His servant Manes, with whom he has a vigorously sadomasochistic relationship, says to Psyllus, one of the other servants in the play, that he will not see his master until midnight, claiming: 'I have a back way into his tub'. Diogenes lives simply in a tub as part of his basic philosophy that nothing should be concealed. Manes' remark might just refer to sneaking in late, were it not for Psyllus picking up on it:

PSYLLUS Which way callest thou the back way, when every way is open?

MANES I mean to come in at his back.

There is no back door to a tub, so Manes will come in behind Diogenes' own back, so as not to be seen. The double meaning of 'I mean to come in at his back' confirms the buggery in all this talk of back ways.

As in *Damon and Pythias*, it is the smaller boys, who presumably played the servants, who get the smuttiest double meanings. This popular contrast of innocence and knowingness, in which those who speak the words can hardly be blamed for any offence they cause, offsets potential objections to such exchanges. This allowed the boys companies' greater satirical licence at the end of the sixteenth century, although this would eventually get out of hand, landing many of their playwrights in prison.

Campaspe is indirectly a play about a great love between men, but it is also the first closet play. It is more noble for the love-struck hero to deny the sexual desire which shames him and sets him apart from his society. Here Lyly uses it as a way to handle a man's choice between the masculine world of statecraft and war, and the feminine world of marriage and sex.

Later playwrights, after the separation of conscious and subconscious desires, would play with the theme as a way to explore self-sacrifice in same-sex love. Terence Rattigan was the supreme dramatist of the closet: Hester Collyer in *The Deep Blue Sea* is an Alexander who does give way to passion, disastrously. There are even unlikely rumours of a secret draft in which she is actually a suicidal homosexual man. Rattigan's own closetedness, however, always feeds his work. Whatever the permutations of gender and plot, the exquisite, lonely torment of a secret love is rarely missing.

Misogyny triumphs in *Campaspe*. Diogenes and Hephestion get their way, and Alexander leaves the woman he loves. He rejoins the men's world of conquest and killing, setting off to attack Persia. Although the theme of masculine friendship goes in and out of fashion, war remains its stronghold. In Shakespeare, men's love is rarely so innocent, and full-blown romantic friendship is usually reserved for women. It makes itself felt from offstage, however, in *Henry V*, with the Duke of Exeter's speech about the deaths of the Dukes of Suffolk and York in battle:

> Suffolk first died, and York, all haggled over
> Comes to him, where in gore he lay insteeped,
> And takes him by the beard, kisses the gashes
> That bloodily did yawn upon his face,
> And cries aloud, 'Tarry, dear cousin Suffolk.
> My soul shall keep thine company to heaven.
> Tarry, sweet soul, for mine, then fly abreast,
> As in this glorious and well-foughten field
> We kept together in our chivalry.'
> So did he turn, and over Suffolk's neck
> He threw his wounded arm, and kissed his lips,
> And so espoused to death, with blood he sealed
> A testament of noble-ending love.

This is a tear-jerker for him, the king and the audience. Imminent espousal to death allows men to appreciate otherwise suppressed passions, as the poetry of the First World War testifies in the twentieth century.

5

Lesbian Double Cherries

Snatches of Poetry

'Were kisses all the joys in bed, One woman would another wed', William Shakespeare is supposed to have written. Whether it was him or not, the quip reflects two notions about women's sexuality popular in the theatre of Shakespeare and his contemporaries. One is still extraordinarily prevalent: that sex requires a penis. This is used to quell any unease caused by the other: that women might well prefer love without men.

Romance and sensual intimacy are regularly portrayed in female relationships which seem to lack nothing, until the problem of the absent dick stops them short. This is perhaps unsurprising in works written by men, and performed by men and boys. Lesbianism requires the absence of the gender exclusively allowed to create theatre at the time. It remains an impossibility on stage, as long as it is unknowable by those who manufacture the illusions. Literally unknowable, in the word's sexual sense, by men, love between women is lavishly represented, but heavily circumscribed, in pre-Restoration theatre.

Like romance between men, passionate female friendship is often idealized. It causes a problem, however, when it suggests that women do not actually need men as a context for their lives. It is therefore imagined as the practice of a better land, but a distant one, an impossible Eden, or the lost playground of childhood. In the absence of potential husbands, fathers become key figures in deciding the fate of such women, who cannot be allowed the freedom of Damon and Pithias, just to run off together.

The passage from love for another woman into wedlock with a man is not a psychological development in this period, but a compulsory social and economic one. Marriage is an inescapable sentence. The pressures on poorer women were greater (see chapter nine), but even the leisured heiresses of Elizabethan comedy frolic beneath its shadow. Its inevitability frames any outburst of female independence.

A toy made for ladies

The original lesbian takes to the English stage in 1582, in John Lyly's second play, *Sappho and Phao*. As in *Campaspe*, he uses classical history as his source, and deliberately stages romance between a man and a woman as his main plot. In *Campaspe* he takes the better-known love between Alexander and Hephaestion for granted, making his play the story of Alexander's love of Campaspe. In his Sappho play, the title makes clear that it is based on the dubious story of her love for a man.

Biographical information about Sappho is sparse and unreliable. She is, nevertheless, without doubt the archetypal Lesbian, having lived on the Greek island of Lesbos around 600 BCE, and lesbian, for her poetry full of passionate love for other women. The story of her unrequited love for Phaon the ferryman is certainly an invention, first recorded in comedies written two hundred years after her death, best known from an even later poem attributed to Ovid. 'No more the Lesbian dames my passion move . . . ' she complains, before launching into the unhappy romance which results in her throwing herself over a cliff. For those uneasy with Sappho's love for women, the story of this disastrous dalliance with a man has proved an easy way to confirm prejudices about the impossibility of love and sex between women.

Lyly used the Ovid poem as the source for *Sappho and Phao* but the play shows his awareness of that other love, which he sets to one side. That Elizabethan poets knew of Sappho's desires for women is clear in a poem by John Donne, twenty years older than Lyly, in which she speaks of her love for Philaenis. James Holstun calls it the first explicitly lesbian love elegy in English but it is too expressive for one modern editor of Donne, who will not believe such sentiments could come to the mind of a man who became Dean of St Paul's Cathedral. 'I find it difficult to imagine him wishing to assume the love-sickness of Lesbian Sappho', she says. The difficulty even carries into the typography: that careful capital on 'Lesbian', which makes the poet a resident of the Aegean island, rather than a practitioner of the love that bears her name. A twentieth-century editor finds herself unable to imagine a seventeenth-century poet imagining the feelings of another poet in the fourth century BCE. What can hardly be imagined, even at one remove – and only with difficulty – is lesbianism, or rather, 'love-sickness'.

Given this continuing pussy-footing, Lyly's treatment of Sappho does not seem so extraordinary. His second play reworks some of the misogyny of his first. In Ovid's poem, Sappho is bored with lesbian love. At the opening of *Sappho and Phao*, Venus the goddess of love sets out to 'yoke the neck that yet never loved', which suggests that women don't count, a philosophy consistent with that expressed by most of the men in *Campaspe*. It is not, however, a simple celebration of the benefits brought by relationships between men and women.

Venus makes the ambitious ferryman Phao beautiful as a tool in her sport with Sappho: an early toy boy. Sappho and Phao hardly meet in the play, whose main appeal is the battle between two strong women. Sappho, surrounded by ladies who come and go talking of men, is an Elizabethan noblewoman, relatively unruffled by the manipulations of the goddess. Even when vexed by Venus, she is still ordering one of her women to give Cupid sweetmeats: 'O Spiteful Venus! Mileta, give him some of that. What else Cupid?' Her languid distraction suggests that Lyly's choir boys managed an elegant realization of the women they played, rather than the rough and tumble of Udall's Dame Custance or Edwards' Gammer Gurton. What they do not approach is the depth of passion in Sappho's own poetry, or even in Donne's impersonation of her.

Just as the violence and sexual complexity of his raw material are evaded in *Campaspe*, Lyly tones down his sources and eases away from potential tragedy here. Cupid tells Sappho that he has been instructed to strike her with disdain of Phao, rather than resolve to throw herself off a cliff as she does in Ovid. In a reversal of a later popular theory about lesbian or gay desire, her love of Phao turns out to be only a passing phase.

If written for a Hollywood studio, *Sappho and Phao* could have starred Bette Davis and Joan Crawford and survived as a classic camp video. Indeed, if staged as a play within the film, Bette Davis could have doubled Venus with Queen Elizabeth I, for whom the play was performed. A recent editor of Lyly's play suggests that the old queen was the reason *Sappho and Phao* evades lesbianism.

About Sappho's supposed 'lesbianism' or 'Sapphism' in the homosexual sense . . . If Lyly was aware of the allegation, as he probably was . . . he seems to have chosen to overlook the matter as entirely unsuited to his project of flattering Queen Elizabeth.

The distaste which drips from this passage reveals the editor's 1991 anxieties about lesbianism, albeit cloaked in the royal drag of the 1580s. There is at least one reference to 'the allegation' in the play. After she has recovered from her misdirected amour for Phao, Sappho sits with Cupid and assures him:

Cupid, fear not. I will direct thine arrows better. Every rude ass shall not say he is in love. It is a toy made for ladies, and I will keep it only for ladies.

Making a speech rich with sexual puns, Sappho sits with desire in her lap. Cupid's pointed love-shafts will be under her control from now on, she promises. Love is 'a toy made for ladies', and one that she will be keeping exclusively for them in future.

Like *Damon and Pithias* and *Campaspe*, other plays for Queen Elizabeth, this one celebrates the unmarried state. For the first time, however, it does so in a world which is predominantly female, with a female protagonist. Campaspe is hardly an active participant in the play to which she gives her name: indeed it was published as *Alexander, Campaspe and Diogenes*, reflecting which roles were most popular in its performance. Using the talents of his single-sex cast, Lyly at least began to explore what late twentieth-century critics would still find agony to imagine: women's passionate love for each other.

Spunky girls

Lyly married a Yorkshire heiress, Beatrice Brown, in 1583 after writing *Campaspe* and *Sappho and Phao*. Following this, his treatment of marriage softens, as does the misogyny, which had already begun to mellow in *Sappho and Phao*. Sappho may have been his first Lesbian, but lesbians 'in the homosexual sense' triumph in *Gallathea* (1584), a play in which two young women are sent off to be married, courtesy of divine intervention. It is one of the most important plays to celebrate love between women in British theatre, despite (or maybe because of) which, it has been virtually ignored for four hundred years.

The all-female hunting band led by the goddess Diana offered male Renaissance painters a rich subject for lesbian fantasy. She appears in Lyly's play to argue against marriage, as Hephaestion in *Campaspe* did. His argument to his king is a condemnation of the snares of women. From the opposite gender perspective, in *Gallathea* a goddess teaches three love-struck nymphs of the inadequacy of boys.

> And how is your love placed? Upon petting boys, perhaps base of birth, without doubt weak of discretion. Aye, but they are fair. Oh ladies. Do your eyes begin to love colours, whose hearts were wont to loathe them. Is Diana's chase become Venus's court? And are your holy vows turned to hollow thoughts?

That she and her nymphs were being performed by boys, who might well be beautiful but also petting, base of birth and indiscreet, was part of the fun. Where she and Hephaestion coincide, nevertheless, is on the disruptive effects of unregulated heterosexual love in a well-run court. Fired with annoyance at Cupid, the nymphs then plan to rip the boy to pieces as punishment for disseminating desire, a far more violent response than the dandling he gets from Sappho for the same offence.

The main plot of *Gallathea* is an explicitly transvestite pastoral, which plays on the cross-dressing conventions of the Elizabethan stage in a way which significantly influences Shakespearian comedy. It is indebted to classical poetry for its world of nymphs and shepherds gambolling with gods, and Lyly's main source was probably Ovid again. Yet, like the Arden of *As You Like It*, the Navarre of *Love's Labour's Lost* or the wood near Athens of *A Midsummer Night's Dream*, its setting is a distinctly English landscape. *Gallathea* has a specific geography, that of north Lincolnshire and Humberside, near Beatrice Brown's home.

This local detail is not just decorative, for the Humber estuary has a dramatic significance in the play. Every five years the fairest and most chaste virgin in all the country has to be taken there and bound to a tree. Leaving aside the question of whether there can be degrees of chastity, her fate is that a monster either drowns her, devours her or takes her to the sea-god Neptune – which amount to much the same thing. The monster, called the Agar, is a sort of tidal wave created by a sudden rush of water into a narrow estuary, and is an observed meteorological event on the Humber.

It is also a vivid example of the sort of suffering once favoured for the pathetic leading ladies of boys' plays, as it was for the similarly wriggling heroines of the early cinema – although they tended to be tied to tracks, and in danger of demolition by mechanical monsters. Both exploit the erotic possibilities of an innocent in sexual danger. The Agar is technically an 'eagre', but also a 'bore'. Even without that pun on piercing, it is hardly over-eager to find a sexual undercurrent in the ravishing of this maiden by a sudden burst of pent-up liquid along a narrow channel. When Leontes in *The Winter's Tale* claims 'And many a man there is . . . holds his wife by th'arm, That little thinks she has been sluic'd in's absence', it is the same watery metaphor, albeit more bitter and explicit.

The shepherd Tityrus brings his daughter Gallathea to the tree and explains the sacrifice to her. He has disguised her as a boy in order to protect her from this terrible fate. Cross-dressing was always a controversial issue, on stage and off. The idea of women dressing as men was particularly subversive, and Gallathea's moral objection to it reflects a well-documented attitude: 'The destiny to me cannot be so hard as the disguising hateful'. She would rather die at the monster's attack than wear male clothing, showing a determined piety which her father's arguments do not impress. If the gods disguised themselves as animals for carnal purposes then, she says: 'They were beastly gods, that lust could make them seem as beasts'. Given the rapacious indifference to consent expressed in most versions of Jupiter's rapes, she has a good point.

Phyllida, another fair, chaste virgin is being urged to the same precaution by her father, Melebeus. She also considers male apparel inppropriate, particulary for the sexual confusions which might arise:

> For then I must keep company with boys, and commit follies
> unseemly for my sex, or keep company with girls, and be thought
> more wanton than becometh me. Besides, I shall be ashamed of
> my long hose and short coat, and so unwarily blab out something
> by blushing at everything.

Her clothing risks accidental revelation: blabbing her sex. Some idea of the crucial way in which clothing creates identity for her can be seen in the way boys' clothes inevitably require her to join boys' company and perform boys' behaviour. Like children entering through the sex-differentiated doorways of their Victorian primary school buildings, Phyllida has learned early that 'Boys' and 'Girls' travel different routes. Gender as performance is not for her a postmodern theory but an obvious fact of life.

Once there are two beautiful virgin girls disguised as boys wandering around the forest, it is only a matter of time before they see each other. Even from their first meeting, they have suspicions that maybe the other is not a boy, but they fall in love anyway. This displeases the gods. Neptune, who has lost his chance to spurt up the Humber estuary as a result of their transvestism, cross-questions them. They acknowledge their fancies burning and desires inflaming for each other, each claiming that she was misled by the other's clothing.

NEPTUNE Do you both, being maidens, love one another?

GALLATHEA I had thought the habit agreeable with the sex, and so burned in the fire of mine own fancies.

PHYLLIDA I had thought that in the attire of a boy, there could not have lodged the body of a virgin, and so was inflamed by a sweet desire, which I now find a sour deceit.

Diana may be against her nymphs loving boys, but she advises Gallathea and Phyllida against loving each other as well: 'Now things falling out as they do, you must leave these fond, fond affections, Nature will have it so; necessity must.' Both the natural order and practicality make love between women an impossibility. This is disappointing from a great lesbian icon but Gazza and Phyll are undaunted. They may have fallen in love thanks to a confusion in clothing, but have no intention of going back on it now that a small matter like physiological gender has intervened.

GALLATHEA I will never love any but Phillida. Her love is engraven in my heart with her eyes.

PHYLLIDA Nor I any but Gallathea, whose faith is imprinted in my thoughts by her words.

This is exasperating for Neptune: 'An idle choice, strange and foolish for one virgin to dote on another'. He may be a god, but he is also male. Diana gives arguments why their love cannot be allowed by nature or law, but he dismisses it as idle, strange and foolish. Besides, he says, how can they 'imagine a constant faith where there can be no cause of affection'? That absent cause being presumably a penis, whether human or divine. He appeals to the goddess of love: 'How like you this, Venus?' hoping perhaps that her record, taunting Sappho with a toyboy during Lyly's earlier play, proves her a persistent scourge of lesbians. Not a bit of it. Venus, who is after all goddess of love, decides to make the two women a test case. 'I like well, and allow it', she pronounces. 'They shall both be possessed of their wishes, for never shall it be said that nature or fortune shall overthrow love and faith.' The argument that neither luck nor nature should deny love remains a radical notion even four centuries later. She continues with what could serve as a good opening for a pagan partnership ceremony:

> VENUS Is your love unspotted, begun with truth, continued with
> constancy, and not to be altered till death?

> GALLATHEA Die, Gallathea, if thy love be not so.

> PHYLLIDA Accursed be thou, Phyllida, if thy love be not so.

Diana has no patience with this nonsense, interrupting with irritation, 'Suppose all this, Venus. What then?' Venus produces a trump card: 'Then shall it be seen that I can turn one of them to be a man, and that I will.' Diana is astonished: 'Is it possible?' Neptune is completely silent. Gender reassignment is a big deal, even for gods and goddesses. Yet Venus is determined to prove her superiority over all of them, and reminds them of the story from which Lyly adapted his: 'What is, to love or the mistress of love, impossible? Was it not Venus that did the like to Iphis and Ianthes?' No one can disagree.

The principle that gender is not necessarily fixed, providing divinity lends a hand, having been established, Venus turns back to the lovers.

> VENUS How say ye, are ye agreed to be a boy presently?

> PHYLLIDA I am content, so I may embrace Gallathea.

> GALLATHEA I wish it, so I may enjoy Phyllida.

At the start of the play, these conservative yong women found the notion of putting on male clothing worse than death. Now they immediately consent to sex-swapping in the service of love. Certainly

Phyllida's anxieties about how she could decently play as a girl in boys' clothes are now irrelevant. As a 'real' boy there should be no conflict between fashion and whom you join in the playground; and now she has met Phyllida she will not want their balls anyway. As for Gallathea, her determination to 'enjoy Phyllida' whatever it takes, uses one of Shakespeare's most frequent smutty puns. Since she thinks becoming a boy is necessary for sex between them, she partly connives with Neptune's notion that some male presence is essential. The *Oxford English Dictionary* decided in 1891 that only women (probably) may have it done to them, giving the relevant definition of to enjoy as 'To have one's will (of a woman)'. The great book does not restrict the gender of those doing the having, however.

Who could fail to celebrate such a delightful conclusion? Their fathers, of course. Tyterus and Melebeus are displeased at these signs of independence from their hitherto dutiful daughters, suspecting maybe that this could lead to a rash of copycat paternal defiance from other Elizabethan heroines.

MELEBEUS (*to Phyllida*) Soft, daughter, you must know whether I will have you as a son.

TYTERUS (*to Gallathea*) Take me with you, Gallathea. I will keep you as I begat you, a daughter.

These are the same men who dismissed their daughters' anxieties about cross-dressing at the start of the play. For them, the whole story becomes a grim warning to fathers of the dire consequences in blurring gender roles for your offspring. One day she is wearing long hose and short coat, the next she is marrying another woman.

More troubling still are the questions of power and ownership. It is not for girls to make crucial decisions about their futures, even with a goddess. Their fathers must make any bargain which is necessary. Since a boy has more rights and independence than a girl, the changing of genders willy-nilly – as it were – can only disrupt the central structures of the family, and raise questions of property and title.

MELEBEUS Tyterus, let yours be a boy, and if you will, mine shall not.

TYTERUS Nay, mine shall not; for by that means my young son shall lose his inheritance.

MELEBEUS Why then, get him to be made a maiden and then there is
nothing lost.

The men's panto-style exchange looks like spiralling into the absurd and
dangerous area where gender means little or nothing. Instead, Lyly gives
them a dirty joke.

TYTERUS If there be such changing, I would Venus could make my
wife a man.

MELEBEUS Why?

TYTERUS Because she loves always to play with men.

In *Damon and Pythias* and *Campaspe*, it is the younger boys who get
the bawdiest jokes to tell. Here the boys playing old men have the
crudest humour. Old women can also be funny in boys' plays, but these
young women are treated with the same sentimental seriousness as their
male romantic counterparts. There may be a slightly patronizing edge in
the portrayals of all these young idealists, but there is no sense that
Gallathea and Phyllida are mocked for their love, in the way their
fathers are for their stupidity. Venus, unimpressed by their smut, simply
tells the dads to shut up:

VENUS Well, you are both fond. Therefore agree to this changing,
or suffer your daughters to endure hard chance.

This immediately silences their objections. With the consent of Diana
and Cupid, as well as Neptune, thus deprived of drowning either chaste,
fair virgin, Venus takes them off to church immediately. 'Then let us
depart. Neither of them shall know whose lot it shall be till they come to
the church door. One shall be. Doth it suffice?' – and it does.

This teasing ending – which girl will it be? – is the more playful
because *both* become boys backstage. The homoerotics of the plot can
be resolved only in a world somewhere between the theatre and real life.
Unlike *Gallathea*, both *As You Like It* and *Twelfth Night* open the
frame of their transvestite plot by first presenting their heroine dressed
as a woman. They end up in a similarly ambiguous realm, however. The
actor formerly known as Rosalind says flirtatiously in his/her epilogue,
'If I were a woman I would kiss as many of you as had beards that
pleased me.' *Gallathea* has a tremendous influence on Shakespeare's

woodland comedies, and makes it impossible to dismiss love between the women in them as many commentators rush to do.

The great lesbian Shakespeare betrayal

The liberal attitudes of the late Eric Partridge are praised by one of the world's leading Shakespeare scholars, Stanley Wells, in a foreword to the reissue of Partridge's book *Shakespeare's Bawdy*. In it, Partridge tells us:

> Shakespeare, by the way, does not speak of Lesbians: Lesbianism was an extremely rare deviation in Shakespearian England. The prevalent well-informed view is . . . that all female passives . . . are . . . exaggeratedly female (. . . impelled . . . by the perhaps masochistic libido to be possessed by *some*body, even if it is only a woman) . . . and the active female homosexual is 'a woman with an excessive contribution of the male'.

Written in 1947, last revised in 1968 and widely used even now, *Shakespeare's Bawdy* is hardly still liberal, even if its compiler once was. It is dangerously easy to sneer at Partridge's homophobia, given that the book was first published the year that Ferdinand Lundberg and Marynia Farnham in *Modern Woman: The Lost Sex* advised banning all unmarried women from teaching for fear of potential lesbian contamination. The research in the book is extensive and useful, and can be helpful even to the scholarly intersexual. That a leading contemporary scholar should endorse the book's treatment of homosexuality as 'straightforward and sensible, if simplistic' in 1990, however, is extraordinary. More troubling to Wells is the fact that the book failed to give 'bud' as a play on the head of the penis in Sonnet One. A recent survey of Shakespearian research could cite Valerie Traub and no one else publishing work on lesbianism and Shakespeare. Is this, as Partridge argues, because there is nothing to say? Or because those who determine the agenda for Shakespeare studies have effectively excluded it from serious consideration? Is that the great lesbian Shakespeare betrayal?

No. The great lesbian Shakespeare betrayal is Rosalind's. She attains heterosexual marriage after a spell as a gay man, but at the expense of the woman who loves her. In *As You Like It* (1600), another pastoral comedy, the paranoid father Duke Frederick banishes his niece Rosalind, daughter of the brother he deposed, in order to prevent her popularity undermining his rule. His daughter Celia's love for her is all that has prevented him sending Rosalind away earlier. We get this information from two contrasting males in the Duke's entourage: his straightforward wrestler Charles, and his overtalkative courtier Le Beau. Their names and professions indicate their differing versions of maleness, but they agree on one thing: Celia and Rosalind's love for each other. Le Beau says their loves 'are dearer than the natural bond of sisters', confirming, with opposite effect, Diana's comment in *Gallathea* that nature excludes passionate love between women. According to Charles:

> the Duke's daughter her cousin [Celia] so loves her [Rosalind],
> being ever from their cradles bred together, that she would have
> followed her exile, or have died to stay behind her. She is at the
> court, and no less beloved of her uncle than his own daughter;
> and never two ladies loved as they do.

Charles' comment that Rosalind is as much loved by Duke Frederick as his own daughter may just be his mistake, given her prompt banishment. The Duke's changeability does, however, link him with the inconsistent fathers of Lyly's play, and the paranoid ones in later dramas exploring erotic possibilities between women.

Celia places her love for a girlfriend above that for a father, and is vexed that Rosalind will not do the same, remaining miserable about her father's banishment:

> I see thou lovest me not with the full weight that I love thee . . . so
> thou hadst still been with me, I could have taught my love to take
> thy father for mine: so wouldst thou, if the truth of thy love to me
> were so righteously tempered as mine is to thee.

This is not over sympathetic, although Celia promises that when she inherits from her father, she will give Rosalind the property which she would have inherited from hers. What Duke Frederick 'hath taken away from thy father perforce, I will render thee in affection', she promises Rosalind, 'by mine honour, I will; and when I break that oath, let me turn monster'. Her economy, based on female affections, will overrule her father's just as Tyterus and Melebeus have their disposition of property disrupted by their daughters' love for each other.

Celia's love is tested and proven when Duke Frederick does banish Rosalind, which she takes as her expulsion too:

CELIA Knowst thou not the Duke
    Hath banished me his daughter?

ROSALIND That he hath not.

CELIA No, hath not? Rosalind then lacks the love
    Which teacheth thee that thou and I are one.
    Shall we be sunder'd? shall we part, sweet girl?
    No: let my father seek another heir.

She is quite determined: 'And do not seek to . . . leave me out; . . . Say what thou canst, I'll go along with thee.'

Shakespeare's main source for *As You Like It* is *Rosalynde*, a prose romance by Thomas Lodge, one of Lyly's fellow euphuists (see chapter four). In the same way as Lyly's *Euphues* books celebrate love between men, Alinda, whose role in the story parallels Celia in the play, uses a classical model of same-sex fidelity to describe her love of Rosalynde:

Thou hast with thee Alinda a friend, who will be a faithful copartner of all thy misfortunes, who hath left her father to follow thee, and chooseth rather to brooke all extremeties than to forsake thy presence . . . As we have been bedfellowes in royaltie, we will be fellow mates in poverty: I will ever be thy Alinda, and thou shalt ever rest to me Rosalynd; so shall the world canonize our friendship, and speak of Rosalynd and Alinda, as they did of Pilades and Orestes.

In Lodge's work, Alinda is banished by her father, rather than choosing to run away as Celia does. Shakespeare also all but removes the parts of Lodge's story which tell of Alinda's romance with a man in the forest. The play takes her devotion to another woman much more seriously, and dramatizes it with an erotic language that tickles the possibilities of sex between women.

Sex is part of Celia and Rosalind's love. It is their first choice as a topic for entertaining dicussion: 'Let me see', wonders Rosalind, 'what think you of falling in love?' Not in earnest, only for sport, and be careful how far you go with men even then, warns Celia. She advocates very safe sex: going no futher 'than with safety of a pure blush thou mayst in honour come off again'. How far you can go and still come off without blushing, she does not specify, but it disappoints Rosalind. 'What shall be our sport then?' she wonders.

Instead of risking sex with men, they make an apparently obscure switch into philosophical debate, discussing the shortcomings of fortune and nature. These are relevant to amorous pursuits: Venus in *Gallathea* allows women's love to triumph over both, commanding 'never shall it be said that nature or fortune shall overthrow love and faith'. Nevertheless, it does seem a dry substitute for a discussion about the possibilities of love.

This is to ignore the erotic themes on which they play as they talk. Celia mocks Fortune as a housewife, meaning either a woman who has gone too far with a man, therefore into marriage; or one who sells sex: wedlock and prostitution are both ways in which economics encourage women to service men's sexual needs. She is an egalitarian feminist, demanding that Fortune's 'gifts may henceforth be bestowed equally'. The specific inequality of which they complain is, says Rosalind, between the sexes: 'the bountiful blind woman doth most mistake in her gifts to women'. If 'gifts' here also means male genitals, the change of subject from sex with men to philosophical speculation is less obscure. Rosalind asks what they are to do if they cannot have sex with men: Celia replies that they should complain about their lack of endowment. The well-endowed men endlessly advertised for in gay contact ads certainly seem to have Fortune's gifts. Admittedly this re-erects the long-standing fallacy also present in *Gallathea*, that penile presence is essential even for women who desire consummation, but this play too is written and originally performed by men and boys.

Sex is the key to staging this otherwise indigestible and out-of-place sequence of metaphysical debate. It retains its ambiguities, however. 'When Nature hath made a fair creature, may she not by Fortune fall into the fire?' asks Celia. The luck of a beautiful woman is to be embroiled in sex: to fall into the fire of lust. Does she mean herself, desiring her friend but short of the gift that allows her to act? More likely, given her status as female lead in the conventional sexual economy of the play, it is Rosalind who is the fair creature. Is Celia then predicting her friend's collapse into love for a man later in the scene, when Orlando enters? Or is it an invitation to fall into her own fire – a seduction immediately interrupted by the very unfortunate arrival of Touchstone.

By the end of the scene, the seed of division between these two inseparable friends has been sown. Once Orlando has wrestled, Rosalind has fallen, and Celia will be emotionally banished, even if, like that of her friend, announcement of her sentence is somewhat delayed. Although her isolation is confirmed only in the final scene, Celia sees in her first scene that she has competition. When the two women leave Orlando, Rosalind turns back to talk to him again. The irritation in Celia's 'Will you go coz?' gets a laugh, but the truth is that she has already lost her friend.

Rosalind to Celia is 'my sweet Rose, my dear Rose'. 'Rose is a rose is a rose is a rose, is a rose' said a later lyric lesbian, Gertrude Stein, perfectly aware that a rose is also a cunt. The climax of one of the commonplace verses Orlando pens and pins up plays on this image of Rosalind's sweet Rose:

> He that sweetest rose will find
> Must find love's prick and Rosalind

There is an extended discussion of the rose as a female sexual symbol in the play Shakespeare wrote with John Fletcher, *The Two Noble Kinsmen*. It is initiated by Emilia, whose love of another girl, Flavinia, is elegized in the play. 'Of all flowers, Methinks a rose is best', she says:

> It is the very emblem of a maid:
> For when the west wind courts her gently
> How modestly she blows and paints the sun
> With her chaste blushes! When the north comes near her,
> Rude and impatient, then, like chastity,
> She locks her beauties in her bud again
> And leaves him to base briers.

Just like Celia, she recommends a maiden going no further in love with a man (or a male wind) than is consistent with chaste blushes, closing her buds to rudeness. Although Emilia here gives no gender to the West Wind, his best known love is homosexual, as a rival to Apollo for the beautiful youth Hyancinthus. Given her belief that 'the true love 'tween maid and maid may be More than in sex dividual', the rival winds can also be different versions of erotic play: gentle courting of the sort she describes with Flavina, compared with the rude impatience of men. Once again, it reinforces a notion of female eroticism as gentler than that involving a man, but explores it nevertheless.

Emilia's Woman brings the sexual imagery of the wind-tossed rose onto a cruder level:

> Yet, good madam,
> Sometimes her modesty will blow so far
> She falls for't – a maid,
> If she have any honour, would be loath
> To take example by her.

'Thou art wanton', scolds Emilia, delighted, and the two women joke about 'laugh and lie down', a card-game with obvious sexual innuendo. The falling rose as a sexual emblem is actually staged in the play, when Emilia goes to pray to Diana to help her. The goddess, far from helpful to Gallathea and Phyllida and their marriage in 1584, is more forthcoming in 1613. A rose tree rises from Diana's altar, and its single rose drops to the ground, symbolizing Emilia's discharge from virginity.

There is one more 'Rose' bedded in Celia's defiant declaration of love for Rosalind, with which she defies her father. I was too young when her father was banished to value her, she says, but now I am a woman of greater experience:

> But now I know her. If she be a traitor,
> Why so am I; we still have slept together,
> Rose at an instant, learn'd, play'd, eat together;

(In chapter seven, the treacherous sodomy of Shakespeare's male 'bedfellows in royalty' will be discussed.) Here Celia denies treason but reveals a language of love. Within three lines, she uses four verbs which imply sex elsewhere in Shakespeare: to know, to sleep together, to play and to eat. To learn, or to gain knowledge of, fits neatly into that pattern. As for 'Rose at an instant': as a metaphor for male sexual arousal it would stick out clearly. In this context, however, the double-meaning is transgendered. They both 'Rose' together: becoming sexual organs themselves 'at an instant'. That instant being simultaneous orgasm, a divine coupling:

And wheresoe'er we went, like Juno's swans
Still we went coupled and inseparable.

Inseparable from Celia's narrative of love with Rosalind is an elaborate sexual story.

Duke Frederick's response, a lecture to his daughter condemning her playmate, also hints at sex:

She is too subtle for thee; and her smoothness
Her very silence and her patience,
Speak to the people and they pity her.

Someone subtle is a prostitute; someone smooth is licentious. Rosalind's 'very' is excess, her 'silence' as sexually treacherous as the *quietus* which prematurely ends Sonnet 126. It is a deadly discharging, there executed on a lovely boy by his sovereign mistress, nature. An excess of patience makes her very *patiens*: the unnatural passivity which makes homosexuals of men (*patientia*) whose mirror is the lesbianism to which it has lured Celia. Rosalind is more a boy whore than a woman companion: Celia's Ganymede.

The Duke justifies his incomprehensible change of heart towards Rosalind by accusing her of treachery. The erotic subtext of this charge is more convincing than its narrative convenience. The sexual double standard is ruthless: Celia is humiliated while her friend pleases all the town. 'Thou art a fool', says her father, 'she robs thee of thy name; And thou wilt show more bright and seem more virtuous When she is gone.' He blames Rosalind for taking away from his daughter what we know she will freely give. If Celia is alienated from her father and the town, it is not Rosalind's persuasion, but her own choice. Following Lodge's Alinda, Celia even names herself for this strangeness in her exile, choosing to be called:

Something that hath a reference to my state.
No longer Celia, but Aliena.

Although he identifies Rosalind as the cause of his daughter's potential ruin, Duke Frederick commands Celia to control herself. His instruction to keep quiet, and retain the natural deference of a woman, is also a command to sexual restraint: 'Then open not thy lips'.

Celia silenced

Celia goes into the woods for love of Rosalind. Yet once they are there, Rosalind seeks and finds a different love. Exhausted by their journey, Rosalind and Touchstone are neverthless inspired by Silvius the shepherd and his talk of love. Celia, although in shepherdess costume, wants only food. Tensions between the two women increase with Orlando's presence. Celia teases Rosalind about his love poems, remains silently on stage through a long scene between the two would-be lovers and then leads the catechism of Orlando's faults which fails to arrest Rosalind's love of him.

The confident lead she took in affairs at home has disappeared in the woods. She snaps at Corin, and hardly speaks when Orlando is present. When she does, it is to mock the charade of wooing in which Rosalind pretends to be Ganymede pretending to be Rosalind. She insults the fake Rosalind and praises the true one: 'he hath a Rosalind of a better leer than you', she puns on her friend's body, leer meaning 'complexion' and 'loin'.

'Ganymede' and Orlando's fake yet all too real marriage chokes her. Pushed by Rosalind to officiate she initially refuses – 'I cannot say the words'. Grudgingly, however, she provides a one-line service, then lapses back into silence, exploding after Orlando leaves:

> You have simply misused our sex in your love-prate. We must
> have your doublet and hose plucked over your head, and show
> the world what the bird hath done to her own nest.

Celia argues that her rage is against Rosalind's betrayal of women in general, but it is a specific sexual treachery which fills the language, that of buggery.

Whenever the idea of lesbian sex is approached in these plays, it disappears. It is unimaginable for even the female characters, because their male creators do not accept the possibility of sex without a penis. That thing which is thought to be lacking is, however, on stage throughout, between the legs of the young male actors, even as they bemoan its absence. Lyly keeps the magic which Venus performs offstage in *Gallathea*, and presents his girls as boys from the beginning. *As You Like It* complicates matters by transforming the body of Rosalind onstage through ever more intricate operations of gender reversal, culminating in this scene with her marriage as a male actor playing a female character playing a male character playing the same female character.

As Ganymede, Rosalind is not just a boy, but a gay boy, and Celia accuses her, following the marriage with Orlando, of anal sex. If Rosalind's doublet and hose are plucked over her head, it reveals her arse, the place which she has fouled, as the bird does its nest. This image comes from Lodge's story, but the play develops its anality further. Celia claims that Rosalind's love has turned her into a boy who can be fucked. Buggery is a way in which she can sexually counterfeit a man, and play Rosalind for Orlando without ceasing to be Ganymede. Rosalind claims that she has not allowed that:

> ROSALIND O coz, coz, coz, my pretty little coz, that thou didst
> know how many fathom deep I am in love! But it cannot be
> sounded. My affection hath an unknown bottom, like the
> bay of Portugal.

> CELIA Or rather, bottomless; that as fast as you pour affection in,
> it runs out.

Despite the deepness of her love, its bottom – and hers – is not (sexually) known. Celia says she is a leaky vessel, her bottom hole dripping. Rosalind has been transgendered, just like either Gallathea or Phyllida, but it does Celia no good. 'Ganymede' desires penetration, just as Rosalind considered love pointless without an endowment.

Another woman then falls in love with Rosalind, this time in her Ganymede disguise. Phoebe sends a love poem to Rosalind/Ganymede, who tries to claim that the poem is a man's letter, then perverts it further: reading out Phoebe's words of love and claiming they are abuse. Phoebe first describes her love by quoting a 'dead shepherd': Christopher Marlowe, whose own amorous shepherds were deliberately ambiguous in gender (see chapter eight). Phoebe the real shepherdess describes her beloved Ganymede as god turned to a man. Celia, as Aliena the fake shepherdess, knows her beloved Rosalind is a woman, disguised as a man. Both cases are hopeless.

Orlando's older brother arrives: previously despised as a villain by everyone, even Duke Frederick, Oliver has abruptly converted from his previous 'unnaturalness', and become a good man. With similarly unlikely speed, Celia is reported to have fallen in love with him. This might fit Phoebe's Marlovian notion of love at first sight, had Celia shown any interest in him when he arrived. In fact she addresses just two lines to him, and those no more than polite. News of their love is reported by Oliver himself, who is unable to explain her sudden acceptance of him. Rosalind confirms their love with the oddly sexual image that 'there was never anything so sudden but the fight of two rams', in a speech about their preparation for marriage that one edition dismisses as textually inauthentic, and another calls 'a pack of lies'. Either way, it does not ring true.

The play must end with weddings, however bogus. Hymen the god of marriage is brought in by Rosalind to order everything to her (and Nature's) satisfaction, for she takes little pleasure in the sexual and amorous confusion. As well as the dubious shotgun pairing of Oliver and Celia, there have been two other parodies of matrimony. One, the wedding of two men, Orlando and Ganymede; the other, the marriage, by Sir Oliver Martext, of Touchstone and Audrey under a bush. There, the bride has no one to give her away but a stand-in, the gloomy sodomite Jaques, and the groom deliberately chooses the priest, whose name means 'bad script':

> for he is not like to marry me well; and not being well married, it
> will be a good excuse for me hereafter to leave my wife.

That Rosalind loves no woman is crucial to the wrapping up: she says it four times, promising 'And as I love no woman, I'll meet', when arranging her theatrical coup. Even more wounding for Celia, if she does marry a woman it will be Phoebe, the real shepherdess, not her old friend. This is a safe promise, however, for the god of marriage will not allow such a disruption. Hymen orders Phoebe to marry a man she despises:

> You to his love must accord
> Or have a woman to your lord

This could sour the happiness so ruthlessly imposed at the end of the play, but Phoebe shows the deference required of a poor woman faced with gods and nobility, and accepts graciously.

As for her other female lover, as well as oldest and closest friend: Rosalind does not address Celia at all. In their husbands' newly acquired separate kingdoms the two women will be separated forever. What does Celia think of all this? We never see her speak to the man she has agreed to marry. In fact, having been lively and talkative at the start of *As You Like It* she never speaks again, remaining silent throughout the last act of the play. Sodomy can just about speak its name in the enchanted forest, but lesbianism must be shut up.

George Sand, a woman who enjoyed taking a male name, male clothes and challenging male privileges, was not satisfied with this treatment of Celia, although fell short, as she did in her own life, of allowing love between women to triumph. Herself preferring unmanly men, she marries Celia to Jaques in *Comme il vous plaira*, her 1856 version of Shakespeare's play.

The two noble kinswomen

The beauty of love between women gets eloquent expression in *The Two Noble Kinsmen* (1613). Emilia talks of her relationship with another girl, Flavina, who died when they were both young.

> I was acquainted
> Once with a time when I enjoyed a playfellow;
> You were at wars when she the grave enriched,
> Who made too proud the bed; took leave o'th moon –
> Which then looked pale at parting – when our count
> Was each eleven.

Eleven is young, but only a year younger than a girl could legally marry at the time. Palamon, when he prays to Venus later in the play, calls the goddess of love 'thou that from eleven to ninety reign'st In mortal bosoms'. The Nurse in *Romeo and Juliet* says she lost her virginity at twelve. Like other treatments of love between women in the period, that between Emilia and Flavina is placed back in time, as a childhood experience. Although such elegy is used in Shakespeare to distance lesbianism as a childhood phase, its retelling as part of the play, albeit in Act One, restores its immediacy, bringing the dead Flavina back to life. Emilia recalls that both girls

> were things innocent,
> Loved for we did, and like the elements,
> That know not what, nor why, yet do effect

> Rare issues by their operance, our souls
> Did so to one another.

Childhood innocence combines with a powerful image of the naturalness of their love: it is elemental, a basic, unpremeditated desire. The balance and peacefulness of this love between equals is celebrated: 'What she liked Was then of me approved; what not, condemned – No more arraignment.'

Emilia describes this love to her sister Hippolyta, who is to marry Theseus. She compares her girlish love for Flavina with the masculine affection between Theseus and Pirithous. The men's love is, she says, more mature and well-judged, described by both her and Hippolyta in terms of their fighting alongside each other, and in images of cunning knots and careful cleaving. In contrasting the evenness and purity of female affections with the vigour and seasoning of that between men, Emilia is caught between a celebration of women and a development of a gender stereotype. In some ways, her eulogy resembles idealized portraits of lesbians which appeared in early gay liberation drama, particularly those created by over-earnest men.

There is, nevertheless, a strain of eroticism which like Celia's sweet rose, uses floral imagery to create a picture of this natural female passion:

> The flower that I would pluck
> And put between my breasts – O then but beginning
> To swell about the blossom – she would long
> Till she had such another, and commit it
> To the like innocent cradle, where, phoenix-like,
> They died in perfume;

The sensuality is unmistakeable, as the flowers and the girls' bodies become one, all sweet scent and beautiful buds. The cleft for the rose between their swelling breasts mirrors the rose they hold between their legs – an innocent cradle. That symmetry is matched by the way the body and desire of each girl mirrors the other, just as they do in the other Shakespeare play featuring Theseus and Hippolyta, *A Midsummer Night's Dream*. There Helena reminds Hermia of their 'childhood innocence' and love for each other:

> We Hermia, like two artificial gods
> Have with our needles created both one flower,

Both on one sampler, sitting on one cushion,
Both warbling of one song, both in one key,
As if our hands, our sides, voices and minds
Had been incorporate.

Here the flower is artificial, created by the prick of needles which Celia
and Rosalind did not have. The sensual imagery continues: sight, sound
and touch are all in unison here, like the smell of Emilia and Flavina's
perfumed flowers. They too shared songs as well as fashions:

on my head no toy
But was her pattern; her affections – pretty,
Though happily, her careless wear – I followed
For my most serious decking; had mine ear
Stol'n some new air or at adventure humm'd one
From musical coinage, why, it was a note
Whereon her spirits would sojourn – rather dwell on –
And sing it in her slumbers.

The two women become one flesh, in a natural marriage which is also
physically transcendental. For Helena, the image of their union takes
her back to horticulture, and thus to sex:

So we grew together,
Like to a double cherry: seeming parted,
But yet an union in partition,
Two lovely berries moulded on one stem.
So with two seeming bodies but one heart,
Two of the first, like coats in heraldry,
Due but to one, and crownèd with one crest.

The crested shield with a line down the middle seems an odd diversion
from the fruity flow of Helena's description, unless it is recognized as a
picture of an adolescent vagina, divided and crowned with early pubic
hair. The cherry is a maidenhead then as now, the 'union in partition'
presumed to be broken only with another union: marriage. Any sex with
men leaves traces, though, argues Donne's Sappho in 'Sapho to Philaenis':

Men leave behind them that which their sin shows,
And are as thieves traced, that rob when it snows.
But of our dalliance no more signs there are
Than fishes leave in streams, or birds in air.

Like the sluicing of the Humber estuary in *Gallathea*, penetration by a penis leaves devastation in its wake: or at least footsteps in the snow, the tell-tale traces of a man's theft. The virgin has been unspotted by blood or semen, if virginity for a woman is taken as the state before penetration by a penis. With such a notion of sexuality, lesbianism becomes not a sin, but an imaginary state before the fall. The signless fish and birds, leaving no trace, are idealized in Sappho's lesbian Eden. The forbidden fruit remains unpicked, just caressed, like Helena's cherries. These two red round fruits tantalizingly unparted suggest further mirroring. Helena and Hermia have two seeming bodies but one heart when physically entwined: the double cherry is a sexual pressing together of their two lovely berries.

In 'Sapho to Philaenis', lines which similarly evoke lesbian sex through a duplication of parts have been omitted from some versions:

My two lips, eyes, thighs, differ from thy two,
But so, as thine from one another do;
And, oh, no more; the likeness being such,
Why should they not alike in all parts touch?
Hand to strange hand, lip to lip none denies;
Why should they breast to breast, or thighs to thighs?
Likeness begets such strange self flattery,
That touching myself, all seems done to thee

Here Sappho complains of the restrictions which prevent her meeting Philaenis' breast or thighs with her own. Donne's impersonation is not mediated through a male performer. The mirroring which he uses in the multiplication of lips and eyes and thighs is, in the plays, performed by actors of the same sex. Theatre before the Restoration had to play on the similarities between boys and women, and explicit comparisons are frequent. In *The Two Noble Kinsmen*, Arcite's misogyny dismisses 'poutings Fitter for girls and schoolboys', and the Wooer of the Jailer's Daughter recognizes a voice that was 'by the smallness of it A boy or woman'.

Given the lesbian eroticism in the Donne poem and its metaphorically expressed version in *A Midsummer Night's Dream*, Emilia's opening begins to seem less innocent. When she says she was 'acquainted', followed by the fact that she 'enjoyed a playfellow . . . who made too proud the bed' there is a play on cunt as 'quaint', a usage which goes back to Chaucer. Thus, when she reaches her climactic end, and the conclusion 'That the true love 'tween maid and maid may be More than in sex dividual', it is not surprising that she is visibly excited: 'Y'are out of breath', says Hippolyta of her 'high speeded pace'. Helena, too, is wrought up by her lesbian speech: Hermia says 'I am amazed at your passionate words'. This passion combines erotic reminiscence and betrayal, however:

> And will you rent our ancient love asunder,
> To join with men in scorning your poor friend?
> It is not friendly, 'tis not maidenly.
> Our sex as well as I may chide you for it,
> Though I alone do feel the injury.

The context is an argument over a man but Helena, like Emilia, considers 'love 'tween maid and maid' should count for more. By joining with men to mock her, as she believes Hermia has, Helena claims her friend has injured women as a whole, and her in particular. More erotically, Donne's Sappho suspects Philaenis of sexually deserting her for men, and calls her back:

> O cure this loving madness, and restore
> Me to me; thee, my *half*, my *all*, my *more*.

Unlike these irreconcilable arguments, however, Emilia and Hippolyta manage quite a polite discussion. They are sisters, and not in any sexual competition, as Helena and Hermia are. Neither is the lesbian love under discussion a romantic dilemma between them, as it is for Celia and Rosalind, or Sappho and Philaenis. They are both Amazons, part of that legendary band of warrior women which 'wast near to make the male To thy sex captive' before the play began. This seems to make Hippolyta more understanding of Emilia's lack of interest in heterosexuality, summarizing her speech as meaning:

> HIPPOLYTA That you shall never – like the maid Flavina –
>   Love any that's called man.
>
> EMILIA I am sure I shall not.

Flavina died, however, which is why she will never now love a man. Unlike her, Emilia seems to be rejecting marriage through choice, although she earlier supports Hippolyta in a successful petition to send Theseus back to war, by swearing she will never marry if he ignores her plea. After this speech, that threat seems simply to confirm what she intended to do anyway. Hippolyta may be sympathetic, but she is not convinced.

> Now alack, weak sister,
> I must no more believe me in this point –
> Though in't I know thou dost believe thyself –
> Than I will trust a sickly appetite
> That loathes even as it longs.

For a woman, even an Amazon, sexually to reject men is weak, even sickly. Like the women's movement in the 1970s, the Amazons are a heterosexual band, unable comfortably to include lesbians. Hippolyta says Emilia is kidding herself: not, however, that she is rejecting what has been said:

> But sure, my sister,
> If I were ripe for your persuasion, you
> Have said enough to shake me from the arm
> Of the all-noble Theseus

This is contradictory, perhaps to soothe Emilia's 'high-speeded pace'. There is a good argument for loving women rather than men, but only if those who hear it are ripe for persuasion. Hippolyta is sure she is not herself, but also doubts that Emilia really is, either. So lesbianism, although a reasonable possibility, is pushed away. Perhaps to confirm this, Hippolyta immediately goes in to pray for her husband:

> HIPPOLYTA . . . for whose fortunes
>   I will now in and kneel, with great assurance
>   That we, more than his Pirithous, possess
>   The high throne in his heart.

> EMILIA I am not
>   Against your faith, yet I continue mine.

The scene ends with neither convinced. Loving women or men are different faiths in Emilia's terms, an intriguing notion of sexual preference as religion. Hippolyta has, however, been convinced by their conversation that Theseus loves her more than Pirithous, a man. Emilia's eulogy of women's love and its qualities has at least challenged the idea that only men can love properly.

As in *A Midsummer Night's Dream*, Hippolyta and Theseus's marriage is an event of extended interrupted coitus. In both plays, the gap between ceremony and consummation provides a frame for the main action. This is only a night in the woods in the former, but *The Two Noble Kinsmen* keeps them waiting for ages. Theseus's ambivalence between Hippolyta and Pirithous symbolizes a conflict between domestic pleasure and military duty, but it is also, as Hippolyta realizes, an emotional and sexual dilemma: choosing between their two bodies. His decision to go back to battle makes a virtue of necessity, just as Emilia does in threatening not to marry, when she has no desire to do so anyway.

Emilia's love for her suitors is low-key, albeit a little more enthusiastic than Celia's. When Arcite and Palamon are about to be killed for fighting over her, she intervenes over what she calls 'The misadventure of their own eyes'. She refuses to choose one of them, which would solve things, saying: 'they are both too excellent For me', and persuades Theseus to banish them instead, offering as a condition that they can never know her again. These are not the actions of someone much in love. By contrast, the Jailer's Daughter in the play has an Ophelia-like madness caused by sexual desire which Palamon has inflamed then dismissed.

Even the reasons Emilia gives for saving Palamon and Arcite are women-based. She asks for mercy because as a woman she pities their fate, telling Theseus that if they die for loving her, she will be hated by 'goodly mothers' and 'longing maids', 'Till I am nothing but the scorn of women'.

Eventually she concedes that she must choose one of them, but becomes so confused by their pictures that she cannot manage it. Her bewilderment becomes ludicrous as the play continues, and finally she has to ask Diana to choose for her whether she marry or not, which is when the rose falls from the tree. Ultimately they have to fight over her again, an event which she refuses to watch:

O, better never born,
Than minister to such harm!

The horror of heterosexuality, which destroys love between women in *As You Like It* and *A Midsummer Night's Dream*, here does the same to that between Palamon and Arcite. Their deadly competition for Emilia requires that the loser die, which horrifies her. She bewails

> this unfriended
> This miserable prince, that cuts away
> A life more worthy from him than all women

In marrying, her husband destroys the greatest love of his life. Although male supremacist in its elevation of one man's life over all women, Emilia's earlier valuation of women's love suggests that separatism would suit her better. Although she does get married at the end of the play, it is an event mixed with the gloom of Arcite's death. He, like Flavina, the woman she loved, will be eternally single.

Women's empty rooms

The most spectacular presentation of lesbian eroticism on the Jacobean stage is in Thomas Heywood's *The Golden Age* (1610), the first in an epic five-play series on the history of the world. It is an eccentric mix of classical mythology and contemporary references, dashed off by one of the most prolific playwrights of the time. Its dramatization of the rape of Calisto by Jupiter disguised as a woman is pornographic, yet troubled by the same difficulties revealed by Lyly and Shakespeare in their attempts to create the impossible: lesbianism on the Renaissance stage. How can love and sex between women be presented in a form which allows only men to create it? The limitations are clear when boy actors joke about lesbian sex in Thomas Dekker's *Satiromastix*:

FIRST GENTLEWOMAN 'tis – O a most sweet thing to lie with a man.

SECOND GENTLEWOMAN I think 'tis a O more more more more
    sweet to lie with a woman

That second O is a vagina, and the over-enthusiasm for it simultaneously that of a boy actor and a woman character. The gentlewoman's foolishness diverts some attention from the lesbian implications of her excitement. Meanwhile the male body which interprets her ensures that there is still a penis present, even when belief in it has been willingly suspended for the duration of the performance.

The Golden Age goes a little further. It starts when, to avoid war, King Saturn promises his brother Titan that he will kill any male child he fathers, so that Titan's descendants will rule after him. He follows this promise once, and when another child is due – the Oracle having predicted not only that it will be a boy but also that it will usurp its father – Saturn (uneasily) orders it killed as well. Sibilla the Queen and Vesta the Queen Mother are with the Nurse when a lord comes in with the sentence. Vesta, whose name recalls Rome's famous all-women priesthood, ejects him:

> VESTA Forbear sir, for this place is privileg'd
> And only for free women

This prefigures later trespasses of female space by men in the play, both geographically and anatomically, of which the rape of Calisto is the worst example. Here the male intrusion is foiled, and the women decide to save the baby, sending him to the care of 'two bright maids', daughters of Melliseus, King of Epirius. Saturn will be shown a young kid's heart, while they counterfeit sorrow. The Chorus, blind Homer, gives equivocal praise to their actions which emphasizes the play's gender divisions:

> What cannot women's wits? they wonders can
> When they intend to blind the eyes of man

Intriguingly, Robert Graves suggests that Melliseus is in fact Melissa, 'the goddess as Queen-bee, who annually killed her male consort', which gives an additional twist to his upbringing by virgin girls and their father in this piece. In any case, having grown up, Jupiter and his soldiers take over the kingdom of King Lycaon, following a disastrous truce attempt. This is the occasion for a second violation of space, when his army burst into the private rooms of Calisto, Lycaon's daughter. Jupiter immediately desires her:

> JUPITER Come, lets ransack further,
> But stay, what strange dejected beauty's this
> That on the sodaine hath surpris'd my heart,
> And made me sick with passion?

Calisto faces an armed gang of enemy male soldiers in her bedroom with no one around to help. With the imperiousness essential for a princess, she orders them out, a brave response:

CALISTO Hence away.
    When we command, who dares presume to stay?

JUPITER Bright lady.

CALISTO You affright me with your steel.

JUPITER These weapons Lady come to grace your beauty
    And these my arms shall be your sanctuary
  From all offensive danger

Jupiter fails to recognize that he is the offensive danger, and his weapon of no interest to Calisto. He tries to woo her, asking 'Are you a queen?' but she rejects him, again with a spirited display of self-assurance:

CALISTO I am myself.
    Uncivil stranger, you are much too rude,
    Into my private chamber to intrude:
    Go call the King my father.

Lycaon has gone, however, and without a father's protection, nothing stands between an unmarried woman and rape, except her own wits. Helena in *A Midsummer Night's Dream* and Emilia in *The Two Noble Kinsmen* are similarly caught outside the roles of daughter and wife. Celia deliberately rejects her father, not in favour of a husband, but for a woman. All face great difficulties as a result, although none so dangerous as a persistent soldier in their private chamber. Jupiter uses the image of women as empty rooms to persuade Calisto that she needs him:

JUPITER Fair, can you love?

CALISTO To be alone I can.

JUPITER Women, fair queen, are nothing without men:
    You are but ciphers, empty rooms to fill,
    And till men's figures come, uncounted still.
    Shall I sweet lady, add unto your grace,
    And but for number-sake, supply that place.

CALISTO You're one too many, and of all the rest,
   That bear men's figure, we can spare you best.

Calisto, like Emilia and Celia, has no interest in men at all. This fails to have any effect on Jupiter however, who offers to give her anything in the world. She sees her chance and asks:

This only freedom to your captive give
That I a nun and professed maid may live.

Just as his own father agreed to a disastrous contract, Jupiter finds himself required to do something contrary to his desires. Desperate, he argues that it is unnatural to keep her empty room an empty womb, just as Shakespeare's first sonnets argue that the young man to whom they are addressed should reproduce:

To live a maid, what is't? 'tis to live nothing:
'Tis like a covetous man to hoard up treasure,
Barred from your own use, and from others pleasure.

It is Calisto's duty to be heterosexual and reproduce. Calisto may find sex with a man unappealing, but it is a socially useful activity in which it is her responsibility to engage. She was born to give birth, he says. Having been born herself, she should provide that service to another.

Oh think fair creature, that you had a mother,
One that bore you, that you might bear another:
Be you as she was, of an infant glad,
Since you, from her, have all things that she had.

Calisto's mother has no role in the play apart from this argument. Jupiter accepts that she might not enjoy sex with him, but it will be worth enduring for this end result. In presenting childbirth not as a natural female urge but as a social duty, the play recognizes that women might feel at best ambivalent about childbirth, a dangerous and often deadly business. Still unable to convince Calisto, Jupiter uses an argument against celibacy which takes it to the extreme:

Should all affect the strict life you desire,
The world itself should end when we expire.
Posterity is all, heavens number fill,
Which by your help may be increased still.

What is it when you lose your maiden-head,
But make your beauty live when you be dead
In your fair issue?

In 1996 reports of falling sperm counts brought similarly *fin de siècle* warnings about the race dying out. Jupiter's desperate argument fits with an apocalyptic tone, sounded by Homer at the start of the play. The conceit which links Heywood's five plays is that the 1610 audience is at the end of the Iron Age, the last after the Gold, Silver and Brazen ones. Homer tells his audience that time is nearly up:

You that are in the world's decrepit age,
When it is near his universal grave

Nothing convinces Calisto, however, having locked Jupiter into the promise which will save her. All he can fall back on is an accusation of religious impropriety:

CALISTO Tush, 'tis all in vain,
    Dian I am now a servant of thy train.

JUPITER Her order is mere heresy, her sect
    A schism, 'mongst maids not worthy your respect.

Later in the century Andrew Marvell's poem 'Upon Appleton House' condemns a Catholic priory, imputing lesbianism to its nuns. James Holstun notes: 'It is difficult to say whether Marvell wishes to denigrate Roman Catholic England, by associating it with lesbianism, or the other way around.' Nevertheless, Calisto does get herself to a nunnery, or the nearest thing available: Diana's cloister:

I claim your oath, all love with men adieu,
Diana's cloister I will next pursue. *Exit CALISTO*

That her parting words are not 'all love adieu', but 'all love with men adieu', fits the rhythm of the line, and the sentiments she has so far expressed.

In Diana's cloister

'What's that Diana?' asks Jupiter, ignoring that he seemed to know perfectly well a few lines earlier, an inconsistency quite consistent with the chaotic composition of the play. One of the lords tells him:

She is the daughter of an ancient King,
That swayed the Attic scepter, who being tempted
By many suitors, first began this vow:
And leaving court betook her to the forests.

Heywood was obsessed with Queen Elizabeth; he wrote a prose history *England's Elizabeth* in 1613 and a heroic poem *The Life and Death of Queen Elizabeth* in 1639, and with his Diana, a virgin queen beset by suitors, he glances back at her reign. Like Sappho's description of Philaenis' body, Diana's virgin world is also a 'natural Paradise'. Heywood combines pagan myth, a little Christian doctrine, and some recent history; Diana's woods, the garden of Eden and Elizabethan England are all Golden Ages.

Unlike Shakespeare's male woodland courtiers of Arden and Navarre, Diana's huntswomen are a tough lot. In Gaveston's imagined masque at the opening of *Edward II*, they tear Actaeon to pieces (see chapter eight). Their order is a strict one:

Her beauteous train are virgins of best rank,
Daughters of kings, and princes, all devoted
To abandon men, and choose virginity.
All these being first to her strict orders sworn,
Acknowledge her their queen and empress

Her women are of high worldly rank, thanks to their fathers, but transfer that status not to a husband, but to a goddess. Their lives consist of treading grass rings, drinking from fountains, eating honey and fruit from trees, and the occasional chase up a steep mountain for some venison: a perfect pastoral idyll. The woods are shared, like the lands where the Amazons lived, by separatist male and female tribes. The satyrs who precede Diana's appearance on stage, singing her praises, seem happy with this arrangement. Diana explains:

These satyrs are our neighbours, and live here,
With whom we have confirmed a friendly league
And dwell in peace.

Years away, but with Diana in spirit, some early mixed gay households developed into a lesbian separatist ideal. Julia L. describes London's Faraday Road commune in the early 1970s: 'The house ended up as just women . . . Mad Lizzie, Sapphire, Lorna, Caroline, Barbara, me, Lynn, there were lots of us. We were still together as a household, we had a lounge and a huge bedroom where women could stay.' A certain political and social idealism also inspires Diana's band, as she explains to Calisto:

> Here is no City-craft.
> Here's no Court-flattery: simpleness and sooth,
> The harmless chase, and strict Virginity
> Is all our practice

There might be quibbles over the definition of virginity, and vegetarianism (the 'harmless chase' hardly being so for the deer), but this radical project is an interesting blueprint for feminist counter-cultural living experiments. It provides exactly what Calisto, disgusted at the corrupt ways of the world, is looking for: somewhere away from man's society, represented by the urban, immoral, lustful court.

> Great Queen, I am sequestered from the world,
> Even in my soul hate man's society,
> And all their lusts, suggestions, all Court-pleasures,
> And City-curiosities are vain,
> And with my finer temper ill agree
> That now have vowed sacred virginity.

Venus, in the Humberside forest with Gallathea and Phyllida, says neither nature nor fortune shall overthrow the women's love and faith. Nature surrounds this band of women, and their ascetic life makes them safe from Fortune because, as Diana says: 'They can lose nothing, that for nothing care'.

The romance of lesbian separatism, like all attempts at an ideal society, is tempered by the context of an unenlightened world. Love is a powerful but potentially disruptive force, which in Diana's wood is ruled by strict pair bonding:

> DIAN Is there no princess in our train,
>   As yet unmatch'd to be her cabin-fellow,
>   And sleep by her?

> ATLANTA Madam, we are all coupled
>   And twin'd in love, and hardly is there any
>   That will be won to change her bedfellow.

The library copy I have has 'WHAT!?' pencilled next to this exchange, presumably by someone surprised at the careful organization of sleeping arrangements for Diana's band. It looks as if Calisto may have to suffer a solitary life among these unshakeable female couples, but the goddess has a practical solution, albeit an imperious one:

> You must be single till the next arrive:
> She that is next admitted of our train,
> Must be her bed-companion; so 'tis lotted.

This edict gives Calisto even less choice in her female partner than she might expect as a princess married off by her father. At least he would know who she was getting. Presumably, however, any woman qualifying to join Diana would be a suitable mate. This submission to the goddess in matters of partnership might have prevented a few of the problems emotional democracy brought to the communes:

> everything was free love and everything else, you can use your imagination. Of course relationships started happening and splitting up and the dramas were out of this world . . . nobody should be jealous and nobody should be monogamous, so of course as soon as somebody became slightly monogamous and then they went off with somebody else, there would be a jealous tantrum so we'd all have to talk about it all night.

Diana's instruction in Heywood's 1610 play coincides with the assertion of the 1994 report into sexual behaviour in Britain that 'there is a tendency for lesbian women to experience relatively stable, long-term relationships'. How much either of these reflects actual practice is impossible to assess, and they are, of course, utterly different creations. One is an admitted work of fiction, although based in the murky area between ancient history and myth. The other claims to be 'The first ever authoritative survey of sexual behaviour in Britain'. The convergence between Jacobean drama and contemporary sociology suggests a persistent set of cultural expectations about female behaviour, even if the methodology and assumptions of the authoritative survey itself are sometimes as questionable as Heywood's history.

Transgender penetration

Jupiter, dressed as a woman, enters Diana's territory: the play's third male intrusion of female space. The goddess is impressed:

> A manly lass, a stout Virago,
> Were all our train proportioned to thy size
> We need not fear mens subtle treacheries . . .

It is, of course, just such a devious betrayal which Jupiter is undertaking. 'Her largeness pleaseth me', says Diana. 'If she have courage Proportioned with her limbs, she shall be champion To all our wrongèd ladies.' Heywood has fun punning on the nature of those services, although the stage directions go along with the deception: '*Her oath is given on Diana's bow*':

> ATLANTA Madam you must be true
> To bright Diana and her virgin crew.
>
> JUPITER To bright Diana and her train I'll stand.

He is joking about his erection, but Diana's response is curious. She takes Jupiter aside and asks 'What can you do?' 'More than the best here can', he promises. There is a sexual double-meaning here, but her secret exchange with him suggests that, having been physically much impressed with her new recruit, there is a private agenda between them. Atlanta has not heard them, and continues the swearing in:

> ATLANTA You shall vow chastity:
>
> JUPITER That's more than I can promise (well proceed)

He must say the first half of that line as an aside, and the rest to Atlanta, since he is not expelled from the ceremony for refusing to promise chastity. The previous aside from Diana suggests that, rather than this simply being Jupiter's joke with the audience, she hears his disavowal of chastity too. If she does, since she does not comment on it, she must be complicit in his sexual intentions. Consistency is not Heywood's strong point, but the rest of the scene is pointless if Diana has secretly realized Jupiter is a man – although it could be played that way. More likely, this adds to the scene's central conceit, of lesbian sex depicted through male impersonation, by giving Diana the desire for her new maiden which

Calisto lacks. The only one of Jupiter's persistent double-meanings here which is definitely addressed to Diana leaves his gender unspecified. The others, however, revel in his concealed penis. Atlanta continues:

ATLANTA You never shall with hated man atone [unite],
  But lie with woman, or else lodge alone

JUPITER Make my oath strong, my protestation deep,
  For this I vow by all the gods to keep.

His oaths are testicles, his protestation his erection, and its deepness stands for itself. He is being sworn to a straight man's sexual paradise, in which playing with ladies is compulsory. This may be a lesbian Eden, but it is created by and for men: writer, performers and, here, the audience, who know that Jupiter is a male actor, playing a male god, pretending to be a woman for sexual advantage.

ATLANTA With ladies you shall only sport and play,
  And in their fellowship spend night and day.

JUPITER I shall.

ATLANTA Consort with them at board and bed,
  And swear no man shall have your maiden-head.

JUPITER By all the powers both earthly and divine,
  If e'er I lose't, a woman shall have mine.

Like Rosalind, he could promise both: 'I will marry you if ever I marry woman' and 'I shall satisfy you if ever I satisfy man'. Although as a character she is his opposite – a woman pretending to be a boy – onstage they are identical, both male actors in women's clothing. For either of these commitments to work out, lesbianism must be impossible. Rosalind cannot marry a woman, and no woman can take another's maidenhead.

Diana, showing either favouritism or Heywood's inconsistency, seems to offer Jupiter the choice of partner denied to Calisto: 'And if with our election, yours agree', she says, 'Calisto here your bed-fellow shall be'. Same-sex bedfellows are not necessarily sexual partners, but Diana's final instructions to them show that Heywood, at least, could imagine such activity between women. She instructs Jupiter and Calisto to greet and get to know each other: 'Then hand each other and acquaint yourselves'. To hand is to masturbate, and to acquaint is to know the cunt. Diana may not intend it, although her earlier knowing exchange with Jupiter implies she could, but she sends her two newest recruits off to finger each other.

This command is immediately followed by a burst of hunting. Bugles aspire to heaven, horns are winded, nimble javelins sing and stags rush up the mountain, pursued by the women, who soon leave them exhausted. Jupiter holds Calisto back from the rest of Diana's train. Her eagerness to get to the hunt shows a certain diverted sexual zest: 'Hie then to stain our javelings' gilded points In blood of yon swift stag, so hot pursued.' Jupiter, however, will not divert his lust, and leads her to a bower where she inadvertently offers him opportunities to pursue his rape, suggesting 'Come shall's lie down a little?' He is determined to have sex with her, whether she consents or not, gripping her and lying on her once she is trapped with him. 'Oh, how I love thee', he says, 'come let's kiss and play'. Calisto, like Rosalind with Celia, cannot understand the point of that. 'How?' she asks. 'So a woman with a woman may', he replies, although she still resists, as his assault continues:

CALISTO I do not like this kissing.

JUPITER   Sweet, sit still.
     Lend me thy lips, that I may taste my fill.

CALISTO You kiss too wantonly.

JUPITER   Thy bosom lend,
     And by thy soft paps let my hand descend.

CALISTO Nay, fie what mean you?

JUPITER   Prithee, let me toy.
     I would the Gods would shape thee to a boy,
     Or me into a man.

This gesture towards the heterosexual imperative is purely for Jupiter's own benefit. Calisto does not want even to be near men, let alone have sex with them. That Jupiter should wish he were a man or that she were a boy, therefore hardly reflects sensitivity to any unease she might feel at sex with another woman. It is nevertheless crucial that, were the gods to answer Jupiter's insincere prayer, Calisto be made a boy, rather than a man.

That he is interested in boys as well as women is enacted at the end of *The Golden Age*. King Tros and his son Ganimed invade Jupiter's Cretan kingdom. Although Jupiter defeats them, he is impressed that Ganimed fights to the end. 'I love thy valour and would woo thy friendship', he says to the boy soldier. This differs from the usual version of the story, which accounts for the god's attraction by Ganymede's extraordinary beauty (see chapter eight). Heywood's use of military and hunting metaphors, which leads up to Jupiter's rape of Calisto, here tries to conceal sexual interest between the two men. Ganimed refuses to accept an offer of freedom unless he fights for it, which excites Jupiter even more. The god says he will try to purchase his love with blows. 'I love him best, whose strokes can loudest sound', says Ganimed. They fight, lose their weapons and embrace. Ganimed accepts the conquest:

JUPITER I have thee and will keep thee.

GANIMED Not as prisoner.

JUPITER As prisoner to my love, else thou art free,
My bosom friend, for so I honour thee.

GANIMED I am conquered by both arms and courtesy.

The play ends with an elaborate dumb-show, in which Jupiter ascends on an eagle to heaven, accompanied not by his wife or the women he has raped, but the boy he has defeated in battle. Psychoanalysis might find in Jupiter's closet homosexual climax an explanation for his compulsive heterosexual promiscuity. What links them more profoundly, however, is the confusion of male sexual conquest and physical violence.

Ganimed and Jupiter understand and respect the martial game which engages them both. Calisto has no desire to play it. Ganimed accepts submission 'by both arms and courtesy', but at no point during Calisto's rape does she neglect her vows. Act Two ends with her desperately struggling and crying for help: 'To do me right Help fingers, feet, nails teeth and all to fight'. After he rapes her, she rejects him, refusing to be his queen.

Further disaster follows, when she becomes pregnant and so is banished from the virgin world as well. Lesbian fundamentalism caused a similar stir in Faraday Road, as Julia L. reports: 'Meanwhile one woman said she had become pregnant and had never fucked anybody.' Carla Toney also remembers the incident: 'I went into the toilet and found "Immaculate Conception" written on the toilet wall.' The expulsion of the pregnant Calisto in *The Golden Age* is a scene which also raises dilemmas in presenting the implausible. Diana and her nymphs prepare to bathe:

> *They unlace themselves, and unlose their buskins: only Calisto refuseth to make her ready. Diana sends Atlanta to her, who perforce unlacing her, finds her great belly, and shows it to Diana, who turns her out of her society, and leaves her. Calisto likewise in great sorrow forsakes the place.*

Mimed, presumably to musical accompaniment, the necessary stylization of the dumb-show allows a display of a pregnant woman's naked belly in a theatre which employed only males. There is pornographic gratuitousness in the display of the female body in this scene, even if it is imagined on the figures of boys.

Peter Paul Rubens painted *Jupiter and Calisto* in 1613, around the same time as Heywood's play. This presents a moment before the rape: Calisto is naked in the bower, Jupiter represented as a woman, but clothed. Another of the god's disguised assaults was painted by Giulio Romano whose *La Fornarina* is intriguingly reworked as one of photographer Cindy Sherman's History Portraits: *Untitled, # 205* (1989). Giulio Romana's picture, of Raphael's mistress, is restaged in Sherman's photograph, Sherman playing the pregnant woman with the blatant use of prosthetics. Like the Jacobean boy actors in Heywood's spectacular, Sherman uses the most effective available technology to effect disguise. The 'great belly' she wears in her picture is simply a plastic refinement of whatever property the boy playing Calisto would have used. Sherman's photograph does nothing to remove the vulnerability of the pregnant woman, her middle ill-concealed by a falling veil. Unlike Rubens' painting, however, where Calisto gazes up and uneasily across the frame at her supposed friend, Sherman's pregnant woman gazes directly at the viewer, implicating those who view the photograph in its exhibition of her (fictional) body. Calisto is triply humiliated: raped, displayed and rejected.

Heywood's narrator, Homer, makes Calisto the criminal in his summary of the events: 'Her crime thus found she's banished from their crew, And in a cave she childs a valiant son'. Equally callous is the father whose flight left her unprotected in the first place. Lycaon describes his daughter's rape only as an attack on him and his brothers the Titans, and even then it comes as a parenthesis, apparently an afterthought, and certainly is not integral to the speech:

> He that expulsed me from Pelagia's crown
> And in my high tribunal sits enthroned
> Is Saturn's son, and styled Jupiter
> (Besides my daughter by his lust deflowered)
> On us the poor distressed Titanoyes
> He hath committed many out-rages.

Male authority deserts Calisto in *The Golden Age*: Lycaon her father; Jupiter the king of the gods, who is also the hero of the play; and even Homer its narrator. She is not even presented as a good mother by Heywood. Her son Archas, brought up by her in the forest, is presented as disturbed by such an upbringing: savage as the tigers, lions, wolves and bears. When she confronts Jupiter with his child, he greets his son enthusiastically, but makes little effort to keep her from heading into the wilderness alone. The violence and determination he showed when raping her is diminished to a token request to stay. Archas is delighted to remain with Jupiter, completing three generations of male humiliation for Calisto.

The Transsexual Empire, Bethnal Green

An East London Labour Party found itself wrangling in February 1996 over the election of Paula (formerly Paul) Thomas to the party's Women's Council. Having had no anatomical alterations, argued her opponents, Paula's only qualification to be a woman was that she said she was. Although no one suggested that she had the sort of nefarious motives present in Jupiter's transgendered penetration of women's space, the same argument has flared occasionally but violently in activist groups for years. At its heart is an irreconcilable difference in theory: between gender as something essentially fixed; and an idea of it as a fluid, performed or constructed notion. That debate is well-aired, but has not solved a series of practical problems. A women-only space or meeting assumes that there is something useful in bringing together women, either because there is inherently something different about women's experience, or because a patriarchal society creates such a difference. Those who believe that the division between women and men's roles has no basis except social convenience are hypocritical to exclude those who not only agree, but actually live in a way which demonstrates the impermanence of gender. Equally, it is hard for essentialists to justify in theory excluding those who, like them, agree that being a woman *is* different, and are prepared to go to extraordinary lengths in pursuit of that conviction. Why should such a reductive question as anatomy be the way to qualify as a woman in progressive circles?

All this theorizing is fine, but look at Jupiter and Calisto. Had Diana had a strict policy on transgender recruitment, Jupiter might have been expelled before causing the trouble he did. The suspicion is that these people may want to be called women in order to penetrate female spaces, but they will behave just like men once they get inside.

Transgender individuals, often pre-operative male-to-female trans-sexuals, have been the subject of furious rows not just in Bethnal Green Labour Party, but also between volunteers on London Lesbian and Gay Switchboard and, in the 1970s, the early Gay Liberation Front. Janice Raymond's *The Transsexual Empire* places transsexuals and lesbians in complete opposition, rather than marching cheerfully under the same proud banner. In this analysis, transsexuals will, like Jupiter, seek to use male powers to colonize all aspects of women's experience. Gay Liberation Front veteran Nettie Pollard is a thoughtful observer of the early debates, when she describes herself as feeling 'extremely torn on the subject':

> There was lots of discussion on whether pre-operative transsexuals should be able to go to the women's group . . . Some of the women felt that these people had very male attitudes and were very patronizing to women and trying to steal women's oppression without giving up their prick power.

The argument of *The Golden Age* is devastating on that point: Jupiter certainly does not give up his prick power. Calisto's surrender of her son to him confirms male superiority: Archas can be raised without his mother, but not without his father. Calisto disappears from the play having proved a convenient means for Jupiter to legitimize conquest of her father's kingdom. He makes her son its new ruler:

Archas, we make thee of Pelagia King,
As King Lycaon's grand-child, and the son
Of faire Calisto. Let that clime henceforth
Be called Arcadia, and usurp thy name.

Arcadia, that land of pastoral idyll, is founded on rape.

The Golden Age confirms some radical lesbians' worst suspicions in its tale of Calisto: threatened, deceived, raped and exploited by a bisexual transvestite sadomasochist paedophile. Its author, however, seems untroubled by her fate, and that of the other women Jupiter mistreats in the course of the play. Given that, it might seem perverse to argue that Thomas Heywood was something of a feminist for his time.

The fact that *The Golden Age* gets as close as any English play before 1660 to recognizing lesbian sex is uncomfortably tied up with its cavalier attitude to exploiting women in any way. Yet it also comes from a dramatist who was unusually prepared to give women importance and independence in his writing. Heywood wrote not only about Queen Elizabeth, but other notable women in myth and history and the titles of his best-known plays indicate an interest in female characters less apparent here, where he is dramatizing classical stories: *A Woman Killed With Kindness* and *The Fair Maid of the West*. Other plays which have women as their titles are the lost *Joan as Good as My Lady* and *The Wise Woman of Hogsdon*. These women are significant characters, without being queens or princesses, even if their treatment hardly seems progressive now. Heywood's mix of exploitation with enthusiasm indicates a man with a real interest in women, at a time when it was possible virtually to ignore them.

When Gallathea's father wants her to dress as a boy, he argues from the precedent of divine shape-changing. 'To gain love the gods have taken shapes of beasts', he explains, which surely means she can dress as a man to save her own life. Jupiter's metamorphoses are never far from lesbian possibility in English Renaissance drama. Valerie Traub identifies two Jacobean plays which 'momentarily stage the temptations of a female-oriented eroticism': *The Golden Age* and James Shirley's *The Bird in a Cage*. They share with *Gallathea* superstitious or over-protective fathers of virgin daughters, but this is hardly unique to works of the period which touch on lesbianism. More unusually, however, they also both feature the real or imagined presence of heaven's most notoriously amorous shape-changer.

Thirty years earlier than the first of these plays, Jupiter's exploits justify the disguise which will embroil Gallathea in love with a woman. In *The Golden Age*, his rape of Calisto is staged until the point he reveals his gender, when it passes off stage. In *The Bird in a Cage*, two women characters act out another episode from the Golden Age: that between Jupiter and Danaë. Passing from the idyllic lesbian Eden of the sixteenth century evoked by Lyly, Shakespeare and Donne, the seventeenth opens with a rougher, more knowing neoclassical scene for female encounters. Jupiter's self-transformations provide the possibility of lesbian sex on stage, albeit a problematic one, in plays written and performed by males. His omnipresent maleness, even in female form, allows the all-male Renaissance theatre tenatively to approach the fact that there is somewhere men are utterly redundant. Only by the end of the century, when women themselves become performers, writers and even managers, can the serious history of the lesbian stage begin.

6

Shakespeare's Sodomite Stage

Tiring House Trade

Ann Bacon had two sons who were keen on the theatre, much to her distress. That they were also keen on young men must have been another cause for concern. Writing to the older brother, Anthony, on his move to Bishopsgate, she notes that the theatres of the district

> infect the inhabitants with corrupt and lewd dispositions. I marvel you did not first consider of the ministry as most of all needful, and then to live so near a place haunted with such pernicious and obscene plays and theatres able to poison the very godly.

Since Anthony escaped a death sentence for sodomy in Montauban only on the intervention of the King of Navarre, Bishopsgate was probably comparatively safe.

If a fraction of what contemporary satirists complain about in the theatres of Shakespeare's London is true, Lady Bacon was not unreasonable in her assessment of the theatre district. Thomas Middleton's *Father Hubburd's Tales* includes advice that at the Blackfriars theatre visitors 'should see a nest of boys able to ravish a man'. The puritan Philip Stubbes asks his readers to:

> Mark the flocking and running to theatres and curtains, daily and hourly, night and day, time and tide to see plays and interludes, where such wanton gestures, such bawdy speeches: such laughing and fleering [sneering]: such kissing and bussing: such clipping and culling: such winking and glancing of wanton eyes and the like is used, as is wonderful to behold. Then these goodly pageants being done, every mate sorts to his mate, every one brings another homeward of their way very friendly, and in their secret conclaves (covertly) they play the *Sodomites*, or worse.

There is a general agreement among the satirists that the theatre is a major haunt of late sixteenth-century gay men. It is one of the places frequented by Michael Drayton's fictional sodomite Mooncalf, and Edward Guilpin complains of the theatregoer 'who is at every play and every night Sups with his ingles, who can well recite'. 'Ingle' usually refers to an older sodomite's younger male companion, often, in these critical works, with an implication of prostitution or some other financial dependence: rent boys, toy boys and house boys.

Like marriage, relations between men involved material as well as sexual and emotional considerations. John Greene condemns the decadence of actors which, he argues, easily slips into prostitution. They:

> find such sweet gains to maintain their idle life, that they might give their whole industry to various and mimical inventions, that they might become men-pleasers, and those of the profanest condition

Lady Bacon's concerns do not end with the audience: plays themselves can poison the very godly. Some years into the seventeenth century, 'Queen's Poet' Francis Lenton has a similar warning for young gallants:

> Plays are the nurseries of vice, the bawd
> That through the senses steals our hearts abroad;
> Tainting our ears with obscene bawdery,
> Lascivious words, and wanton ribaldry;
> Charming the casements of our souls, the eyes,
> To gaze upon bewitching vanities,
> Beholding base loose actions, mimic gesture
> By a poor boy clad in a princely vesture,
> These are the only tempting baits of hell,
> Which draw more youth unto the damnèd cell
> Of furious lust, than all the devil could do
> Since he obtainèd his first overthrow.

Boys and young men played female roles on the Elizabethan and Jacobean stage: and there were some companies composed only of boy performers. Lenton warns that, for a young man attending the theatre for the first time, the sight of boys in costume will be quite enough to inflame lust. John Rainolds is more specific about the sort of dressing up that causes this unhealthy inflammation, in his condemnation of the theatre: offering 'sparkles of lust to that vice the putting of women's attire on men may kindle in unclean affections as Nero showed in Sporus'.

Stephen Gosson's *School of Abuse* goes further, arguing that young men should go into the military rather than the theatre, just as Lady Bacon would rather Anthony joined the ministry. Neither of these seems entirely free of risks for an impressionable lad. Ovid in Ben Jonson's *Poetaster* is another parent dismayed by the homosexuality of the profession:

What? Shall I have my son a stager now, an ingle for players?

One great love of Anthony Bacon's brother Francis was the younger Tobie Matthew, who, although he appeared on stage at Gray's Inn as a youth, was hardly rough trade. His father was Bishop of Durham at the time of his theatrical appearance, and later Archbishop of York. Matthew grew up to be a courtier and diplomat, considered by some to be a spy. There are extensive affectionate letters between the two, and he inspired Francis's influential essay 'On Friendship' which includes the metaphorically theatrical observation that 'If a man have not a friend, he may quit the stage'. His other gay friends at court included James I's lover George Villiers. Indeed, the court of King James was so full of sodomites that Francis Osborne could only compare it, with a shudder, to the stage:

In wanton looks and wanton gestures they [King James and George Villiers] exceeded any part of womankind. The kissing them after so lascivious a mode in public and upon the theatre, as it were, of the world prompted many to imagine some things done in the tiring house [dressing room] that exceed my expression no less than they do my experience.

The most celebrated playwright of this notoriously sodomite theatre was William Shakespeare.

Shakespeare's gay lovers

Let us get one thing clear: there are no heterosexuals in Shakespeare's plays. Nor are there homosexuals or bisexuals. The terms were not invented until three hundred years later. This did not, however, prevent him from writing about characters who express and enact sexual desire. The presence of particular characters or behaviour in the plays or poems tells us nothing concrete about Shakespeare's sex life: attempts to recruit him as heterosexual, homosexual or bisexual are meaningless. The plays, however, offer interesting scope for interpretation, their resonances changing over the centuries they have been performed.

Because of Shakespeare's status as a national monument, discussion of the relationships between men and between women in his plays tends to be fraught with the need to prove that he belongs to one side or another. Oscar Wilde's favourite of his own stories, *The Portrait of Mr W. H.*, imagines a love affair between Shakespeare and a boy actor, Will Hughes. He commissioned a portrait of the fictitious Hughes from gay painter and theatre designer Charles Ricketts in the style of Clouet, which is lost, but may one day turn up just as a forged portrait of Hughes does in the story. Shakespeare's *Sonnets*, which address both a female and a male love, have been used for all manner of biographical speculation.

If some commentators have been over sentimental in such interpretations, against a background of the criminalizing and persecution of homosexuality, they have been more than matched by the homophobia of their detractors: some of them homosexual themselves. Eric Partridge, in a 1947 book he intended to call *Sexuality, Homosexuality and Bawdiness in the Works of William Shakespeare* approvingly quotes Hesketh Pearson's ungenerous complaint that 'Pederasts and pedants have been the curse of Shakespearian biography and criticism', and offers 'I am neither pederast nor pedant' as a qualification for writing such a book. He dismisses homosexuals as 'pathetically eager to prove that Shakespeare is one of *us*'. His own, presumably neither pathetic nor eager, conclusion is that Shakespeare is, like himself, a heterosexual and 'extremely tolerant' in his attitude to homosexuality. Fifty years later it is unfair to berate Partridge too much for his foolishness, but it is extraordinary to read a passage of literary mind-reading which he retained even in the last, 1968, revised edition of his book. It asserts that Shakespeare would

have subscribed in full to the sentiments expressed in the following brief passages from Kenneth Walker's excellent *The Physiology of Sex* . . . '. . . There, in the unfortunate intersexual whose method of expressing his urge disgusts us, walk ourselves, but for the grace of a more satisfactory complement of hormones.'

Looking at how Shakespeare and his contemporaries depicted loving and sexual relationships in the context of Elizabethan and Jacobean society reveals a web of erotic and emotional ties. Many of these are between men or between women and are often ignored or belittled in discussion or production of the plays. It bewilders the guardians of Shakespeare as a monolith of English heritage that he should write about people in whom lesbians and gay men can recognize themselves. Deep-seated homophobia disfigures the teaching and production of his work. Those who insist on Back to Basics in the curriculum should reflect that an honest and historically accurate account of Shakespeare's theatre proves the enduring existence of love and sexual desire between men and between women.

Rehearsing Shakespeare's plays today also benefits from an understanding of the context in which they were written. The simple and widely known fact that the plays were originally performed by all-male casts has clear implications for the sexual interpretation of the works. Revivals cannot recreate the circumstances of those first productions, whether in a reconstructed Globe theatre or with a single-sex company – although such experiments can be revealing and entertaining. This is not an argument for theatrical archaeology – the plays live only through persistent reinterpretation – but for an understanding of the differences and similarities between the imaginary worlds of the plays and our own. Love and sex between men and between women is a significant part of those imaginary worlds, as it is of the world in which those plays are taught and revived. It is as complex and open to interpretation as any other aspect of the plays, but that cannot happen while it is ignored.

Sex As You Like It

Gay director Declan Donnellan has said that 'Shakespearian comedy is quite a homosexual thing'. His all-male production of *As You Like It,* designed by his lover Nick Ormerod for their company Cheek by Jowl, has toured the world bearing out that claim. A 1967 National Theatre production was also performed only by men, with Ronald Pickup as Rosalind, Charles Kay as Celia and Anthony Hopkins as Audrey, but this twentieth-century experiment began in 1920, appropriately enough at the Central London YMCA, with an all-male Elizabethan dress version. Such productions simultaneously draw attention to and ignore the gender of performers: a double response which need not be limited to all-male experiments.

It is at a performance where Rosalind is played by a woman that Oscar Wilde's Dorian Gray begins his fall into vice:

> Sibyl was playing Rosalind. Of course the scenery was dreadful and the Orlando absurd. But Sibyl! You should have seen her! When she came on in her boy's clothes she was perfectly wonderful. She wore a moss-coloured velvet jerkin with cinnamon sleeves, a dainty little green cap with a hawk's feather caught in a jewel, and a hooded cloak lined with dull red.

The night Sibyl Vane plays Rosalind, Dorian Gray first kisses her backstage, and tells her he loves her. It is, however, her performance as the boy Ganymede, the role Rosalind takes in the forest, which he describes. In her boy's clothes, says Dorian Gray: 'She had never seemed to me more exquisite', and it is those clothes on which his description dwells. The cross-dressing allows Dorian to fall in love with a boy and a woman simultaneously. Within the transvestite conventions of Shakespeare's theatre, clothes created gender on stage, costume being a much more significant part of the spectacle than scenery on the open stage of the Globe. The definitions of sexuality which assume gender to be unbending fit uneasily with such performances. A century after Dorian Gray and Sibyl Vane, a woman in the audience of Cheek by Jowl's *As You Like It* might be sexually attracted to Adrian Lester as Rosalind as Ganymede. Is that a lesbian fantasy? A heterosexual one?

> ROSALIND [disguised as Ganymede, pretending to be Rosalind]
> Come, woo me, woo me, for I am in a holiday humour, and
> like enough to consent.
>
> ORLANDO I would kiss before I spoke . . .
>
> ROSALIND Nay, you were better speak first.

There is no word in the banal division of experience into hetero- homo- and bi-, for what we witness. Four hundred years before the breakdown of sexual categories announced by queer, a mass audience is watching two male actors: one playing a woman dressed as a boy; the other playing a youth who imagines he is making love to a boy pretending to be a woman. Of course, such erotic experimentation cannot be sustained, even if it is imaginary. When Hymen, god of marriage, arrives to say 'Peace, ho, I bar confusion', it is not just the complexities of the plot he sorts out, but the forest's jumble of sexual desires, now to be ordered and regulated by wedlock.

The weakest kind of fruit

Pairs of characters named Antonio and Sebastian occur in three of Shakespeare's comedies. In *The Tempest*, they are villainous younger brothers: Antonio has usurped Prospero as Duke of Milan and encourages the plot against his friend Sebastian's older brother, Alonso, King of Naples. In *Twelfth Night*, Antonio is the sea captain who rescues Sebastian, Viola's twin brother, from drowning. In *The Merchant of Venice*, Antonio borrows money from Shylock for his friend Bassanio, the name a version of Sebastian. In *Twelfth Night* and *The Merchant of Venice*, part of the plot hinges on Antonio's devoted love for Sebastian/Bassanio, and in both these plays Antonio, like Jaques in *As You Like It*, is a gloomy figure left out of the final symmetry achieved through marriage, in which his beloved pairs off with a woman.

In all three plays, Antonio, more worldly than his companion, rescues, supports or encourages Sebastian/Bassanio, who may well be younger than him. Other common factors between all three pairs are the characters' Mediterranean origins, which certainly could suggest sexual unorthodoxy to Shakespeare's audience, but which they share with many others; and the odd significance of shipwrecks in the plays, which presumably has no bearing on their treatment of sexuality.

This depiction of male devotion coincides with a tradition in visual art since the medieval period, of homoerotic attachment between Saint Antony and Saint Sebastian. Richard Ellmann in his biography of Oscar Wilde claims that the tradition of a gay Sebastian survived well after the Renaissance:

Sebastian, always iconographically attractive, is the favourite saint among homosexuals. André Raffalovich, when admitted to the third order of Dominicans, took the name Brother Sebastian, and Wilde took Sebastian as his Christian name for his alias in France.

Derek Jarman's 1976 film *Sebastiane* takes the gay interpretation of the saint's story into the twentieth century, while Hugh Sebastian in Keith Winter's 1933 *The Rats of Norway* and Sebastian Venable in Tennessee Williams' 1953 *Suddenly Last Summer* are different stage gay martyrs. Excessive sexual desire causes the downfall of Shakespeare's 'amorous surfeiter', his most famous Antony: for a woman who bitterly predicts that their story will be transformed by theatrical convention:

> Antony
> Shall be brought drunken forth, and I shall see
> Some squeaking Cleopatra boy my greatness
> I'th' posture of a whore.

These words are, of course, originally spoken by just such a boy actor.

The pairing of Antony and Sebastian characters is used by Shakespeare in these three plays from different stages of his writing: relatively early, middle and late in his career. In *The Merchant of Venice*, probably written around 1597, Antonio and Bassanio are the male heroes of the play. In *Twelfth Night*, probably written around 1601, Antonio and Sebastian are less prominent, not appearing until Act Three, and only in four scenes each altogether: Sebastian is still a romantic lead, marrying Olivia in place of his sister Viola/Cesario, with whom Olivia has fallen in love, but Antonio is an old enemy of Orsino, the Duke who will marry Viola. By the time of *The Tempest*, around 1611, the couple are simply wicked. Whether this progression from heroism to villainy is coincidence or design is impossible to know, but it does indicate a flexible use of this conventional relationship.

All three female characters in *The Merchant of Venice* dress as boys at some point. Two use the disguise to encourage their husbands into a technical infidelity: asking for and getting the rings from which the men promised never to part. The third is Shylock's daughter, Jessica, who looks 'sweet, Even in the lovely garnish of a boy' according to her lover Lorenzo. Her transvestite moment is also an occasion of religious crossing: 'Now, by my hood, a gentile and no Jew', says Gratiano as she gets some more of her father's money. John Boswell argues that there was

> a much more powerful medieval *moral* tradition against usury than against homosexual behaviour. Unlike homosexuality, usury had been condemned almost unanimously by philosophers of the ancient world as uncharitable, demeaning, and contrary to 'nature'.

In allowing love between a Christian man and a Jewish woman, the world of *The Merchant of Venice* is more liberal on miscegenation than a thirteenth-century lawbook which decrees:

> Those who have connexion with Jews or Jewesses or are guilty of bestiality or sodomy shall be buried alive in the ground, provided they be taken in the act and convicted by lawful and open testimony.

The activities of unnatural sex and moneylending are also linked. According to the medieval historian Matthew Paris, the French called usurers buggers. In Shakespeare's sonnets four and six, the young man loved by the poet is encouraged to reproduce, through various sexual puns on usury. Is this Venice, which allows certain limited religious freedoms, therefore also softer on sodomites? Antonio has his coterie of male flatterers, but no one, including Portia, seems to find his adoration of Bassanio inappropriate. The only critic of their relationship is his business rival, the other merchant of Venice. Shylock the Jew watches Antonio the man-lover with his young companion and sneers: 'How like a fawning publican he looks.' It is Shylock, however, who makes the catastrophic discovery that the state's tolerance of minorities has its limits.

The love between Antonio and Bassanio is not depicted with the same cynicism or playfulness which characterizes the portraits of houseboy Ganymedes and their wealthy patrons. There is a material interest in the relationship nevertheless: the older, richer Antonio financing the younger man's romantic endeavour; but with no reference to him doing so in return for sexual favours. The contract on which the plot of the play hinges is, however, a fleshy one. At the heart of *The Merchant of Venice* is not a religious dispute, but a voluntary legal undertaking, in which Antonio offers his own flesh for love of Bassanio. This is a gruesome version of the melancholy self-sacrifice which characterizes their relationship. It also binds two men's lives legally, with marriage a secondary result: the hazard of Antonio's body enables Bassanio's to be united with Portia's. Faced with the consequences of his promise, Antonio, who excels in self-pity from the start of the play, argues that his sterile pursuit of a male love-object is in part to blame:

> I am a tainted wether of the flock,
> Meetest for death. The weakest kind of fruit
> Drops earliest to the ground; and so let me.

Even allowing for his constant melancholy, the image of himself as a diseased, castrated ram is pungent.

Antonio's most spirited moments are in rivalry with Portia, the woman he has financed Bassanio to woo. He may be wealthy, but she also has money (some of it his, by the end) and is a woman, so there is no chance of them exchanging roles. He can only be Bassanio's friend, she his wife. Which of them means more to him may still be in the balance, nevertheless. There is comedy in the disguised Portia's response to Bassanio's promise that he would give his wife to the devil if it would save his friend.

> Your wife would give you little thanks for that
> If she were by to hear you make the offer.

In fact it is Antonio who insists that a combination of his own love and the deservings of the boy lawyer Balthasar outweigh Portia's instruction to Bassanio always to keep her ring. That Balthasar is Portia allows this legalistic balance of responsibilities to be ultimately comic rather than tragic. That the rings are sexual tokens heightens the off-colour banter of the closing scene, in which, before all is revealed, Antonio makes a promise to the wife of his beloved youth:

> ANTONIO I once did lend my body for his wealth
> Which, but for him that had your husband's ring
> Had quite miscarried. I dare be bound again
> My soul upon the forfeit, that your lord
> Will never more break faith advisedly.

> PORTIA Then you shall be his surety.

In the delight of Antonio's discovery a few minutes later that his ships and fortune are safe, he, and the audience, can forget that he has just offered his soul as a guarantee of Bassanio's sexual fidelity. It ups the stakes in a strange parody of his previous choice to hazard himself, this time on a promise it is not within his power to keep, for an end he will never enjoy. As King Lear's Fool could have told him:

> He's mad that trusts in the tameness of a wolf, a horse's health, a boy's love, or a whore's oath.

His fancy's queen

The thwarted desires of men for their protégés need not always be melancholy. In *Twelfth Night*, Orsino's mood is fuelled, like Jaques' in *As You Like It*, by music. The Duke of Illyria abruptly puts aside Olivia, for whom he has been pining since the first sounds of the play, in order to propose marriage to Viola, whom he had thought a boy until only a few minutes before. He proposes marriage, *then* asks her to change her clothes:

> Give me thy hand,
> And let me see thee in thy woman's weeds.

The fact that the woman he is about to marry has just converted from being his page Cesario is a matter for joking, rather than agonizing:

> Cesario, come –
> For so you shall be while you are a man;
> But when in other habits you are seen,
> Orsino's mistress, and his fancy's queen.

Comedy allows a safer enjoyment of gender confusion: just as in 1959 *Some Like It Hot* could end with Osgood E. Fielding II assuring Daphne/Jerry that he might not be a woman, but 'Nobody's perfect'. This line, with its implication that Joe E. Brown would be happy with Jack Lemmon, whatever he wore, did not stop Billy Wilder and I. A. L. Diamond getting an Academy Award nomination for the screenplay. Drama is more dangerous: the following year a more veiled scene, in which Lemmon's co-star Tony Curtis is a stripped slave boy helping Laurence Olivier from the bath, was snipped from the film *Spartacus*.

Wilder's infamous tag-line is also the title for a fascinating essay by Stephen Orgel on the convention of boys as women on the Elizabethan and Jacobean stage. He points out that Viola wants her old clothes back, which are with the captain who brought her safely to shore: her version of Sebastian's Antonio. Since the captain has been locked up by Malvolio, and Malvolio has just run off in rage, converting Cesario to Viola will be harder than it might seem. The conventions of comedy erase such practical anxieties in both Shakespeare's play and Wilder's film.

Buddies: Two gentlemen and two noble kinsmen

There are other Sebastians in Renaissance Comedy: Sebastian Wengrave, for example, intrigues with the man-woman Moll Cutpurse in Thomas Middleton and Thomas Dekker's *The Roaring Girl*, a play which also features the character Sir Beauteous Ganymede. Shakespeare's only other Sebastian is both male and female: the girl-boy created by Julia when she disguises herself and becomes a page to her treacherous lover Proteus in *The Two Gentlemen of Verona*. This 'Sebastian' watches the man he loves wooing another woman and, like Viola/Cesario in *Twelfth Night*, becomes an agonized go-between in the affair.

The Two Gentlemen of Verona is an early Shakespeare play, another Mediterranean comedy like *Twelfth Night* and *The Merchant of Venice*. It too has an Antonio: he is not, however, in love with Julia/Sebastian, but the father of Proteus, her beloved. The devoted male friendship this play explores is between Proteus and the other gentleman of Verona, Valentine. It is not the type of love exemplified by the Antonio and Sebastian stories, in which the affections of the former are made secondary to the marriage of the latter. The relationship between Valentine and Proteus is closer to that in Richard Edwards' play *Damon and Pithias*, or John Lyly's story *Euphues*. In these accounts of pure friendship between male equals, their love for each other may be tested by rivalry over a woman, but emerges triumphant.

The Greeks were best at this sort of thing, of course. So it appears from a play written at the other end of Shakespeare's career: a collaboration with John Fletcher, half of the most famous male partnership of the Jacobean theatre. *The Two Noble Kinsmen* contains two pairs of devoted men friends, as well as an adoring female duo. The

two male couples, Palamon and Arcite – the ones in the title – and
Theseus and Pirithous, are both notorious for their great friendship.
This comes from classical literature, including Plutarch's *Lives* – 'They
both wondered at each other's beauty and courage' – and the medieval
sources for the play.

When Emilia observes of Theseus and Pirithous 'How his longing
Follows his friend!', Hippolyta, Theseus' queen, agrees:

> Their knot of love,
> Tied, weaved, entangled with so true, so long,
> And with a finger of so deep a cunning,
> May be outworn, never undone.

Emilia describes what is different between men's love and women's:

> Theirs has more ground, is more maturely seasoned,
> More buckled with strong judgement, and their needs
> The one of th'other may be said to water
> Their intertangled roots of love

Her love for a girl when young was innocent, but that between Theseus
and Pirithous is more adult. Since root also means penis, the watering
and intertangling of them she praises is a lively image, as is that of the
finger which knots them so deep and so long. This may seem an over-
zealous reading, but this is a play which is self-conscious about
dramatic bawdy, including a schoolmaster who is ridiculed for his
lewdness and possibly sodomy: 'Stop no more holes but what you
should', he is advised. He appears in the context of a performance,
eccentric for classical Athens, of a British folk play, a form whose
appetite for filthy *double entendre* is insatiable, the troupe being given
money to paint their pole.

The language of Renaissance friendship meanwhile sets up Palamon and
Arcite as pure in their love. Arcite encourages his friend to leave Thebes
with him, before the moral corruption of the city drags them down:

> Dear Palamon, dearer in love than blood,
> And our prime cousin, yet unhardened in
> The crimes of nature, let us leave the city,
> Thebes, and the temptings in't, before we further
> Sully our gloss of youth.

And here to keep in abstinence we shame
As in incontinence; for not to swim
I'th' aid o'th' current were almost to sink –
At least to frustrate striving; and to follow
The common stream 'twould bring us to an eddy
Where we should turn or drown; if labour through,
Our gain but life and weakness.

Here a retreat into male love is actually a route to greater purity. The specific temptings to crimes of nature which Thebes offers are not specified, but the fact that Palamon is yet unhardened in them confirms suspicions that the options of abstinence or incontinence are substantially sexual. Military matters overtake, however, as the friends' city comes under threat from Athens, thwarting their departure.

The two end up in prison, trapped in a scene Fletcher is assumed to have written, whose sexual undertones erupt through the language of finer sentiments. It veers between the high-flown and the ludicrous, as their devoted pure declarations to each other are quickly tossed aside at the sight of a woman. Palamon is sad at their exclusion from the physical world: they will never see 'The hardy youths strive for the games of honour', be praised and rewarded for 'the wagging of a wanton leg', never fight, use their swords or 'shake / Our pointed javelins' again. Arcite, in the language of the Sonnets, bewails the world of adult maleness which they will never know. They will never marry, therefore never have sex with a woman, therefore never have children; and as a result time has no meaning. 'We shall know nothing here but one another', he regrets, but there is a possible double meaning in 'know'. For there are comforts: at least they have each other:

ARCITE Yet cousin,
　　　　Even from the bottom of these miseries . . .
　　　　I see two comforts rising . . .

PALAMON . . . 'Tis a main goodness, cousin, that our fortunes
　　　　Were twined together. 'Tis most true, two souls
　　　　Put in two noble bodies . . . so they grow together
　　　　Will never sink

Like Theseus and Pirithous' intertangled roots of love, there is something here in the rising from the bottom, twining, growing together and never sinking of the two men's most vital parts. It is not, however, the imagery of the other men's maturely seasoned love; the sexual imagery peeking through here is more of unconscious frustration than deliberate execution. Prison is, after all, one of the places where men regularly have sex with each other.

This might all seem like reading beneath the text to avoid the surface, but Arcite makes an overt declaration of the possibilities of their love, separated from 'worse men' and liberty which might corrupt them, as if they were women.

> ARCITE We are an endless mine to one another:
> We are one another's wife, ever begetting
> New births of love; we are father, friends, acquaintance;
> We are in one another, families –
> I am your heir, and you are mine; this place
> Is our inheritance: no hard oppressor
> Dare take this from us. Here, with a little patience,
> We shall live long and loving. No surfeits seek us –
> The hand of war hurts none here, nor the seas
> Swallow their youth. Were we at liberty
> A wife might part us lawfully, or business;
> Quarrels consume us; envy of ill men
> Crave our acquaintance. I might sicken, cousin,
> Where you should never know it, and so perish
> Without your noble hand to close mine eyes,
> Or prayers to the gods. A thousand chances,
> Were we from hence, would sever us.

> PALAMON You have made me –
> I thank you cousin Arcite – almost wanton
> With my captivity . . .

> PALAMON Is there record of any two that loved
> Better than we do, Arcite?

> ARCITE   Sure there cannot.

> PALAMON I do not think it possible our friendship
> Should ever leave us.

> ARCITE   Till our deaths it cannot.

Out of context, this could serve as a fine basis for a gay partnership ceremony. This pure male romance is about to be completely undermined, however, by the arrival of a woman. Underneath the high-flown sentiment is indeed material to make Palamon almost wanton. Verbal sex penetrates the rhetoric of pure friendship as a string of double meaning threads through Arcite's speech. Lust is on his tongue, even if he negates it: they are each other's endless mines; wifes ever begetting new births; but there will be no hard oppressor, no surfeits, no swallowing of youth, no sickening and perishing. This is the rhetoric of self control.

It is to no effect, however, since Palamon is immediately overcome by the sight of a woman, Emilia. From this point the love between the men, and Arcite's own life, are doomed. As in the rest of the play, there is an uneasy mixture of tragedy and comedy, expressed in part by the capacity of the poetry to be simultaneously high-minded and smutty. It is a play of homosexual romantic ideals contradicted by heterosexual lust: two men who say they will never love anyone as much as each other, both of whom then fall for a woman who says she will never love anyone so much as her childhood girlfriend. In the garden beneath them, Emilia, also having a saucy scene with a woman attending her, offers an ironic critique of the men's position, and thus indirectly her own:

EMILIA What flower is this?

WOMAN 'Tis called narcissus, madam.

EMILIA That was a fair boy, certain, but a fool
    To love himself. Were there not maids enough?

Not in prison, certainly.

The sexual triangle of the *Sonnets'* two men and one woman plays itself out. Here is what Leontes thinks he sees in another late Shakespeare, *The Winter's Tale.* When he watches his wife, Hermione discuss with Polixenes the two men's boyhood devotion, it is the spring for the jealous rage which nearly destroys them both. Here there is a strange comedy in the youths' friendly discussions before they fight viciously over Emilia. Two youths who love each other prepare to penetrate each other with weapons instead. It is another anachronistic phallic event, after the strolling players and their pole, the rules being:

which can force his cousin to touch the pillar, he shall enjoy her

Arcite wins, but is fatally injured when the horse Emilia has given him overturns, arse over face. The story of his death has a vocabulary appropriate for a pornographic story: plunging, rooting, between the legs, standing on end, coming over and rider's load:

> When neither curb would crack, girth break, nor diff'ring plunges
> Disroot his rider whence he grew, but that
> He kept him 'tween his legs, on his hind hooves –
> On end he stands –
> That Arcite's legs, being higher than his head,
> Seemed with strange art to hang. His victor's wreath
> Even then fell off his head; and presently
> Backward the jade comes o'er and his full poise
> Becomes the rider's load.

This equine climax having dispatched his rival, Palamon is spared execution to accept Emilia from his dying friend. As he watches his cousin's dead body taken off, he muses on the fact that his marriage has cost them their love and Arcite's life.

> O cousin,
> That we should things desire which do cost us
> The loss of our desire! That naught could buy
> Dear love, but loss of dear love!

Each man kills the thing he loves.

Beatrice and Benedick: the gay couple

Oscar Wilde once played Benedick in *Much Ado About Nothing*, a play which teaches a man and a woman to settle down together. 'Who is his companion now?' asks Beatrice about Benedick, 'He hath every month a new sworn brother.' His friendship may not be fatal to young men, but it is hardly healthy:

> BEATRICE Is there no young squarer now that will make a voyage
>   with him to the devil?
>
> MESSENGER He is most in the company of the right noble Claudio.

BEATRICE O Lord, he will hang upon him like a disease. He is
sooner caught than the pestilence, and the taker runs pres-
ently mad. God help the noble Claudio. If he have caught the
Benedick, it will cost him a thousand pound ere a be cured.

The debaucheries to which Benedick leads his young men are not
specified, and Beatrice is probably exaggerating for effect. The plot of
their romance hinges, however, on her demand that Benedick kill
Claudio to prove he loves her. He must destroy his former male
companion before she can believe him. The reason is Claudio's
treatment of Hero, but Benedick's dilemma is heightened by his loves
for both Claudio and Beatrice.

Not that he starts the play with any avowed love for her. His rejection
of women is extreme, as it needs to be for the comedy of his romantic
fall. He is 'a professed tyrant to their sex'. He laments, 'Shall I never see
a bachelor of three-score again?' Don Pedro calls him 'an obstinate
heretic in the despite of beauty'. In the laws of the time, crime against
the kings of heaven and earth had two forms: heresy and buggery or
sodomy. His bawdy comments suggest he has sex with women, but he
rejects marriage: 'I will live a bachelor.'

Benedick is set up as a man's man, Beatrice as a woman who can
match men. She 'fathers herself' and will not marry 'till God make men
of some other mettle than earth'. She wants a husband who is both
youth and man, or she will end up in heaven sitting with the bachelors.
Claudio is pretty: 'exquisite' and shallow. Benedick compares him to a
calf, after he has rejected their friendship for love of Beatrice.

In one, entirely anachronistic, sense *Much Ado About Nothing* is
heterosexual propaganda. The soldiers' world of masculine affection is
what Benedick and Claudio must leave to choose effeminate
domesticity. Promiscuous attachments with men must be replaced by a
steady contract with a woman, even if, as in this play, both Benedick
and Beatrice are tricked into accepting what we know they really want
but are too proud to admit.

Once married, Benedick seeks to share his state with others.
Contradicting his own experience, he tells Don Pedro that to be an
unmarried man is a cause for melancholy: 'Prince, thou art sad, get thee
a wife, get thee a wife.' Don Pedro is left out of the final marrying, like
the other melancholiacs, Jaques and the Antonios. His world is a man's

world, that of the army, just as the others live in piracy, monasticism or the exchange.

That's my boy

Francis Flute, the bellows mender, may be named for his high voice, but resists the obvious casting he is given in the tedious brief scene of *Pyramus and Thisbe*:

> Nay, faith, let not me play a woman: I have a beard coming.

He is not much better served by a 1979 editor of *A Midsummer Night's Dream*, who classes Flute 'a sexual defective' on the evidence of his pitch and beardlessness, comparing him to Hardy's Christian Cantle: another such man 'not unsympathetically laughed at'. Given that Flute is far more likely to be a boy than a eunuch, this is perhaps not the place to wonder quite how pleasant being sympathetically laughed at might feel to a sexual defective. In fact even bearded youths can get away with playing women, it seems. In John Fletcher's *Monsieur Thomas*, Hylas kisses Thomas, who is disguised as a girl, and says:

> Her lips are monstrous rugged; but that surely
> Is but the sharpness of the weather

His lack of perception is considerable, since he later marries this hirsute bride.

Not only is Flute made to play Thisbe, but his performance before Duke Theseus includes the most inadvertently obscene moments of Peter Quince's script. Separated from her lover, Pyramus, by Wall, played by Tom Snout the tinker, Thisbe becomes embroiled in a mounting sequence of filthy double meanings. Firstly, Pyramus curses Wall's stones for hiding Thisbe from him. That stones can also mean testicles is surely not lost on both the onstage Athenian audience and the theatre one. In *The Merchant of Venice*, Salerio jokes at Shylock's loss of his daughter and his wealth:

> Why, all the boys in Venice follow him,
> Crying, 'His stones, his daughter, and his ducats!'

Thisbe's own pathetic address to Wall piles up even more accidental *double entendre*:

My cherry lips have often kissed thy stones,
Thy stones with lime and hair knit up in thee.

The vaginal opening of her cherry lips kisses his stones, which taste of
the sticky sap of lime – semen – and (pubic) hair. Boy/woman and
man/wall are sexually knit up in a murotic fantasy which reaches climax
when the actors Flute and Bottom attempt to kiss each other through
Snout's hole. The 'crannied hole or chink' in the wall is created by
Snout's hand: 'let him hold his fingers thus', Bottom demonstrates in
rehearsal. If these are held, accidentally or by design, not at arm's
length, but at crotch level, there is even more fun to be had from the two
lovers' attempts to make contact. If Wall has his back to her, Thisbe's
lament, 'I kiss the wall's hole, not your lips at all', needs no more
explanation.

The potential sexual allusion in the Athenian workmen's play
disproportionately involves Flute as Thisbe. As a woman, he is
inevitably crucial to the romance of the story it tells. The convention
that a boy can represent a woman is not played upon in the body of
A Midsummer Night's Dream, in which Hippolyta, Titania, Helena and
Hermia do not cross dress. Only in the play within the play, which
places the audience at another remove, is the transvestism explored.
Here it is funny, even obscenely so, to watch a boy playing a boy playing
a woman, while the integrity of the other onstage female characters is
unchallenged. As a former Amazon queen and two bosom girlfriends,
the 'real' women in this play come from worlds which exclude maleness
entirely.

Meanwhile in fairyland, Oberon, who seems to maintain an open yet
stormy marriage with Titania, has decided to put his foot down. He
may grudgingly accept her other sexual relationships, as she does his,
but will not tolerate her possession of a 'lovely boy'. Puck, presumably
following his master's line, claims the boy was stolen from an Indian
king. Titania maintains the boy's mother was a votaress of her order
who died in childbirth. Both stories could be true, but this custody
battle is having disastrous effects on the weather and the seasons.
Titania refuses to let Oberon have the boy as his henchman, and so he
makes her fall in love with the grotesquely sexualized Bottom with his
ass-head. This passion makes Titania happy to give up the boy, and
possession of him satisfies Oberon and calms the supernatural discord.

The battle for ownership of a lovely boy is central to the plot and the characters of the fairy king and queen, yet is kept offstage. The boy is an obscure object of desire, part of that obscurity being the sexual element in his pursuit, by this husband and wife who are not his parents. Bestiality on stage is one thing, it appears, paedophilia with a hint of incest quite another. The former can be tamed by comedy; the latter never.

Cupid's Butt-Shaft

'Ganymede' claims he has cured a man of love by making him woo him as his mistress:

> At which time would I, being but a moonish youth, grieve, be effeminate, changeable, longing and liking; proud, fantastical, apish, shallow, inconstant, full of tears, full of smiles, for every passion something, and for no passion truly anything, as boys and women are, for the most part, cattle of this colour; would now like him, now loathe him; then entertain him, then forswear him; now weep for him, then spit at him; that I drave my suitor from his mad humour of love to a living humour of madness, which was, to forswear the full stream of the world, and to live in a nook merely monastic.

Which last absurdity is of course what the men around Rosalind's father are doing.

Going into the woods appeals to Ferdinand, King of Navarre and his noblemen in *Love's Labour's Lost*. Like the exiled Duke Senior in *As You Like It*, he creates an enclave purified from worldly corruption. His troupe of warriors against society's temptations make the choice which Palamon and Arcite will discuss, but not take, in *The Two Noble Kinsmen*. Berowne is dismayed, however, by some of the points he has to sign:

> Item. 'That no woman shall come within a mile of my court . . .
> On pain of losing her tongue' . . .

> Item. 'If any man be seen to talk with a woman within the term of three years, he shall endure such public shame as the rest of the court can possibly devise.'

The woodland settings for these all-male experiments may be named the Forests of Arden or Navarre, but sound more like a cross between Radical Faery encampments outside San Francisco, and the hotbed of nudist academic misogyny, Oxford's Parsons Pleasure.

The most diligent observer of the No Ladies rule is Don Adriano de Armado, whose first action in the play is to send the idiot Costard to be punished by the king for heterosexual activity. Armado is the model of a Renaissance London sodomite: a vain, tawny Spaniard, 'fashion's own knight', who describes himself as

besieged with sable-coloured melancholy

He claims the king is his 'familiar':

it will please his Grace, by the world, sometime to lean upon my poor shoulder, and with his royal finger, thus dally with my excrement

by which he means his moustache. He is inseparable from his tender juvenile, the precocious and cheeky pageboy Moth, who sings to make his sense of hearing passionate. His hypocrisy is exposed when he falls for Jaquenetta, the very woman with whom Costard has dallied. She is not at all sure what to make of him. 'Man?' she asks on their first meeting. Like the other men in the play who have forsworn women, Don Armado cannot keep his vows. The only thing more ridiculous than a sodomite is a sodomite in love with a country wench.

This sexually punning comedy of men and women in physically separated worlds is at one level a demonstration that love of men for women will always win through. As Don Armado puts it, in typically affected style:

Cupid's butt-shaft is too hard for Hercules' club, and therefore too much odds for a Spaniard's rapier

Despite this, it has the most equivocal ending of all Shakespeare's comedies, as the men are sentenced to another year's waiting for marriage. Berowne points out the peculiarity:

Our wooing doth not end like an old play;
Jack hath not Jill . . .

Instead Armado, brought low by his devotion to a social inferior, introduces a final dialogue of the owl and the cuckoo. It is written by the real men's men in *Love's Labour's Lost*, those who seem to have had no interest in women to give up: the curate Sir Nathaniel and the schoolteacher Holofernes. The latter, according to Moth (who should know) 'teaches boys the hornbook'. Their concluding entertainment derides marriage as a state for men, as the play preceding it has mocked the celibate life. In his last prosaic words of the play, Armado divides the company, presumably by gender once more, with a wry venereal reference to the classic cure for syphilis:

> The words of Mercury are harsh after the songs of Apollo. You,
> that way; we, this way.

Shakespeare's likely model for the court of Navarre's refined traveller of Spain is Philip II's former favourite, Antonio Perez. He was indeed a former resident of Navarre, escaping there before arriving in England, having been condemned as a homosexual by the Inquisition. His reputation seems to have been even less savoury than Don Armado's.

> Your brother . . . keepeth that bloody Pérez, as I told him then,
> yea as a coach-companion and bed companion.

Ann Bacon again, writing to Anthony, this time about Francis, who, you may remember, escaped execution for sodomy thanks to the real King of Navarre. If anything, real life was more depraved than the theatre.

7

Wearing the Trousers

Renaissance Women Go Butch

A goddess like Diana or a queen like Elizabeth may be praised yet not married, but these are exceptions. For most late sixteenth-century women, remaining single doomed them to join with an ape after death. Beatrice in *Much Ado About Nothing* resists all marriage, but knows the proverb:

> I will even take sixpence in earnest of the bearherd and lead his
> apes into hell.

As Elizabeth's reign over England ended and James' began ('the king is dead, long live the queen' some wits are supposed to have said), some of the men who wrote for the stage show signs of feminism. The final scene of Shakespeare's *The Taming of the Shrew* (c. 1594), with Katherine's eloquent speech of self-abasement, is an ugly celebration of male supremacy. John Fletcher's sequel *The Woman's Prize, or, The Tamer Tamed* (c. 1611) has its revenge on Shakespeare's brutalizing husband, as Petruchio's second wife and a band of other women subdue him instead. The women sing in praise of this gender revolution, symbolized as a change of clothing:

> A health for all this day,
> To the woman that bears the sway,
> And wears the breeches;
> Let it come, let it come!
> Let this health be a seal,
> For the good of the common-weal
> The woman shall wear the breeches!

Maiden bachelors and virgin maidens

A more substantial manifesto against marriage occurs in a play written by three men, Thomas Dekker, Henry Chettle and William Haughton, *Patient Grissil* (1599). Based on the tale also found in the *Decameron* and *The Canterbury Tales*, it shows a poor but honest woman cruelly tested by her husband. While Grissil bears the humiliations of matrimony, however, her sister-in-law Julia resists the advances of three suitors: Farneze, Onophrio and Urcenze.

> URCENZE Would you not have men love you sweet mistress?
>
> JULIA No not I, fie upon it sweet servant
>
> ONOPHRIO Would you wish men to hate you?
>
> JULIA Yes rather than love me, of all saints I love not to serve mistress Venus.
>
> FARNEZE Then I perceive you mean to lead apes in hell
>
> JULIA That spiteful proverb was proclaimed against them that are married upon earth . . .

Julia sets herself up against the proverbial wisdom and, far from becoming less appealing to her suitors as a result, has them eating out of her hand, Her notion of female intergrity offers an antidote to the relentless passivity of the title character.

> JULIA . . . for to be married is to live in a kind of hell.
>
> FARNEZE Aye as they do at barleybreak.
>
> JULIA Your wife is your ape, and that heavy burden wedlock, your jackanape's clog, therefore I'll not be tied to't. Master Farneze, sweet virginity is that invisible god-head that turns us into Angels, that makes us saints on earth and stars in heaven. Here virgins seem goodly, but there glorious. In heaven is no wooing yet all there are lovely. In heaven are no weddings yet all there are lovers.

Her success in arguing that marriage benefits neither men nor women convinces the potential husbands. Rather than marry her, they become a sort of fan club, an earthly answer to Diana's court – and perhaps a flattering reflection of Queen Elizabeth's. Chettle was certainly a fan, publishing an elegy, *England's Mourning Garment*, when the Queen died, three or four years after this play was first performed.

> ONOPHRIO Let us sweet madam turn earth into heaven, by being
> all lovers here too.
>
> JULIA So we do: to an earthly heaven we turn it.
>
> ONOPHRIO Nay but dear Julia, tell us why you so much hate to
> enter into the lists of this same combat matrimony?
>
> JULIA You may well call that a combat, for indeed marriage is
> nothing else but a battle of love, a friendly fighting, a kind of
> favourable terrible war: but you err Onophrio in thinking I
> hate it. I deal by marriage as some Indians do the Sun, adore
> it and reverence it, but dare not stare on it, for fear I be stark
> blind. You three are bachelors, and being sick of this maiden-
> head count all things bitter which the physic of a single life
> ministers unto you: you imagine if you could make the arms
> of fair ladies the spheres of your hearts, good hearts, then
> you were in heaven. Oh but bachelors take heed, you are no
> sooner in that heaven but you straight slip into hell.

Chastity is the alternative Julia offers; and as the play progresses it seems frankly the most desirable of the three possibilities dramatized. Julia's brother the Marquess cruelly tests his wife Grissil; meanwhile a Welsh couple, Gwenthyan and Sir Owen ap Meredith, fight relentlessly. Given the choice between a cruel husband in one marriage, or a shrewish wife in the other, Julia maintains her resistance through four acts. She is the most articulate woman in the play, and her rejection of matrimony is vigorously written.

> Gwenthyan's peevishness and Grissil's patience make me here to
> defy that ape Cupid. If your love stand upon his laws, I charge
> you leave it. I charge you never to sigh for love, nor speak of love,
> nor frown for hate. If you sigh I'll mock you, if you speak I'll stop
> mine ears, if you frown I'll bend my fist.

She cannot completely subvert the conventions of Renaissance comedy, however: like *As You Like It* the play climaxes with a song to Hymen, god of marriage. Grissil is released from her torments and Gwenthyan, like Katherine at the end of *The Taming of the Shrew*, promises her husband a sort of truce. It is Julia, however, who disrupts this neat ending, interrupting before the Marquess can lead off the happy couples. She addresses the company and the audience with a stirring restatement of her theme:

> besides ourselves there are a number here, that have beheld
> Grissil's patience, your own trials, and Sir Owen's sufferance,
> Gwenthyan's frowardness, these gentlemen lovertine [addicted to
> love], and myself a hater of love. Amongst this company I trust
> there are some maiden bachelors and virgin maidens. Those that
> live in that freedom and love it, those that know the war of
> marriage and hate it, set their hands to my bill, which is rather to
> die a maid and lead apes in hell, than to live a wife and be
> continually in hell.

Gwenthyan contradicts her by making a speech about the importance of marriage, but advising wives who would bridle their husbands to follow her example in the play. This leaves the Marquess anxious to know who will take the part of patience as the third option for women. This is the one the play might be expected to endorse given the choice of subject. Ironically, the expected eulogy for submissiveness is impossible, since Patient Grissil herself does not speak. Her supposed sentiments are left for the buffoon Sir Owen to express. Thus the play ends with the case for being a patient wife put by an idiot man speaking on behalf of a mute woman. If that was not enough to undermine its effect, Sir Owen eventually gets completely confused about what he is trying to say. The argument for 'maiden bachelors and virgin maidens' to remain unmarried hangs persuasively over the end of the play.

Praise for a woman choosing the single life might be appropriate for a woman in the time of Elizabeth I. Twenty years after *Patient Grissil*, the court of James I is satirized for its decadence, with hints of the horrors to which women may turn in the absence of men. Philip Massinger's play *The Bondman* (1623) tells of a decadent Sicilian aristocracy threatened by a slave revolt. The absence of its army in a foreign war makes Sicily vulnerable, but also leaves Corsica, one of its noblewomen, flirting with sexual alternatives to men:

> . . . Fie on these warres,
> I am starv'd for want of action, not a gamester left
> To keep a woman play; if this world last
> A little longer with us, ladies must study
> Some new found mystery, to cool one another,
> We shall burn to cinders else; I have heard there have been
> Such arts in a long vacation; would they were
> Revealed to me

The heavily hinted holiday activities of which Corsica has heard are clearly lesbian. Unlike Julia in *Patient Grissil* these women are not renouncing sex in the absence of men. If they can only work out how, they will be cooling each other's heated passions all summer long.

The Bondman is not an isolated example of early seventeenth-century anxiety about the possibilities for female behaviour. Three years before the play's premiere, the pamphlet *Hic Mulier* berated the women of London for sexual excessiveness of a different kind: that resulting from dressing in clothes designated for men. That this was a serious issue is confirmed by the king's instruction that cross-dressing by women be condemned from the pulpit.

Prostitution, and perhaps witchcraft or piracy, were risky possibilities for independent employment by women at the time. Androgyny was implicated in all of them, inevitably since any independent action by a woman revolted against the codes which bound her behaviour to her gender. If such rebellions were depicted in contemporary drama they were less roundly condemned than in the broadsides. Since the theatre was itself a transvestite activity, and often under attack from the same moralists, a certain sympathy might be expected.

Thomas Dekker, one of the *Patient Grissil* playwrights, consistently contributes to plays which, while hardly proto-feminist, concede a wider range of opportunities to the women presented on stage – and therefore in the audience. In his two-part play *The Honest Whore*, the title gives some sense of such sympathies. The title character Bellafront is not just a tart with a heart, but a major heroine. She dabbles in cross-dressing in order to see see Hippolito, the man she loves. On her arrival, disguised as a page, Hippolyto's servant comments on her androgynous appeal.

Dekker's most lasting spunky woman, however, was not his own creation. Together with Thomas Middleton, his collaborator on part one of *The Honest Whore*, he wrote a seventeenth-century biopic partly based on the life, and greatly inspired by the fame, of Jacobean London's remarkable gender-bending celebrity, Mary Frith.

The Toms' Tomrig Moll

Mary Frith's father was a shoemaker in the Barbican area of the City of London, where coincidentally the Royal Shakespeare Company's new London theatre opened in 1982. The following year, in a belated local tribute four centuries after her birth, the company staged the first major revival of Middleton and Dekker's *The Roaring Girl* (1611). An account of Frith's Barbican childhood can be found in the anonymous book *The Life and Death of Mrs Mary Frith. Commonly Called Mal Cutpurse*, published in 1662, around the time of her death. How much of it was invented, or altered with hindsight, is impossible to assess, but it depicts her as a tomboy from her early years:

> A very Tomrig or Rumpscuttle she was, and delighted and sported only on boys' play and pastime, not minding or companying with the girls: many a blow and bang this hoyting procured her, but she was not so to be tamed or taken off from her rude inclinations; she could not endure the sedentary life of sewing or stitching, a sampler was as grievous as a winding-sheet, her needle, bodkin and thimble, she could not think on quietly, wishing them changed into a sword or dagger for a bout at cudgels. . . . She would fight with boys and courageously beat them, run, jump, leap or hop with any of them, or any other play whatsoever. . . . above all she had a natural abhorrence to the tending of children

This account goes on to describe her as a notorious thief, fortune-teller and bully, but the other references to her life which survive relate to her early popularity in the theatre, as a performer in her own right as well as a character in plays.

The cluster of appearances between 1610 and 1612, on stage and in court, as herself and performed by others, while Mary Frith was in her late twenties, suggests a considerable reputation. She may have been seen on stage as early as 1605, but these two years are the high-point of her celebrity. As well as *The Roaring Girl*, first performed in 1610, she is presumed to be the title figure of the play *Mad Pranks of Merry Moll of the Bankside* by John Day in the same year. In 1612 she appears as a character in Nathan Field's play *Amends for Ladies*, and is herself in court for real, accused, among other things, of performing on stage.

This Moll-mania was part of the marketing used by the theatres and Frith: the plays stimulated interest in seeing the woman herself, who made people keen to see plays about her. The epilogue to *The Roaring Girl* explicitly invites the audience back to see the real woman, live on stage:

> for such faults, as either the writers' wit
> Or negligence of the actors' do commit,
> Both crave your pardons: if what both have done
> Cannot full pay your expectation,
> The Roaring Girl herself, some few days hence,
> Shall on this stage give larger recompense;
> Which mirth that you may share in, herself does woo you,
> And craves this sign: your hands to beckon her to you.

There are modern-day parallels in the rush of competing biographies, authorized and unauthorized, which cash in on celebrities. Frith seems to have survived and even thrived on this exploitation, by herself and others, remaining confident even when in trouble with the law.

A roaring girl inherently crosses gender lines: the term is a twist on roaring boys, the name for notorious gangs of riotous youths. The prologue to Middleton and Dekker's play suggests that early seventeenth-century London had no shortage of roaring girls, but that their Moll is something special.

> I see attention sets wide ope her gates
> Of hearing, and with covetous listening waits,
> To know what girl, this Roaring Girl should be.
> (For of that tribe are many.) One is she
> That roars at midnight in deep tavern bowls;
> That beats the watch, and constables controls;
> Another roars i'th day time, swears, stabs, gives braves
> Yet sells her soul to the lust of fools and slaves.
> Both these are suburb-roarers. Then there's (besides)

A civil city-Roaring Girl, whose pride,
Feasting and riding, shakes her husband's state,
And leaves him roaring through an iron gate.
None of these Roaring Girls is ours: she flies
With wings more lofty.

These women must have been either individuals recognizable to the
audience by such descriptions, or representative of common types of
behaviour. It is a shame that their stories are not recorded as well as
Frith's. Even allowing for dramatic overstatement, this catalogue of
outspoken brawlers, whores and husband-tamers suggests a range of
intriguing possibilities for tough women at the time.

Although the title character, Moll Cutpurse has a subsidiary role in
the main plot of *The Roaring Girl*. She is the object of a bogus romance,
invented by young Sebastian Wengrave. Sebastian's father, Sir
Alexander Wengrave, has sworn to disinherit his son if he marries Mary
Fitz-Allard. Since Young Wengrave has no intention of marrying
without money, he follows instead what he calls his 'crooked way'. He
hopes to horrify his father by pretending love for the wrong Mary (Moll
Cutpurse) thus weakening his father's opposition to the right one. He
describes the plot, and her namesake, to Mary Fitz-Allard:

There's a wench
Called Moll, mad Moll, or merry Moll, a creature
So strange in quality, a whole city takes
Note of her name and person, all that affection
I owe to thee, on her in counterfeit passion,
I spend to mad my father: he believes
I dote upon this Roaring Girl

Young Wengrave is right to choose Moll Cutpurse as a way to shock his
father. Sir Alexander considers her totally unsuitable for his family,
describing her to his friends as a monster:

A creature . . . nature hath brought forth
To mock the sex of woman. It is a thing
One knows not how to name: her birth began
Ere she was all made. 'Tis woman more than man,
Man more than woman

He blames nature for Moll's mixture of genders: the pun on 'made' and 'maid' is in keeping with his theory that she was born prematurely, before she became a fully fledged female.

Old Wengrave's horror and disgust is not presented as the play's interpretation of Cutpurse by Dekker and Middleton. Their Moll is sympathetic, unlike the only other surviving dramatic treatment of her. *Amends for Ladies* (1612), written by Nathan Field, follows Sir Alexander's more conservative line. In this play for a boy company, Moll Cutpurse arrives at a shop to be mocked by its owner as 'Mistris *hic & haec*'. Her function is as accessory to adultery: delivering a love-letter from another man to the shopkeeper's wife. To emphasize her sexual disruptiveness, the play has a brush with lesbianism, as she flirts briefly herself with the letter's recipient.

MOLL . . . pretty rogue I have longed to know thee this twelve
    months, and had no other means but this to speak with thee,
    there's a letter to thee from the party.

GRACE What party?

MOLL The knight Sir John Love-all.

GRACE Hence lewd impudent
    I know not what to term thee man or woman,
    For nature shaming to acknowledge thee
    For either; hath produced thee to the world
    Without a sex, some say thou art a woman,
    Others a man; and many thou art both
    Woman and man, but I think rather neither
    Or man and horse, as the old Centaurs were faign'd.

MOLL Why how now Mistress what lack ye? are you so so fine
    with a pox? I have seen a woman look as modestly as you,
    and speak as sincerely, and follow the friars as zealously, and
    she has been as sound a jumbler as e'er paid for 't, 'tis true
    Mistress Fipenie; I have sworn to leave this letter.

GRACE D'ee hear, you sword and target (to speak in your own key)
    Marie Umbree, Long-Meg,
    Thou that in thy self (me think'st) alone
    Look'st like a rogue and a whore under a hedge:

Bawd, take your letter with you and begone,
When next you come (my Husband's Constable)
And Bridewell is hard by, y'ave a good wit,
And can conceive.

The terms with which Grace rejects Moll are similar to those employed by Old Wengrave, which may indicate a borrowing between the two plays, but more likely represents a conventional line on the unnaturalness of cross-dressing. Nearly a decade later, as the debate about women in men's clothing heated up, such arguments would be used in the printed diatribes.

The appearance of the Moll Cutpurse character in *Amends for Ladies* is the only point to a crude and gratuitous scene, which seems entirely intended to play on Mary Frith's notoriety. Whether this is for her stage performances or the legal troubles which resulted from them is not clear. Certainly Frith was a selling-point, whatever the opinions about her. As late as 1639, twenty years after Nathan Field's death, an edition of *Amends for Ladies* boasted that it was a play 'With the merry pranks of Moll Cut-Purse'.

The difference in sympathy between *Amends for Ladies* and *The Roaring Girl* may reflect a change in attitudes between productions of the two plays, but they were staged at around the same time. More likely they stage a different viewpoint, perhaps one held by the authors, but equally likely to be inspired by an idea of what might suit their audience. Field, formerly a leading boy actor, is also writing for a company of boys, which may ironically have enhanced the desire to spice up the sexuality of the presentation. His play also includes, albeit offstage, a comic bed-sharing scene between two 'women': Bold, a man cross-dressed, and Lady Bright. When she discovers the discrepancy, she drives him out, naked, in another moment irrelevant except for the purposes of titillation.

In his Moll Cutpurse scene Field also throws in allusions to two famous tough women of the previous century: Marie Umbree, heroine of the Siege of Ghent 1584, and Long Meg of Westminster. Some idea of the implications in those references can be deduced from Dekker's play *Satiromastix*. In that play the blustering homophobe Captain Tucca abuses Mistress Miniver when she resists his advances with the same images as Field's pious City wife, comparing her to both Long Meg and

Mary Umbree. Grace the shopkeeper's wife uses the comparison in her treatment of Moll as a sexually threatening whore with lesbian tendencies. For Tucca, however, a woman who resists him sexually is like the legendary viragos. The fictional portraits may resist definition of Cutpurse's sexual interests, but lewdness towards women is a distinct possibility. Field's play uses Moll's familiarity with another woman to imply a lesbianism which Middleton and Dekker evade. They, the more sympathetic of her portraitists, instead provide her with various male admirers.

The sexual possibilities in Moll Cutpurse's mix of man and woman are soon articulated in *The Roaring Girl* during the sexy shop scene. Cutpurse visits a tobacco shop, where the only role for a woman should be behind the counter. Master Laxton, watching Moll, can hardly contain his excitement at her:

> LAXTON Heart I would give but too much money to be nibbling
> with that wench, life, sh'as the spirit of four great parishes,
> and a voice that will drown all the City, me thinks a brave
> captain might get all his soldiers upon her, and ne'er be
> beholding to a company of Mile End milk sops, if he could
> come on, and come off quick enough. Such a Moll were a
> marrowbone before an Italian: he would cry bona-roba till
> his ribs were nothing but bone. I'll lay hard siege to her,
> money is that aqua fortis, that eats into many a maidenhead,
> where the walls are flesh and blood I'll ever pierce through
> with a golden auger. . . . She slips from one company to
> another, like a fat eel between a Dutchman's fingers: I'll
> watch my time for her.

> MISTRESS PRUDENCE GALLIPOT Some will not stick to say she's a
> man, and some, both man and woman.

> LAXTON That were excellent, she might first cuckold the husband
> and then make him do as much for the wife!

Laxton's pornographic eulogy gives Moll a mixture of what are considered masculine and feminine attributes: she has a great spirit, a loud voice, and the ability to breed soldiers as fast and as often as a man is able to come inside her. Like marrowbone she is an aphrodisiac as well as a phallic symbol to the notoriously unmanly Italians. Laxton's wealth is his phallus, or golden auger (for his 'hard siege'), which he considers invincible where the walls around the maidenhead are of flesh and blood. Moll is also like a fat eel, however, which excites him still more, but makes the conquest less certain. His fantasy becomes complete with the final double cuckolding: in his imagination Moll becomes less a lesbian and more a transsexual porn star.

There is no suggestion, as there will be in later texts dealing with lesbian sexual desire, that Moll does have a penis, or the 'overgrown clitoris' popular in later seventeenth-century depictions of unnatural women. She may, however, given Sir Alexander's description of her as 'a codpiece daughter' have one of those as part of her costume, which would make the presentation of her genitalia identical with that of the men on stage. Since the role was also originally played by a male actor, such a codpiece would play the dual role of concealing what was there and what was not, depending on how you chose to imagine it. Imagining it, however, is clearly what the play encourages its audience to do.

As if to illustrate the role of clothing in making Moll Cutpurse, the next scene takes place at a tailor's. It has little value in terms of advancing the main plot, but offers ample opportunities for bawdy humour. The tailor, a stock character of both effeminacy and lecherousness, provides the manly and apparently indifferent Moll with the trappings of manhood in her well-filled breeches. As the conservative Sir Alexander observes, while secretly watching this scene, the blurring of gender boundaries is infectious: mannish women breed womanish men:

SIR ALEXANDER WENGRAVE What age is this? If the wife go in
    breeches, the man must wear long coats [petticoats] like a
    fool.

MOLL CUTPURSE What fiddling's here, would not the old pattern
    have served your turn?

TAILOR You change the fashion, you say you'll have the great
    Dutch slop [wide breeches], Mistress Mary.

MOLL CUTPURSE Why sir, I say so still.

TAILOR Your breeches will then take up a yard [also meaning
    penis] more.

MOLL CUTPURSE Well, pray look it be put in then.

TAILOR It shall stand round and full, I warrant you.

MOLL CUTPURSE Pray make 'em easy enough.

TAILOR I know my fault now: t'other was somewhat stiff between
the legs; I'll make these open enough, I warrant you.

This is bawdy enough for a boozy drag cabaret night. Here is an
effeminate tailor, fiddling around with the crotch of a woman (played
by a boy) and discussing openings, insertions, stiffenings and standings
out with more excessive innuendo than a scene from *Are You Being
Served*. For sheer concentration of obscene *double entendre* it is a
classic of comic writing.

It is not just the tailor who is less than an ideal male in *The Roaring
Girl*. A lack of manliness affects many of those around Moll Cutpurse,
including Laxton, the man who finds her mixture of male and female so
thrilling. Sir Alexander jokes crudely at Laxton's expense on his first
appearance:

SIR ALEXANDER WENGRAVE . . . furnish Master Laxton
with what he wants – a stone – a stool, I would say,
A stool.

LAXTON I had rather stand, sir.

SIR ALEXANDER WENGRAVE I know you had, good Master Laxton.

Laxton's name suggests he lacks balls (stones), and Sir Alexander also
mocks his desire to stand – get an erection. In an essay on the play
Stephen Orgel observes that:

Moll is surrounded by men who are less than men; the play is full
of references to impotence, castration, false phalluses, counter-
tenors; it even includes a character called Sir Beauteous Ganymede.

Clearly Moll Cutpurse would be the one wearing the trousers in any
heterosexual relationship. She is not clear, however, that, being able to
take on any man, she would wish to, famously declaiming:

I scorn to prostitute myself to a man,
I that can prostitute a man to me!

She is too butch to love a man – so who does that leave?

The gender confusion of *The Roaring Girl* reaches its peak when Sebastian is on stage with his two Molls: his 'crooked' love Moll Cutpurse, dressed as a man; and his 'straight' love Mary Fitz-Allen, dressed (well, naturally) as a pageboy. Here are three young men, dressed as three young men, portraying one man and two women. Mary hardly speaks in the scene, leaving the talking to the two 'men', but she does kiss her lover, causing Moll to comment on such strangeness.

MOLL CUTPURSE How strange this shows, one man to kiss another.

SEBASTIAN WENGRAVE I'd kiss such men to choose Moll,
　　Me thinks a woman's lip tastes well in a doublet.

Whilst two men kissing may look peculiar on the surface, it is all quite normal underneath, where the doublet conceals 'a woman's lip'. That it does not of course, since all the actors are actually male, allows the audience a complex journey through various erotic levels of clothing and meaning.

For the last word on kissing, the words of a modern heiress to Mary Frith's tradition of outrageous women in popular entertainment:

[CARRIE FISHER] You've been photographed kissing women. Do they kiss the same as men?

[MADONNA] Sometimes better. I've kissed girls that are horrible kissers. I've only kissed women, though.

[CARRIE FISHER] Well you've done the finger-fucking thing.

[MADONNA] Okay, okay.

[CARRIE FISHER] But that's it.

[MADONNA] Let me put it this way: I've certainly had fantasies of fucking women, but I'm not a lesbian . . .

[CARRIE FISHER] You express yourself in crass langauge. Like the woman in your documentary that you say finger-fucked you when you were schoolmates.

[MADONNA] But that's what really happened!

[CARRIE FISHER] Well she denied it in the film. But I wanted to ask about that. Who is that girl?

[MADONNA] She was a girl that I grew up with when I was little.
She lives in North Carolina now; she moved there with her
family. She recently had a baby and named it after me.

So that's that cleared up.

Drawing women to lewdness

Like Madonna Ciccone, Mary Frith found that some of her public
performances got her in trouble with the law. Male transvestism on
stage was ubiquitous, but also criticized. Cross-dressing in the other
direction proved much more threatening, however. For a woman to
dress as a man was not just a sign of potential immorality, but
perversion itself: Venetian law banned it as 'a kind of sodomy'. In the
years leading up to the pamphlet wars and James I's 1620 prohibition,
Mary Frith's defiance of convention was bound to get her into trouble.

Cross-dressing was one of the accusations made against Frith when
she appeared in ecclesiastical court on 27 January 1612 on charges of
immorality:

> she had long frequented all or most of the disorderly and licentious
> places in this City as namely she hath usually in the habit of a man
> resorted to alehouses, taverns, tobacco shops and also to play-
> houses there to see plays and prizes [competitions] and namely
> being at a play about three quarters of a year since at the Fortune
> in man's apparel and in her boots and with a sword by her side, she
> told the company there present that she thought many of them
> were of opinion that she was a man, but if any of them would come
> to her lodging they should find that she is a woman, and some
> other immodest and lascivious speeches she also used at that time.
> And also sat there upon the stage in the public view of all the
> people there present in man's apparel and played upon her lute and
> sang a song. . . . And then she being pressed to declare whether she
> had not been dishonest of her body and hath not also drawn other
> women to lewdness by her persuasions and by carrying herself like
> a bawd, she absolutely denied that she was chargeable with either
> of those imputations.

Frith may not deny her public appearance in man's clothes, but she does claim not to have drawn other women to lewdness. This presumably refers to prostitution, but has the hint of the lesbian possibilities which are also present in both dramatic treatments of her. Like Madonna's old school-friend, she claims not to have gone all the way.

Mary Frith's punishment was to do public penance at Paul's Cross on 9 February 1612, under the disapproving eyes of John Chamberlain, who suspected she was drunk:

> she wept bitterly and seemed very penitent she had the daintiest preacher or ghostly father that ever I saw in pulpit, one Ratcliffe of Brazenose in Oxford, a likelier man to have led the revels in some Inn of Court than to be where he was, but the best is he did extreme badly, and so wearied the audience that the best part went away, and the rest tarried rather to hear Moll Cutpurse than him.

As Stephen Orgel points out, poor Ratcliffe of Oxford seems to have been one of the age's petticoated men, those of whom Chamberlain's fellow conservative Sir Alexander Wengrave despairs in *The Roaring Girl*. As the epilogue to the play says: if neither the men who wrote the play, nor the men who performed it have satisfied you, come back for the real thing. Once again, Moll triumphs over the men, making a performance of her punishment which proves more popular than the thing itself.

King's Favourite

Gay Prince Edward and His Family

Touchstone comments in *As You Like It* that 'When a man's verses cannot be understood . . . it strikes a man more dead than a great reckoning in a little room'. Tradition has it that this refers to Christopher Marlowe's death, stabbed in a row at a Deptford bar. Certainly Phoebe quotes from his poem 'Hero and Leander':

Dead shepherd, now I find thy saw of might.
'Who ever loved that loved not at first sight?'

Thus Shakespeare pays tribute to his late contemporary, whose comedies include a far more provocative version of Ganymede than the disguised Rosalind, and who places sodomy at the centre of the English state.

Outing kit

Why don't they teach any of this in the schools? If they did, maybe he wouldn't have killed himself and maybe you wouldn't be so terrified of who you are.

Marlowe is a consistent number two, after Shakespeare, in the Golden Age of Elizabethan Dramatists' Hall of Fame, safely inside the canon of literary achievement as one of the Great Playwrights. All such lists are preposterous, and more susceptible to fashion than their proponents will ever admit. Yet for those who qualify, such canonization brings a taste of immortality. Impressionable young people are set to read their works, discovering the ways in which they enrich our cultural heritage.

Ned Weeks, in Larry Kramer's *The Normal Heart*, rightly observes that some things tend not to be taught in schools. The extent of Marlowe's contribution to the development of British drama may be on the curriculum: his contribution to the development of British sodomy will not. Weeks characteristically overstates his case: gay male suicides hardly hang on the issue of whether or not John Maynard Keynes was a practising homosexual. Kramer's play does, however, identify a vicious prejudice masquerading as objectivity. For some of those responsible for promoting Marlowe's work, the involvement of sexuality in the discussion is indeed odious. The editor of a popular modern edition of Marlowe's plays complains:

> Readers of *The Times* on 18 September 1963 were told that 'Marlowe was a well known homosexual' – and for that there is no evidence at all.

None at all? What, however, would constitute hard evidence? In the absence of Elizabethan equivalents for Mary Applegate and Jane Cotter, it is difficult to imagine what could prove the point.

Those two women featured in a real life drama: another trial of another playwright on the same subject. Applegate was a housekeeper, Cotter a chambermaid at the Savoy Hotel; both reported to the Old Bailey that Oscar Wilde's sheets were on occasion 'stained in a peculiar way'. The identical formulation might lead cynics to suspect coaching of the witnesses, but it was the closest to hard evidence available. As Wilde's prosecutor pointed out to the jury: 'There is not likely to be an eye-witness of the facts.' For the defence, Edward Clarke's flourish as his summing-up reached climax may have received applause from Wilde's supporters in court, but he picked an unfortunate metaphor when hoping that the jury 'in clearing him, will clear society from a stain'. The semen-encrusted linen of the Savoy has presumably long worn thin, never to hang in the proposed Wilde Museum in the former Bow Street Police Court. Without the discovery of a similar Turin shroud as holograph witness to Christopher Marlowe's sexual activities, the imperfect science of forensic literary criticism is the only way to unearth the evidence demanded.

Even with that evasive hard proof of the erotic and emotional activities of artists, there is no equation which neatly links their biographies to their creative work. If Marlowe is a potential gay role model, he can also be cited as a noble practitioner of drunken thuggery. Ned Weeks fails to understand that replacing the authorized canon with the revised (closet-free) version repeats the error. Being a Great Writer is not the same thing as being a good person, in whatever way you define those two roles.

A refreshing attempt to address those problems of reclamation comes in Noel Greig's 1989 play *The Death of Christopher Marlowe*. An important strand in Greig's work, from *As Time Goes By*, written with Drew Griffiths in 1977, has been the ambition simultaneously to explore and interrogate gay history. In plays grappling with self-contradictory historical figures, he suggests the roots of a contemporary politics. *The Dear Love of Comrades* (1979) celebrates and gently chides visionary gay socialist Edward Carpenter. In an introduction to some of Carpenter's writings, he explains the attraction of a remarkable man outside the canon:

> The history of homosexuality seemed the usual tedious list of 'famous names' . . . here was this man Carpenter 'coming out' in the Labour movement of the late 19th century, not as a wealthy renter of boys, but as an equal partner with a working-class man, and as a literary advocate of homosexuality.
>
> I later came to realise that the picture was less simple and rosy. Carpenter was limited by his class, his temperament and the times he lived in . . . All the same, that first brief description of Carpenter and [George] Merrill [his lover] fired my imagination.

The play opens with the indisputably canonized E. M. Forster, telling cheerfully how Merrill touched his bottom and made him aware of his homosexuality. What it did not inspire him to do – nor any of the Bloomsbury Group's other closeted, male, middle-class homosexuals – was make any effective political connection with the working-class men they loved. Greig draws on his own experience of the distrust between left and gay movements in the 1970s in his exploration of Carpenter's life and work. Even greater contradictions surface in the life of Roger Casement, subject of Greig's 1993 play *Raising Roger*. Hanged for treason by the British government he once served as an imperial official, Casement's status as an Irish martyr and national hero is problematic for some, given the thorough detailing in his diaries of his sexual adventures with men around the world. Greig uses the story to explore personal and political treachery, and contemporary arguments about sexuality, race and empire.

The Death of Christopher Marlowe is a more flamboyant piece of historical romance: a sort of 'Kiss Me Kit'. In this Canterbury Tale of upward mobility, a Kent tradesman's lad goes off to Cambridge, then finds theatrical success and downfall in his sideline as a secret agent. In the play, Greig pays homage to the glories of Elizabethan drama, yet locates the diversities of women's, black or lesbian and gay experience at the centre of a common heritage. Marlowe's life and work are reclaimed, but not without serious questioning.

Wilde is never centre stage in Greig's work, but his trials echo from the wings. Greig and Gay Sweatshop were not the first to stage the scattered individual biographies of 'homosexuals of genius' which had previously constituted gay history. What they did was place those figures in a political context, dramatizing not just 'famous names' but also the social forces shaping gay identities. The trials of Wilde and Marlowe are not isolated incidents, but themselves theatrical set-ups amid a wider set of events.

Oscar Wilde had to be tried for indecency, according to Queensberry's lawyer, in order to prevent the suggestion that 'exalted personages' were shielding a sodomite to protect their own reputations. The posthumous inquiry into Marlowe also implicates people in high places. Testimony from Richard Baines appeared days after Marlowe's death in 1593: *A Note containing the opinions of one Christopher Marly concerning his damnable judgement of religion and scorn of God's word*. It lists a selection of heretical statements supposedly made by Marlowe and ends with an early threat of outing:

> he hath quoted a number of contrarieties out of the Scripture which he hath given to some great men who in convenient time shall be named. When these things shall be called in question the witness shall be produced.

Incorporated in Baines's eighteen allegations is the suggestion of Marlowe's sexual heresy: that he claimed 'All they that love not tobacco and boys were fools'. Whether or not he ever did say it, the phrase has become a pederastic proverb. Notorious celibate Stephen Fry used 'Tobacco and Boys' as a provocative subtitle for his extended sketch *Latin* (1980), set in a boys' preparatory school.

Baines is an unreliable witness, although fellow playwright and collaborator Thomas Kyd, who lived with Marlowe at one point, made similar charges of outraging sexual and religious orthodoxy. He testified to the Privy Council in the year of Marlowe's death that

[Marlowe] would report St John to be our saviour Christ's Alexis,
I cover it with reverence and trembling, that is Christ did love him
with an extraordinary love.

Kyd's 'reverence and trembling' suggest his own fear at expressing such heresy, or perhaps the tortures used to extract the accusation. It uses more poetic imagery than Baines, who confirms the drift of Marlowe's argument, that 'St John the Baptist was bedfellow to Christ and leaned always in his bosom, that he used him as the sinners of Sodoma.'

Alexis, in Virgil's *Second Eclogue*, is a beautiful youth pursued by the shepherd Corydon. Marlowe's best-known poem, 'The Passionate Shepherd to his Love', takes its cue from the Latin, but avoids specifying the gender of the shepherd's object of passion:

The shepherd swains shall dance and sing
For thy delight each May morning.
If these delights thy mind may move
Then live with me and be my love.

This flirtation with ambiguity persists to the androgynous 'kirtle, Embroidered all with with leaves of myrtle', which the shepherd promises he will make for his loved one. A kirtle is both a man's coat and a woman's gown. Nevertheless, Walter Ralegh, one of the 'great men' to whom Marlowe allegedly preached atheism, insists on a heterosexual interpretation in his companion poem, 'The Nymph's Reply'.

How outrageous the Privy Council or the inquiry into Marlowe's opinions considered these particular sexual heresies is impossible to assess. 'Christ had his John, and I have my Steenie', said James I about George Villiers, who apparently reminded him of a portrait of Saint Stephen. The man who commissioned the Authorized Bible said: 'I am neither a god nor an angel but a man like any other, and confess to loving those dear to me more than other men. You may be sure that I love the Earl of Buckingham more than anyone else.'

This was said in 1617 at the time Lord Chief Justice Edward Coke was recalled to the Privy Council, with his daughter's wedding to John, elder brother of 'Steenie'. Coke opposed James persistently, and had been suspended two years previously, the year George was made Gentleman of the Bedchamber. Despite the marriage, or perhaps because of its notable lack of success, Coke maintained his attacks on the Villiers family.

Coke was a scourge of other leading reputed sodomites, including Francis Bacon, but it was a politics of faction rather than personal morality. He does, however, still persecute lesbian and gay activity three centuries after his death, through his massive project to codify English Law. Many years and many miles away from Jacobean England, another Chief Justice, the United States' Warren Burger, would use his predecessor's words to justify anti-gay legislation in the twentieth century:

> The cop stood there for like . . . thirty-five seconds while I was engaged in mutual oral sex. When I looked up and realized he was standing there, he *then* identified himself. He said I was under arrest for sodomy. I said, 'What are you doing in my bedroom?'

Coke surely did not have Georgia on his mind when he clarified the to-ing and fro-ing which had seen buggery briefly taken off the statute books when Mary Tudor repealed her father Henry VIII's laws *en masse*, only for her sister Elizabeth to reinstate the offences when she became queen. The colonial state was not even founded until 1732, seventy five years after Coke confirmed as felony 'the detestable sin of buggery with mankind or beast'. Yet as Janet E. Halley points out, these words were the basis for the United States Supreme Court's 1986 decision that thirty-five seconds of mutual oral sex between consenting adult males in private were indeed illegal in this corner of the land of the free.

> both Justice White writing for the majority and Justice Burger concurring in his own opinion trace Georgia's statute to the state's reception of English law, posing an unmediated codification of Henry VIII's statute prohibiting buggery and Elizabeth I's reinstatement of it in the criminal law of the United States.

Plump boys indeed

Captain Pantilius Tucca in Thomas Dekker's *Satiromastix* makes Richard Baines sound positively restrained. His abuse of the sodomite poet Horace has extraordinary virulence, but amid the play's catalogue of sex-related epithets comes another charge. He calls the despised playwright 'the little atheist', just as sodomy and heresy combine in the charges against Marlowe.

Dekker's play comes nine years after Marlowe's death, and attacks another writer, Ben Jonson, but Tucca and Baines both draw on a common perception that the crimes are linked. In assessing possible punishments for debauchery, Coke quotes a law written in the time of Edward I, father of Marlowe's tragic king, which 'sayeth that sorcerers, sodomers and heretics shall be burned'. Alan Bray's classic of gay history, *Homosexuality in Renaissance England*, also cites Coke's connection of sodomy with other offences:

> *crimen laesae majestatis*, a sin horrible, committed against the King; and this is either against the King Celestial or Terrestrial in three manners: by heresy, by buggery, by sodomy

Bray explores the links between the unholy trinity of heresy, homosexuality and treason which are blended in the charges against Marlowe. He also identifies a recurring notion that the sodomite is the child born as a result of sex between a witch and the devil. 'Such men must be the children of the devil' says the satirist 'R. C.' of sodomites in *The Times' Whistle*. Michael Drayton's satire *The Moon Calf* provides its sodomite with similar parentage: sinful Earth and the devil.

Thomas Dekker's *If This be not a Good Play, the Devil is in It* (1612) has Pluto, god of the underworld, asking:

> . . . Is not the world as t'was?
> Once mother of rapes, incests and sodomies,
> Atheism and blasphemies, plump boys indeed,
> That suck'd (our Dam's breast) is she now barren? Ha!
> Is there a dearth of villains?

To which his saucy devils reply 'More now than ever'.

There may be no smoking gun, or steaming sheets, to prove Marlowe's practice of the crimes attributed to him. What is clear, however, is the way in which the linked offences of heresy, sodomy and sorcery persist as themes in his plays. *Dido, Queen of Carthage* (c. 1587) is a pagan tale, framed by the legendary love affair between Jupiter and Ganymede. The two parts of *Tamburlaine* (c. 1587–8) also revel in their freedom from a Christian setting, encapsulated in pampered jades of Asia's flamboyant drag, and flirt with sodomy in the characters of Mycetes and Tamburlaine himself. *Doctor Faustus* (c. 1592) is the archetype of sorcerers, *The Jew of Malta* (c. 1589) of one major group of heretics, supported by Machiavelli and a moor. *Edward II* (c. 1592) was England's most notorious sodomite monarch. *The Massacre at Paris* (c. 1593) uses the minion-packed court of Henri III, France's most notorious sodomite monarch, as the setting for a play which stages the bitter divisions between Catholics and Protestants. It is impossible to know whether Marlowe himself loved tobacco and boys, or when, if ever, he identified with the characteristics of his cynical, sceptical, deviant and subversive creations. It is, however, beyond dispute that the subjects of sodomy, heresy and treason interested him.

King Edward's on a skewer

The revival of interest in *Edward II* over the last thirty years coincides with the gay liberation movement, whose radical and reform wings both celebrate it. The first major modern revival came in 1969, the year of the Stonewall riots. A then-closeted young gay actor, Ian McKellen, played Marlowe's king alongside Shakespeare's Richard II for the touring Prospect Theatre Company. In Edinburgh, the police were called to see if the performance was legal: the limited decriminalization of the 1967 Sexual Offences Act did not apply to Scotland. Twenty-five years later, now as an openly gay man, and co-founder of the campaigning Stonewall group, McKellen looked back on the play from the city which hosted those riots.

> *Edward II* was really the first gay play ever written . . . since Marlowe predates most of Shakespeare, I think it would be fair to say he invented modern drama in the sense of character and storytelling. It was perhaps his greatest play, and it was clearly about a gay man and the difficulties of being gay.

This is charming and plausible, but risks sentimentalizing author and play. It is probably fairer to give John Bale the credit for inventing the form of the History play with which Shakespeare started his career, and Bale's only overt concern with sodomy was to stamp it out. There are earlier, if less well-known, contenders for the title of first gay play, but there is dispute about whether *Edward II* is even eligible as a nominee. Doubts about such categorization are not limited to reactionary anti-gay traditionalists:

> the many who have written of the apparently openly 'homosexual' nature of the play have not grasped its irony or that the intense emotion, the passionate language, and the embraces we see between these two men have ready parallels in Elizabethan England in the daily conventions of friendship without being signs of a sodomitical relationship.

This sceptical passage is by Alan Bray, from an essay in a 1994 volume of work in lesbian and gay studies. The debate over *Edward II* is an interesting example of the way in which intellectual reflection on the complexities of sexuality and politics diverges from the popular agenda. A leading spokesman gives an interview to an important newspaper, which makes the case for the play as a gay classic. Meanwhile a serious writer, with an even longer track record of exploring gay history, rejects that classification as simplistic.

A play which in 1969 had the Edinburgh police considering prosecution could by 1990 be staged by British theatre's heritage flagship: the Royal Shakespeare Company in Stratford upon Avon. During that period, ideas of pro-gay reform had surfaced in many other national institutions, a process for which the Stonewall Group now lobbies. McKellen himself was knighted in 1991, an award from the state seen by some as symbolizing greater acceptance for those in public life who were openly gay. Others criticized McKellen for accepting an honour which in effect came from a government committed to diminish lesbian and gay rights. The most prominent critic was artist and film-maker Derek Jarman, and the two men became identified with crudely 'reformist' and 'revolutionary' divisions in lesbian and gay political tactics. Ironically, Jarman's approach to *Edward II*, which he adapted and filmed at the time, is as sentimental at heart as McKellen's, despite a more provocative gloss, clear from the title: 'Edward II improved by Derek Jarman', and the slogans decorating the book of the film:

How to make a film of a gay love affair and get it commissioned. Find a dusty old play and violate it.

. . . Marlowe outs the past – why don't we out the present? That's really the only message this play has.

For McKellen the play is 'clearly about a gay man and the difficulties of being gay'. For Jarman it is a 'gay love affair'. Edward as gay lover and martyr is an appealing interpretation, with which both men were successful. The play is more equivocal, however: a deeply political work about the nature of power and leadership, in which sodomy is a key factor in the examination of Edward's role as king. Without these complexities, the play risks becoming a sorry tale of star-crossed sodomites, reducing Marlowe, as Phoebe the shepherdess does, to a sentimental lyricist. Of course *Edward II* is a play about sodomy, but not a simple celebration of it. It flirts with the conventions of Elizabethan friendship, but this is to confuse, rather than clarify, the nature of Edward's loves.

Sweet prince I come

Sometime between the death of James I in 1625 and the assassination of George Villiers in 1628, a prose account was completed of *The History of the Life, Reign and Death of Edward II, King of England and Lord of Ireland, with the Rise and Fall of his great Favourites, Gaveston and the Spencers*. Its author is identified as 'E. F.', thought to refer to Elizabeth Cary, Viscountess Falkland, a closet Catholic married to one of James's other gentlemen of the bedchamber. The book was not published until 1680, well after Cary's death and the Restoration of the monarchy, but shows that examination of Edward's reign, and the lessons which might be drawn from it, continued well after Marlowe's play was produced.

The book acknowledges the existence of unsuitable royal passions, suggesting that these might be embarrassing, but need not be disastrous:

If by heat of youth, height of fortune, or the corruptions of nature, the royal affections fire loosely and at random; yet if it extend no farther than the satisfaction of the private appetite, it may obscure the glory, but not supplant the strength and safety of a sceptre.

It is a pleasingly phallic image of monarchy, that slightly tarnished yet still sturdy sceptre. The Carys were well placed to observe the intrigues of James and his favourites, and it is tempting to draw comments on contemporary events from passages in the *History*. Realistic, if sensually expressed, advice on the treatment of favourites is offered:

> Let the favourite taste the King's bounty, not devour it; let him enjoy his ear, but not ingross it; let him participate his love, but not enchant it.

Its colourful expression also livens up a portrait of Edward I: 'that brave and valiant monarch, had thrice with his victorious arms run through the bowels of Scotland, and brought that stubborn nation (that denied him fealty and homage) into an absolute subjection'. Fisting as a metaphor for imperial conquest suggests that the author knew perfectly well how Edward's son was killed, although the book itself avoids description of the red-hot poker in the anus which had been graphically dramatized by Marlowe. It is more coy than a fourteenth-century monk, who recorded laconically that the cause of Edward's death was 'too much sodomy'.

Although Edward I, whom Coke records as wanting sodomites burned to death, introduced his son to Piers Gaveston, he later banished him as a bad influence, one of what the *History* calls

> those tainted humours of his leprosy, that seduced the easiness of his nature and misled his unripe knowledge, too green to master such sweet and bewitching temptations. Gaveston his Ganymede, a man as base in birth as in condition, he commandeth to perpetual exile.

Young Prince Edward is Eve in Eden, not yet ripe to master fruits. Leprosy here has the implications of venereal infection usual in Edward's time, rather than simply skin disease. In its account of the younger Edward's love for Gaveston, the *History* repeats the link between sorcery and sodomy, although with a medical tone:

> Such a masculine affection and rapture was in those days without precedent, where love went in the natural strain, fully as firm, yet far less violent. Of the circumstances of this passionate humour, so predominant in this unfortunate king, we shall find them as far

short of possibility as reason; which have made many believe, that they had a supernatural operation and working, enforced by art or witchcraft . . . Bridle his affections he could not, which were but bare embryons without possession; alter them he cannot.

In its description of Edward as unable to restrain the urges within himself, the *History* offers an early example of a pathological model for homosexuality, two hundred and fifty years before Richard von Krafft-Ebing's *Psychopathia Sexualis*. It is a 'humour': that word then in transition from denoting a vital physiological component, as it did in medieval medicine, to a looser sense of mental disposition. Here it is 'passionate': Mortimer in Marlowe's play describes Edward's love for a favourite as 'wanton humour'. The *History* even offers a diagnosis of the political result of the illness: 'a sick state, where the head is so diseased'.

A report of the death of Edward I opens *Edward II*, just as Edward III will close it with the funeral of his father. The first line is Gaveston's, reading a letter from the King with its fatal invitation: 'My father is deceased. Come Gaveston'. Less ambiguous than the equivocal Latin which will condemn Edward to death, this letter has its own bawdy double meaning, with which Gaveston sexily toys:

Sweet prince I come; these, these thy amorous lines
Might have enforc'd me to have swum from France,
And like Leander gasp'd upon the sand,
So thou wouldst smile and take me in thy arms.
The sight of London to my exil'd eyes
Is as Elysium to a new-come soul
Not that I love the city or the men,
But that it harbours him I hold so dear,
The king, upon whose bosom let me die

Edward's amorous lines are also the contours of his body, which will embrace Gaveston, not just as a friend, but as a sexual partner. Marlowe's own account of Leander, to whom Gaveston compares himself here, confirms the erotic implications of the text. In *Hero and Leander* (c. 1587), 'amorous Leander, beautiful and young' adores Hero, priestess to Aphrodite, goddess of Love. The poet Marlowe claims his 'rude pen' and 'slack muse' are inadequate to describe the beauty of Leander. Like Gaveston in the *History*, the youth is so beautiful he should be a woman, an argument which may discreetly offer mitigation for those he inspires to sodomitical passion:

> Nature in his [Gaveston's] outward parts had curiously expressed her workmanship, giving him in shape and beauty so perfect an excellence, that the most curious eye could not discover any manifest error, unless it were in his sex alone, since he had too much for a man, and perfection enough to have equalled the fairest female splendour that breathed within the confines of this kingdom.

> Some swore he [Leander] was a maid in man's attire
> For in his looks were all that men desire

And not just men, for the god Neptune is also driven to embrace him. Hero and Leander are parted, like Gaveston and Edward, by a narrow channel of water. Leander must swim the Hellespont to reach his desire, which gives the water god his chance:

> [Leander] stripp'd him to the ivory skin,
> And crying , 'Love, I come', leapt lively in.
> The sapphire-visaged god grew proud,
> And made his cap'ring Triton sound aloud,
> Imagining that Ganymede, displeas'd,
> Had left the heavens; therefore on him he seized . . .
> The lusty god embraced him, called him love . . .
> He clapp'd his plump cheeks, with his tresses play'd,
> And smiling wantonly, his love bewray'd.
> He watch'd his arms, and as they open'd wide
> At every stroke, betwixt them would he slide
> And steal a kiss, and then run out and dance,
> And as he turn'd, cast many a lustful glance,
> And throw him gaudy toys to please his eye,
> And dive into the water, and there pry
> Upon his breast, his thighs and every limb,
> And up again, and close beside him swim,
> And talk of love.

Crying, like Gaveston, 'I come', Leander plunges in to reach his love. The water god 'grows proud' and has his trumpet sounded the moment he sees the beautiful youth, whom he swears to protect, but whose body becomes a site of erotic play for him. Marlowe weaves a description of Leander's naked body swimming through the sea together with a detailed account of the very sexual harrassment of every part of him by an embodied male god, who mistakes him for the archetypal gay toyboy Ganymede. Leander endearingly suggests Neptune has made a mistake: 'You are deceiv'd, I am no woman I'. The god replies with a story, maybe like one of those scandalous ones Marlowe himself is accused of spreading:

> How that a shepherd, sitting in a vale,
> Play'd with a boy so fair and so unkind
> As for his love both earth and heaven pin'd;
> That of the cooling river durst not drink,
> Lest water-nymphs should pull him from the brink;
> And when he sported in the fragrant lawns
> Goat-footed satyrs and up-staring fauns
> Would steal him thence.

Here is the loving shepherd of Marlowe's poem once again, this time definitely wooing a beautiful boy. Leander interrupts Neptune's tale of the delights of masculine love, saying he will be late for Hero, and the angry god throws his mace at his departing body as punishment. Love, however, overcomes anger, and Neptune calls back his large three-pronged dart before it can stick into the boy. It wounds his hand on the rebound, and the sight of the blood makes Leander look sorry for the god. Deluded by his own desires, Neptune interprets pity as love, and rushes off to find rich gifts to shower on Leander. As Marlowe wryly observes, in practical rather than supernatural mode:

> 'Tis wisdom to give much, a gift prevails
> When deep persuading oratory fails.

Many handsome boys before and since have proved that point. Marlowe's early death means we only have two of *Hero and Leander*'s sestiads, so we can only speculate whether Neptune would have had his way in the end.

What the poem does confirm, however, is that Gaveston's gasping on the sand is not simpy the result of a vigorous swim. He 'comes' for the prince, to 'die' upon the king: the verbs which frame the quotation above are both puns on orgasm.

In the first scene of *Edward II*, Marlowe creates problems for a purely romantic reading of the play. Gaveston is indifferent to the sufferings of the poor men who approach him for help, one of them at least a member of that army which buggered the Scots for Edward I. Their inclusion is based on the accounts in Marlowe's sources of the deprivations which supposedly drove Edward's subjects to eat horses, dogs and even their own children, while their king and his boyfriend lavished money on luxuries: banquets, clothes and entertainment.

He mocks the poor, including a man who has risked his life for England – 'These are not men for me'. Like the sodomite subtext of the opening speech, this is a deliberate provocation, but it shows no attempt to create a noble role model out of Gaveston.

Having used material from the history books to emphasize the decadence of the fourteenth century court, Marlowe makes a flamboyantly anchronistic switch to describe the Elizabethans' most fashionable spectacle: the masque.

> I must have wanton poets, pleasant wits,
> Musicians that with touching of a string
> May draw the pliant king which way I please:
> Music and poetry is his delight;
> Therefore I'll have Italian masques by night,
> Sweet speeches, comedies, and pleasing shows;
> And in the day, when he shall walk abroad,
> Like sylvan nymphs my pages shall be clad;
> My men, like satyrs grazing on the lawns,
> Shall with their goat-feet dance an antic hay;
> Sometime a lovely boy in Dian's shape,
> With hair that gilds the water as it glides,
> Crownets of pearls about his naked arms,
> And in his sportful hands an olive tree,
> To hide those parts which men delight to see,
> Shall bathe him in a spring; and there, hard by,
> One like Actaeon, peeping through the grove,
> Shall by the angry goddess be transform'd,
> And running in the likeness of an hart,
> By yelping hounds pull'd down and seem to die:
> Such things as these best please his majesty.

It is a one-sentence masterpiece: decadent, camp, pornographic, and witty. The deliberate arousal and encouragement of a youth's sexual enthusiasm which can be read in *Hero and Leander* is staged in *Edward II*, with Gaveston as master of the revels for these erotic court entertainments. He stages the pastoral scene in which Neptune's tale of shepherdly love is set: the cooling river, sylvan nymphs, fragrant lawns and goat-footed satyrs. Pageboys play the nymphs, male servants the satyrs, and a lovely boy takes the role of virgin goddess of the hunt, Diana. His only costume is a few pearls and some foliage, to conceal his genitals: 'those parts which men delight to see', just as all men desired Leander's beauty.

Maybe all men do desire these imaginary boys. Maybe all men did around 1592, when *Edward II* was staged. Gaveston is presumably exaggerating, however. It is impossible to guess how many men, or women, would have been excited by such an image – or how many would have been repulsed or indifferent. It suggests the potential of an extraordinary sexual charge from a theatrical performance, however, even those less perfectly executed than this imaginary event.

The story it enacts is not that of the devoted Corydon and Alexis, the original gay male romance, but a grim one more appropriate to the tragedy of *Edward II*. Actaeon is ripped to pieces for seeing sexual secrets: he peeps to see Diana bathing, and is punished by her with transformation into a deer, that is torn apart by his own dogs. Lustful looks will end in death – a grim message for the audience of a pornographic masque.

Gaveston's actor, 'one like Actaeon', gets off more lightly. He sees not Diana, but a beautiful boy playing her, and therefore only seems to die – a faked orgasm recalling the double meaning in Gaveston's earlier speech. Such things as this best please King Edward, who will in real life be dragged by his own dogs, the English nobles, down to 'a vault up to the knees in water'. But this is only a play within a play, an imitation of an imitation of life, which warns of the perils of erotic spectatorship, but incites the viewer nevertheless.

Come on Dapper Jack

Cynical commentators on the young favourites of King James I often exaggerated their low birth, just as the English nobles are appalled by 'that base and obscure Gaveston'. The propaganda sources for the play make Gaveston low-born, a characterization which Marlowe follows. Mortimer complains that it is not the king's love for Gaveston which annoys him, but the impropriety of a jumped-up commoner spending the country's wealth on fancy clothes while soldiers are not paid. Gaveston and Edward make an elementary mistake of statecraft in alienating the English army, an institution still officially traumatized by the thought of penetration by homosexuals:

> But this I scorn that one so basely born
> Should by his sovereign's favour grow so pert,
> And riot it with the treasure of the realm
> While soldiers mutiny for want of pay.
> He wears a lord's revenue on his back,
> And Midas-like, he jets it in the court,
> With base outlandish cullions at his heels,
> Whose proud fantastic liveries make such show
> As if that Proteus, god of shapes, appear'd.

One piece of shape-changing in the speech, which may be unintentional by Mortimer, is the transformation of Gaveston into a literal prick. Like his proud followers, he grows pert with Edward's favour, testicles ('cullions') hanging beneath him, as he sticks out ('jets') through the court. 'Jet' seems not to have meant 'spurt' until a century after Marlowe, but the 'treasure of the realm' and the 'lord's revenue' on Gaveston's back are puns on regal semen.

Clothes, however, are Mortimer's real sore point. Gaveston wears hugely expensive items, and mocks, with the king, the attire of the nobility:

> I have not seen a dapper Jack so brisk.
> He wears a short Italian hooded cloak,
> Larded with pearl, and in his Tuscan cap
> A jewel of more value than the crown.
> Whiles others walk below, the king and he
> From out a window laugh at such as we,
> And flout our train, and jest at our attire.
> Uncle, 'tis this that makes me impatient.

By the end of this speech, Mortimer is so worked up that even the way he speaks disintegrates. The regular rhythm of the verse collapses entirely in his final line. Although extravagance is indeed a complaint about Edward's reign in Marlowe's sources, the attention to sartorial offence here is a deliberately Elizabethan touch. Outrage about fashion, on stage and in the street, was a topical issue. Gaveston's dapperness and briskness are not just effeminate, they are another flouting of the established order. Pamphleteer and fellow playwright Thomas Nashe called England 'the players' stage of gorgeous attire, the ape of all nations superfluities, the continual masquer in outlandish habiliments', a place of 'wanton disguising'. There were laws which made the wearing of specific items or materials illegal to particular income groups, but these were rarely enforced. Gaveston's clothes are illegally extravagant, displaying wealth from which his low birth should exclude him. Marlowe's stage, of course, whose main source of spectacle was its costuming, was one place where vagabonds had licence to dress like kings.

Gaveston's rascally followers are also flamboyantly dressed, base, and outlandish, which for Marlowe's audience would have still had the sense of its original meaning, 'foreign'. Continental in his verbal affectation – '*Tanti*!' – Gaveston's Italian coat and Tuscan cap mark him out as a potential sexual deviant. Italy was a location from which Elizabethans expected depravity, as we shall see later on. Indeed, the author of the *History* of Edward II wrongly claims Gaveston was Italian, although she or he acknowledges the other, correct, theory, that 'This siren (as some write) came out of Gascoigne [Gascony]', an English possession in France at the time. Foreign clothes were another subject for sartorial outrage: John Marston makes a direct connection between elaborate, continental modishness and sodomy (although, as Gregory Bredbeck points out, sodomy in this context has several meanings).

> Seest thou yon gallant in the sumptuous clothes,
> How brisk, how spruce, how gorgeously he shows,
> Note his French-herring bones, but note no more,
> Unless thou spy his fair attendant whore,
> That lackies him. Mark nothing but his clothes
> His new stamped complement, his cannon oaths,
> Mark those, for naught but such lewd viciousness
> Ere graced him, save Sodom beastliness.
> *Is* this a *Man*? Nay an incarnate devil,
> That struts in vice, and glorieth in evil.

Mortimer's dapper Jack physically resembles Marston's brisk gallant of 1599 much more than the historical Piers Gaveston.

Mortimer's uncle has tried to reassure him that a minion-mad monarch need not be a security risk with a list of historical precedents (see chapter three).

> The mightiest kings have had their minions;
> Great Alexander lov'd Hephaestion . . .

Certainly the relationship risks political and social disruption, as Marlowe dramatizes, but 'minion' carries the hint of other – sexual – disruption as well. The nobles discuss the disturbing influence of Gaveston, manifested in his public physical intimacy with the king:

> LANCASTER Thus arm in arm the king and he doth march –
> Nay more, the guard upon his lordship waits,
> And all the court begins to flatter him.

> WARWICK Thus leaning on the shoulder of the king,
> He nods, and scorns, and smiles at those that pass.

In the same scene, Marlowe lets Queen Isabella contrast Edward's treatment of his her, his wife, and Gaveston. Once again, the play echoes images of Neptune caressing Leander, specifically the clapping of cheeks, a pun on the mechanics of buggery:

> For now my lord the king regards me not,
> But dotes upon the love of Gaveston.
> He claps his cheeks and and hangs about his neck,
> Smiles in his face and whispers in his ears;
> And, when I come, he frowns, as who should say,
> 'Go whither thou wilt, seeing I have Gaveston'

Alan Bray points out the similarity between the descriptions of Edward's behaviour, and that by Thomas Howard of Robert Carr, a Scottish lad and former pageboy of James, who came to London with the King:

> The Prince [King James] leaneth on his arm, pinches his cheek, smooths his ruffled garment . . . This young man doth much study all art and device; he hath changed his tailors and tiremen [dressers] many times, and all to please the Prince, who laugheth at

the long grown fashion of our young courtiers, and wisheth for change every day . . . this fellow is straight-limbed, well-favoured, strong shouldered and smooth-faced, with some sort of cunning and show of modesty.

Although written in 1611, twenty years after Marlowe's play, the behaviour of a Jacobean favourite is remarkably consistent with his descriptions of Gaveston at Edward's side: public embrace, flashy clothes and even mockery of the fashions worn elsewhere at court. The description given in chapter six of James with George Villiers, who succeeded Carr as his favourite, compares their 'wanton looks and wanton gestures' to the horrors of the stage (where 'tiremen' like Carr's would also work).

Marlowe died before James became King of England, but he was already King of Scotland when *Edward II* was written. Ten years earlier, James had been pressed by his nobles to banish Esmé Stuart from his court, an incident Jonathan Goldberg suggests Marlowe may have had in mind. Stuart was more than twenty years older than the teenage king at the time of his exile, so one convention of royal favouritism would have been reversed. Gaveston's birthdate is unknown, but he cannot have been more than a few years younger than his royal lover.

The classical model for a monarch and his favourite is the love between Jupiter, king of the gods and Ganymede. The *History* calls Gaveston Edward's Ganymede, and in Michael Drayton's verse account *Peirs Gaveston* the favourite says:

> Some slanderous tongues, in spiteful manner said,
> That here I liv'd in filthy sodomy,
> And that I was King *Edward's Ganamed*,
> And to this sin he was entic'd by me.

This makes the connection with Ganymede and sodomy, if only to evade it, or imply that the responsibility for inticing to sin may be with Edward, not himself. Queen Isabella is quite clear that her husband is engaged in the ultimate dotage, half playing on the similarity in the two minions' names:

> For never doted Jove on Ganymede
> So much as he on cursed Gaveston.

Although the dating of all Marlowe's plays is debatable, his brief career means he must have written his play featuring Jupiter and Ganymede around the same time as *Edward II*, probably a year before.

God's own houseboy

In deciding to take 'no worse a name than Jove's own page' while disguised as a man in the forest, Rosalind in *As You Like It* transforms herself not simply into a man, but into a gay archetype. The bond between the king of the gods and his cupbearer had long been recognized as a sexual and loving one. Medieval texts have Ganymede debating with Helen the relative merits of women and boys as lovers for men, and the love between Jupiter and his page was often used as a noble precedent in the Renaissance, as it had been in classical Greece. Accused by rival sculptor Baccio Bandinelli of being a 'dirty sodomite', Cellini in his autobiography records his surely disingenuous reply:

I wish to God I did know how to indulge in such a noble practice; after all we read that Jove enjoyed it with Ganymede in paradise, and here on earth it is the practice of the greatest emperors and the greatest kings of the world.

As discussed in chapter three, reference to notable figures in history is a timeless manoeuvre of gay self-defence.

Given the implications of the boy's name, there is something more than casual in Jaques' approach to Ganymede: 'I prithee, pretty youth, let me be better acquainted with thee.' Some of Jaques' characteristics certainly suggest a Renaissance sodomite: the continental travels for which Ganymede mocks him as he departs are suspicious:

Farewell, Monsieur Traveller. Look you lisp and wear strange suits . . . or I will scarce think you have swam in a gondola.

He rejects the wedding festivities at the end of the play; and he shows none of the interest in Rosalind as a woman that he has done in her whilst disguised as the boy Ganymede. His misogyny is another stereotypical attribute, and his words as he departs the play are carefully shared between the men present: Rosalind, Celia and Phoebe are ignored. His name allows Touchstone a pun on jakes, meaning toilet, an anal play on words appropriate to Jaques' sense of his own purgative mission, to:

through and through
Cleanse the foul body of th'infected world.

Ben Jonson, in *Every Man in his Humour*, makes an equally scatalogical pun: 'Have you a stool there, to be melancholy upon?'

Jaques is no flamboyant minion, indeed one of his complaints against city women is their wearing of expensive clothes. As someone who sees his role as exposing wickedness and corruption, Jaques is aligned with the satirists who verbally assaulted Renaissance sodomites. A. H. Gray's 1928 book *How Shakespeare 'Purged' Ben Jonson* is not an account of enemas among Elizabethan playwrights, but uses a purging reference from the satirical *Parnassus* plays to argue that Jaques is modelled on Ben Jonson, also caricatured as the sodomite poet Horace in Thomas Dekker's *Satiromastix*.

These opposing attributes of sodomite and anti-sodomite may be deliberately combined in Jaques. Duke Senior states that Jaques has previously been a libertine 'As sensual as the brutish sting itself', which, if it is true, makes his railing a new-found disgust after his own debauches. He is at least less of a hypocrite than Jonson's Sir Voluptuous Beast, who draws on his sexual pleasure with boys to teach his wife erotic tricks:

Beast instructs his faire and innocent wife,
In the past pleasures of his sensual life . . .
And how his Ganymede moved.

Another suggested model for Jaques is satirist and playwright John Marston, also posing as a purger:

O that a satyr's hand had force to pluck
Some floodgate up, to purge the world from muck:
Would God I could turn Alpheus river in
To purge this Augean oxstall from foul sin.

Marston makes more complaints than anyone about 'Ganymedes': the boy companions fancied by Elizabethan men about town:

Alack, alack, what piece of lustful flesh
Hath Luscus left, his Priape to redress?
Grieve not good soul, he hath his Ganymede,
His perfumed she-goat, smooth kembed and high fed.

. . .
Yon effeminate sanguine Ganimede
Is but a beaver, hunted for the bed
But ho, what Ganymede is that doth grace
The gallant's heels. One who for two days space
Is closely hired. Now who dares not call
This Aesop's crow, fond, mad, fantastical?
Why, so is he, his clothes do sympathize,
And with his inward spirit humorize.
An open ass, that is not yet so wise
As his derided fondness to disguise.

Marston's Ganymede is over-dressed, effeminate and presumably a prostitute: 'One who for two days space Is closely hired.' As with Gaveston and his followers, the elaborate costuming probably transgresses class boundaries as well: here too is the sexual menace of 'a poor boy clad in a princely vesture'. The pun on 'An open ass' leaves little doubt as to what goes on between a gallant and his 'beaver, hunted for the bed'.

Although Marston's satires express disgust, other dramatists' references to the love affair between Jupiter and Ganymede are more amiable. The second part of Thomas Dekker's *The Honest Whore* opens with an exchange in which Lodovico claims that the weather is so good it might even interest the king of the gods in changing preferences and rolling the opposite sex in the grass:

Oh, a morning to tempt Jove from his ningle Ganimed, which is
but to give dairy wenches green gowns as they are going a milking

Dekker uses a similar image in his earlier court play *Old Fortunatus*, but here exclusively between males. Fortune offers the title character an embrace with Jupiter, as naked boys float in his sight:

Wish but for beauty, and within thine eyes,
Two naked Cupids amorously shall swim,
And on thy cheeks I'll mix such white and red,
That Jove shall turn away young Ganymede,
And with immortal arms shall circle thee.

The classic Ganymede scene is Marlowe's however, in *Dido, Queen of Carthage*. It has a deliberately provocative opening which could even today raise eyebrows, especially if performed by the cast of adolescent boys for whom it was written.

ACT ONE, SCENE ONE

Here the curtains draw; there is discovered Jupiter dandling Ganymede upon his knee and Mercury lying asleep.

JUPITER Come, gentle Ganymede, and play with me.
    I love thee well, say Juno what she will.

GANYMEDE I am much better for your worthless love,
    That will not shield me from her shrewish blows!

Despite its Olympian setting, which presumably exempts it from some moral strictures, this is an extraordinary image. Here is a married man with his sulking boyfriend on his knee. The boyfriend complains about the jealousy of his lover's wife. Then as now, the best response is for the adulterer to calm his lover with valuable gifts: Jupiter's brother Neptune's seductive strategy in *Hero and Leander*. Marlowe emphasizes the outrage by making the favours Juno's wedding jewellery:

Hold there, my little love; these linkèd gems
My Juno ware upon her marriage day,
Put thou about thy neck, my own sweet heart
And trick thy arms and shoulders with my theft.

Decorated with the spoils of love, this is the same abuse of crown jewels with which Mortimer charges Edward's minion. Ganymede, like Gaveston, knows that diamonds are a boy's best friend, particularly in ear-rings. Thomas Howard complains that a way to advancement at James I's court would be to say 'That the stars are bright jewels fit for Carr's ears.'

GANYMEDE I would have a jewel for mine ear
    And a fine brooch to put in my hat,
    And then I'll hug with you an hundred times.

JUPITER And shall have, Ganymede, if thou wilt be my love.

As a picture of love in action this pouting and doting verse is not idyllic like the lyrical pastoral of Alexis and Corydon, but no less effective. It might not be classed as a positive image of a gay relationship, but the pattern is easily recognizable. Marlowe is not dealing here with classical reconstruction, but a mischievous mockery of social mores that have persisted until today. His wry picture of mutual exploitation between an older, powerful man and his younger, prettier lover has been reproduced in same- and-opposite sex partnerships many times since.

Another reference can be seen in the complaint of Venus, who scolds the king of the gods for losing his sense of priorities

Ay, this is it, you can sit toying there,
And playing with that female wanton boy,
Whiles my Æneas wanders on the seas

Like many of Marlowe's other rulers – Edward II, Henri III in *The Massacre at Paris* and Mycetes in *Tamburlaine* – Jupiter is a king who fails to rule properly, in part because of his expensive tastes, effeminate preferences and indulgence of favourites. These plays are an early introduction of a theme which would be taken up by almost every writer in London from 1603, after the arrival of King James from Scotland.

Close shaves

Barbie's friend Ken has passed puberty. I know this because on my desk is the 'Shaving Fun™ Ken® Doll' (although 'Doll' is written in letters one-eighth the size of the others, presumably because male figures aren't supposed to be dolls). Using 'all the great accessories Ken® doll has', I can 'Have fun shaving Ken the easy way!' Trade secrets preclude giving here the composition of the substances which combine with Ken's 'magic Color-change® beard' to allow this innocent fun. A warning that 'This Product May Stain Some Surfaces' on the side of the box above the list of ingredients suggests they are serious stuff, however. Had those chemicals been available in the Elizabethan theatres, the question of how to stage Act Five, Scene Three of *Edward II* would be easily answered.

The play's more notorious staging problem is usually the next scene but one, in which the direction '*King Edward is murdered*' avoids specifying the mechanics of the King's viciously parodic sodomizing. Before he is fucked with a red-hot poker, however, Edward is forcibly shaved: 'Lest you be known, and so be rescued' claims Thomas Gurney, one of his jailers. Edward, now literally in the shit, imprisoned deep in a filthy dungeon, resists Gurney and his Sir John Matrevis as *'They wash him with puddle water and shave his beard away'*. Was this achieved with make-up, carefully selected to dissolve in water? Or was the image of the English king struggling as two men play barbers with dirty water, evocative enough?

Shaving is a sort of emasculation, here forced but elsewhere undergone voluntarily: the climax of Michael Drayton's attack on one gallant is his delight in 'his smooth-chinned, plump-thighed catamite'. The association was still current in 1620, when the pamphlet *Haec-Vir; or, The Womanish Man* appeared, complaining that for men: 'to cut the hair of your upper lips, familiar here in England, everywhere else almost [is] thought unmanly.' The somewhat mannish-woman Beatrice in *Much Ado About Nothing*, however, finds either version offensive:

BEATRICE I could not endure a husband with a beard on his face. I
 had rather lie in the woollen.

LEONATO You may light on a husband that hath no beard.

BEATRICE What should I do with him – dress him in my apparel
 and make him my waiting gentlewoman? He that hath a
 beard is more than a youth, and he that hath no beard is less
 than a man; and he that is more than a youth is not for me;
 and he that is less than a man, I am not for him.

Within the general point, that she has no intention of marrying, Beatrice manages to mock the effeminacy and lack of sexual potency of the beardless youth. Since she was herself played by such a beardless youth, the archness is almost intolerable. She ends up with Benedick, who is a man, and has a beard, but shaves it, making him both man and youth. This is an ideal compromise for Beatrice, if a suspicious sign of unmanliness in him, especially as he also seems to wear make-up and perfume.

The head of Mortimer, presumably bearded, is presented to the boy king Edward III at the climax of *Edward II*. In Marlowe's play he seems even younger than the fifteen years old he actually was when his father was killed. The final lines of the play, as he talks to his father's shaven and sodomized corpse, have a childish pathos:

Sweet father, here unto thy murder'd ghost,
I offer up this wicked traitor's head;
And let these tears, distilling from mine eyes,
Be witness of my grief and innocency.

At the other end of his life, Edward III refused a Commons petition to expel foreign merchants, which used the argument that they had introduced sodomy to England:

The Commons beg that all the Lombards who follow no other calling but that of merchant be made to leave the country . . . They are wicked usurers and employ all the subtle wiles of such men . . . They have now lately introduced into the land a very horrible vice which is not to be named, because of which the realm cannot fail to be destroyed if swift punishment be not ordained.

By this time he was old and senile, and his relations with Parliament terrible, so there are many reasons why he might have rejected the request. Might he, however, have been irritated at a reference to his father's rumoured 'passionate humour'? Only the wilfully sentimental could interpret it as a tribute to a gay martyr. Romanticism triumphs, however, at the end of Derek Jarman's *Queer Edward*, with the boy king lying on top of a cage containing his mother and Mortimer, relishing her make-up and ear-rings.

9

Strange Bedfellows

Ten miles to Pomfret and still no sign of Dick.

Edward III's grandson Richard II succeeded him to the throne. Green
room gossip had old stagers muttering complaints during rehearsal of
the National Theatre's 1995 production of Shakespeare's *Richard II*.
Swiftly circulating apocrypha sustained a fogeyish complaint that
casting Fiona Shaw in the title role was taking political correctness Too
Far. The long history of transvestite performance of which Shakespeare's plays are a part failed to convince doubters, who harped on
gender despite the last hundred years' many celebrated female Hamlets,
and recent King Lears played by actresses in Germany and the United
States.

The programme cover for the National Theatre production shows
Shaw and David Threlfall, who played Bolingbroke, in a near smooch.
The performance played on this sexuality and dependency between boy
friends Dick and Harry, raised together in a precocious hothouse of
gilded youths (dressed by designer Hildegard Bechtler in pleated skirts).
Their male bonding and competitiveness became paradoxically more
homoerotic with Shaw's cocky, Peter Pan-ish Richard. The monarch has
two bodies: the physical and the symbolic. For Richard II's first
audience, ruled by a weak and feeble woman with the spiritual organs
of divine right, this was a major issue of state. Shaw and her partner-
director Deborah Warner explored that duality with theatrical relish.

England's Sun King was crowned at ten and dead by thirty-three.
Extravagant, fastidious and a great patron of the arts, he, like his great-
grandfather Edward II, was deposed and killed. *Richard II* was paired
with *Edward II* for the young Ian McKellen, who says he was pleased to
be 'breaking with the recent tradition of a limp-wristed playboy,

cocking an elegant leg over the throne', but sobered when told later that the performance he considered innovative resembled those of Michael Redgrave and John Gielgud, among others. A young gay actor, doubling Richard II with the 'clearly . . . gay' Edward II, works to find an interpretation which releases the role from the trappings of a stereotypical homosexual. Having done so, he finds that the gay and bisexual stars of the post-war British stage have been there before him. It's a queer business.

Falstaff in love

The troubled family life of the English Royal family never stops. Hardly is he crowned, but Henry IV is worried about his son, that 'young wanton and effeminate boy' whom he has not seen for three months. Rumoured to be hanging around the bars of London's twilight world with 'unrestrained loose companions', he shows signs of going the way of his great-great-grandad. Indeed, the end of *Henry IV Part Two* is like the opening of *Edward II*, as the new king tells his brothers: 'My father is gone wild into his grave'. Edward summons back his exiled lover with 'My father is deceased. Come Gaveston', but Hal responds differently to the same opportunity, rejecting his former playmates, and banishing them himself, 'on pain of death . . . not to come near our person by ten mile'.

The banishment is a grim conclusion to a friendship which has spanned the two parts of *Henry IV*, but not as grim as the fate suffered by both Gaveston and Edward. Jonathan Goldberg has written 'Desiring Hal', a witty and detailed analysis of the Prince and his 'stain', 'riot' and 'rebellion': sodomy. He points out that when the prince becomes king, 'one of the king's betrayers turns out also to have been his bedfellow: their physical intimacy was supposed to have kept Scroop ever from turning traitor to the king'. In *A Knack to Know a Knave* (1592) Philarchus disobeys 'the laws both of God and nature' by being 'once bedfellow to the king'. Goldberg climaxes his account of Hal as object of desire with a reading of the scene in *Henry V* in which Henry confronts that bedfellow 'and attempts to cast off the treasonous "English monsters"'. Treason being, like Coke on sodomy, 'a sin horrible, committed against the King', there is a telling anal ambiguity in Hal's words:

Scroop knew 'the very bottom of my soul' (97), Hal declares; he held the 'key' to Hal's treasure and 'almost might'st have coin'd me into gold / Would'st thou have practis'd on me for thy use' (98–99).

Gus van Sant's 1991 film *My Own Private Idaho* blends parts of the Falstaff and Hal plot from *Henry IV* with a romantic story of a contemporary hustler gang. Goldberg's analysis explores many of the problems in using the anachronistic language of twentieth-century sexuality to describe Elizabethan drama. He cites Alan Bray for his claim that 'much in the ordinary transactions between men in the period, in their negotiations of the social hierarchies, took place sexually'. He then uses Hal as an example:

> while Hal is ever casting off his companions, it is not bedfellows per se that are called into question. Hence there is no reason not to suppose that Hal and Falstaff were bedfellows too. In what situation, after all, does Falstaff ask his first question – 'Now, Hal, what time of day is it, lad' (*1 Henry IV*, 1.2.1)? If he is just waking up, what is Hal doing? What should be made of the fact that the next time we see Falstaff asleep (at the end of act 2, scene 4), Hal is in . . . his pockets? Is this attraction to his sleeping companion what the critics claim, a sign of infantilism? What *is* Hal talking about when he charges Falstaff with being an exorbitant 'bed-presser' (2.4.238)?

P. H. Davison's 1968 edition of the play inadvertently supports Goldberg's thesis. 'Shakespeare does not state a location for this scene . . . What is much more important than location is that Hal and Falstaff should be seen and heard together, without the intervention of their cronies, so that the the audience can gauge the nature of Hal's association with Falstaff.' There is a neat balance if our first sight of Hal and Falstaff, in the pair of plays which show them together, is of them getting out of bed with each other. Falstaff and Hal parody Jupiter and Ganymede, or at least one comic version of them: 'What is't, sweet wag, I should deny thy youth?' asks the besotted king of the gods in Marlowe's play. The first time we see Prince Hal, he could be a boisterous child dandling on Falstaff's knee:

> I prithee sweet wag, when thou art king . . . Marry then sweet
> wag, when thou art king let . . . us that are squires of the night's

body . . . be 'Diana's foresters', 'gentlemen of the shade', 'minions of the moon'.

Falstaff's image of Harry as a boy-child gets more virulent expression when they argue. Then the prince is a (very) little prick: 'you starveling, you elf-skin [or eel-skin], you dried neat's tongue, you bull's pizzle, you stockfish – O, for breath to utter what is like thee! – you tailor's yard, you sheath, you bow-case, you vile standing tuck'. Hal's under-endowment temporarily exhausts Falstaff's vocabulary.

Here, however, the 'mad wag' is told a fairy story of how he will grow up to be king and have a single-sex company of followers like Diana. The androgynous twilight band will be 'gentlemen of the shade' and 'minions of the moon', going a step further than the experimental all-male courts of Arden and Navarre. The telling of the fantasy is disastrously inverted, however: the dream is not the child's but his father-figure's, and will be destroyed when the sweet wag is indeed transformed to father of the country. The two will be 'squires of the (k)night's body' no longer.

For the betrayal at the end of those plays is, just as Edward's was, a choice between bodies. Falstaff's must be removed: 'Make less thy body hence', commands the new King . The expulsion puts a permanent ten-mile channel between them, across which Falstaff, unlike Gaveston, can never swim back. Falstaff must be amputated, for Harry has a new man, with a great body and noble limbs: England.

> And let us choose such limbs of noble counsel
> That the great body of our state may go
> In equal rank with the best-governed nation.

The two plays of *Henry IV* stage Prince Hal's enjoyment of, and departure from, the twilight world of the sodomite, in that term's loosest form. *Henry V* will end with his marriage to France, in the person of Princess Catherine. As a trilogy, the plays dramatize through historical example the journey Benedick and Claudio have to take in *Much Ado About Nothing* (see chapter six). It anticipates a popular later theory of sexuality in 'passing phases'. Benedick and Claudio, like Hal, must reject the freedom and licence of a masculine world and contract to a wife. In Hal's case that piece of paper is also a major international treaty. For all of them, the journey between the two worlds is mediated by a passage through male love at what some would see as its purest state: a warrior band. Harry nearly weeps when he hears about the last moments of the Duke of York, who embraced and kissed the slain Earl of Suffolk until himself 'espoused to death'.

Amputating Falstaff is not enough: Hal cannot marry until his past has been eliminated. Just as he sends one former bedfellow to execution, the other dies too. Falstaff is 'very sick' in Act Two, Scene One of *Henry V*. During the next scene, the king confronts and condemns Scrope. Simultaneously, the 'exorbitant bed-presser' makes his fine end, described by Hostess Quickly in the scene immediately after. Nim has his theory on the cause of death: 'The King hath run bad humours on the knight'. Quickly is more direct:

The King has killed his heart.

Falstaff is the descendent of the medieval tempter whose wickedness, often disguised as virtue, leads Everyman astray: 'that reverend Vice', says Hal. Yet he is not in 'reverend' disguise – his nature is all too plain. No one is deceived by Falstaff, indeed the pleasure is in mocking his boasts and lies. He is punished, while Hal escapes unharmed. Mistress Quickly warns: 'if his weapon be out, he will foin [thrust] like any devil, he will spare neither man, woman, nor child'. He is 'a honeyseeed, a man-queller, and a woman-queller'. The scene is packed with bawdy allusion: such puns on debauchery are funny, not horrific. Hal is convinced that Falstaff has corrupted the page he gave him, from Christian to ape, but does not immediately ring Eastcheap Social Services.

John Dover Wilson sees a longer pedigree, which allows a more benevolent side to mischief, in the origins of theatrical delight with inversions of status and gender discussed in chapter one:

as heir to the Vice, Falstaff inherits by reversion the functions and attributes of the Lord of Misrule, the Fool, the Buffoon and the Jester, antic figures the origins of which are lost in the dark backward and abysm of folk-custom.

Falstaff's androgyny is the final element of this inheritance. He compares himself to a sow overwhelming her children; his womb undoes him. Hal imagines a transvestite role for Falstaff in which they are married: Harry plays his rival Hotspur, and 'that damned brawn shall play Dame

Mortimer his wife'. In *The Merry Wives of Windsor* his folk roots are to the fore, disguised not only as Herne the Hunter (Diana's forester and gentleman of the shade, at last) but, more prosaically, 'the old woman of Brentford', considered to be 'a witch, a quean, an old, cozening quean'. Again, he resembles both the Bessey of the folk play, and an affectionate version of a wicked type in medieval drama. Acknowledging this dual nature, and reversing the conventions of the Elizabethan stage, there have been female Falstaffs since the eighteenth century, including the gender-bending Charlotte Charke in the 1734 *The Humours of Sir John Falstaff, Justice Shallow and Ancient Pistol*. In a further variation on the theme, 'Spy' of *The Weekly Journal* writes in 1724 of his visit to a masquerade dressed as a woman, but 'padded out to the size of Sir John Falstaff': a man as a woman as a man.

'Show me Falstaff in love' said the Queen, supposedly, commissioning Shakespeare to write *The Merry Wives of Windsor*. It is tempting to add the equally apocryphal condition ' . . . with a woman'. The two parts of *Henry IV* are Falstaff's real love story. His attempt at respectable heterosexual adultery is punished by the fairies, who dance around him singing 'Fie on sinful fantasy'. They pinch him, according to the stage directions: as Falstaff himself points out, the pox pinches lechery.

The comic conclusion to the play is not Falstaff's punishment, however, but the revelation that the other suitors have taken boys for women. Slender seems to have just discovered in time that his potential bride is 'a great lubberly boy', and his protestations are comic:

> If I had been married to him, for all he was in woman's apparel, I would not have had him.

Slender is a fool, and his literal-mindedness is mocked, but he has at least not gone through with the ceremony, unlike the French Doctor Caius, who is furious: 'I ha married *un garçon*'. The two fools desire A. (Ann) Page, but get a page instead, a play on words tucked inside the tortured pronunciation of Caius': 'A boy! It is not Anne [*un*] Page, by Gar.' The mistake must be intended to amuse, rather than disgust, the audience, particularly when the play continues with the climax of a bawdy running joke:

> PAGE . . . did you take her in green?

> CAIUS Ay be Gar [God], and 'tis a boy.

Doctor Caius has misrecognized Anne Page by her green clothes, but to 'take in green' also means to fuck a virgin. The last joke in the play, before the romantic conclusion, is an image of inadvertent buggery between a Frenchman and an English boy. In this, Shakespeare's only play set in Elizabethan England, the figure of the continental sodomite, bugbear of the satirists, makes a comic appearance.

Saucy bon companions

The French were good for a laugh. Although allies, they were still Catholics and continentals, both characteristics which Elizabethan and Jacobean playwrights exploited. Just across the channel which had failed to keep out Gaveston, the court of Henri III (reigned 1574 to 1589) was notorious for its *mignons* and extravagance. It inspired Marlowe's greatest hit, *The Massacre at Paris*, and must be partly behind other portraits of weak, sodomite kings. The vogue for plays about recent French history lasted well after Henry's death. Even in 1976, New York dramatist of the ridiculous Charles Ludlam was finding inspiration in Henri for his *Isle of the Hermaphrodites: or The Murdered Minion*:

> Catherine's son Henry III was a homosexual king who had an entourage of minions who were flaming, semi-transvestites as well as expert swordsmen and homicidal maniacs. They were dandies who wore tons of makeup and extremely fancy dress. It was all very decadent. They all vied for Henry's attention, and they used to kill each other regularly in very savage duels. Sudden death was the code. None of them ever lived past thirty.

Jacobean writers found in the French court a useful guise (and a useful Guise, of whom more later). This corrupt world beset by favourites could easily be criticized, yet provided handy parallels with that of James. There was also plenty of opportunity for filthy jokes, particularly from the dangerously satirical and persistently bawdy boy players.

Thomas Dekker and John Webster's *Northward Ho* (1605) introduces the self-styled poet Old Bellamont, based on another writer, George Chapman. Bellamont tells the swaggering fool Captain Jenkins that he is writing a tragedy which is to be presented 'in the French court, by French gallants':

BELLAMONT It shall be sir at the marriages of the Duke of Orleans, and Chatilion the admiral of France, the stage –

CAPTAIN JENKINS Ud's blood, does Orleans marry with the Admiral of France now?

BELLAMONT O sir no, they are two several marriages.

It is a simple joke, which relies for its effect not just on Jenkins' gullibility, but also the hilarity of male marriage among the French nobility. As in *Henry V* and *The Merry Wives of Windsor*, swipes at the French do not preclude jibes at the Welsh as well. Bellamont returns to describing his play:

BELLAMONT As I was saying the stage all hung all with black velvet, and while 'tis acted, myself will stand behind the Duke of Biron, or some other chief minion or so, – who shall . . . step to the French King, and say *Sire, voila* . . . a very worthy man to be one of your privy chamber, or Poet Laureate.

CAPTAIN JENKINS But are you sure Duke Peppernoon will give you such good words, behind your back to your face?

There was no official Poet Laureate when this was first performed, although Ben Jonson would get the job in all but name some years later. Jonson collaborated with Chapman and John Marston on *Eastward Ho*, to which this play responds, and there is mockery of his self-promotion here as in *Satiromastix*. Here sodomy is Bellamont's inadvertent subtext as he describes his projected advancement in the French court. Standing behind one of the king's minions is the best route to his privy chamber – his anus. Captain Jenkins once more jumbles the sense, unable to work who faces which way in this manoeuvre.

Chapman wrote many of his own plays about the French court, the best known of which have as their central character Bussy D'Ambois. Bussy, originally played by Nathan Field, is the favourite of King Henri III's younger brother the Duc D'Alençon or 'Monsieur'. Born poor, Bussy is no innocent. On his first encounter in the play with Monsieur, he observes:

Like to disparking noble husbandmen,
He'll put his Plow into me, plow me up

Parks are ruined by disparking: their character is changed, or coverted to other use: Bolingbroke complains of it in *Richard II*. For Bussy, however, this change of use will be beneficial. In the next scene, when Monsieur says to Bussy, 'Come mine sweet heart I will enter thee', it is quite clear how a handsome young lad gets ahead in the French court. Monsieur is encouraged in his pursuit of Bussy by his brother, who during a bawdy scene gives the advice: 'If you have woo'd and won, then brother wear him'. Whether the play on 'wear him' is 'get inside him' or 'exhaust him', the King must imply the sexual use of Bussy to follow naturally from wooing and winning.

Here Henry is essentially a good but weak king, made more sympathetic by Chapman. Rather then have Henry betray Bussy, whom he apparently loathed, in *Bussy D'Ambois*, Monsieur reveals the adulterous affair with Tamyra which leads to Bussy's death. This gives an additional twist of sexual jealousy to the spunky Bussy's destruction.

The play proved sufficiently popular for Chapman to write a sequel, *The Revenge of Bussy D'Ambois*, some years later. In this, the ghost of Bussy spurs on his brother Clermont to revenge his death. Clermont, too, is taken on by Monsieur, but the cynicism of court advancement contrasts here with a romantic friendship between Clermont and the Duke of Guise. This great love becomes the central relationship in the play, to Monsieur's dismay.

Clermont and Guise are resented from the start. Bussy's brother-in-law Baligny describes Clermont to Guise as 'your creature' and indicates to Monsieur, 'The Guise and his dear minion, Clermont D'Ambois / Whispering together'. Monsieur responds 'See how hee hangs upon the ear of Guise / Like to his jewel'. Ganymede and Robert Carr demand ear-rings from their patrons: Clermont *is* one. The distaste expressed by Baligny and Monsieur resembles that of Mortimer and the English nobles over Gaveston. Closer to Chapman, it shares the image of the public fawning and minion's ear-ring with the report of King James and Robert Carr written by Thomas Howard. The letter containing Howard's comments was written in 1611, around the time *The Revenge of Bussy D'Ambois* was first performed, suggesting that these were then typical attributes on stage and at court, even if one does not directly influence the other.

The major difference between Monsieur's comments on Clermont and those by Mortimer on Gaveston or Howard on Carr, is that

Monsieur is himself a man with minions. The first *Bussy* play rewrites history, giving the betrayal of Bussy a strong taste of Monsieur's sexual jealousy. So in the sequel, Monsieur's comments on Clermont and Guise sound less like general distaste at court corruption – in which he is intimately involved – than envy. That impression is confirmed when Monsieur offers to take on Clermont as he did his brother. He criticizes them being together and stakes a prior claim to Clermont:

> Come, you two
> Devour each other with your virtue's zeal,
> And leave for other friends, no fragment of ye:
> I wonder Guise, you will thus ravish him
> Out of my bosom, that first gave the life
> His manhood breathes, spirit, and means and lustre.
> What do men think of me, I pray thee Clermont?
> Once give me leave (for trial of that love
> That from thy brother Bussy thou inherit'st)
> T'unclasp thy bosom.

Monsieur virtually rips the two friends apart, complaining of their unseemly mutual devouring and ravishment. Yet their friendship is hungry with virtue. There is no such contrast between physical appetite and higher thoughts in Monsieur's account of his claim on Clermont. His imagery evokes the way Clermont's manhood has been given breath and vigour by Monsieur; how it has been shined up and filled with spirit by him. 'Th'expense of spirit in a waste [waist] of shame Is lust in action' puns Shakespeare's sonnet. The play distinguishes virtuous love between men from the sexual favours used to gain advancement at court. Monsieur is furious with Clermont:

> Why do I love thee then? Why have I raked thee
> Out of the dung-hill? Cast my wardrobe on thee?
> Brought thee to court too, as I did thy brother?
> Made ye my saucy bon companions?
> Have I blown for nothing to this bubble?

Tempting though it is to connect Monsieiur's bubble-blowing with his earlier giving breath to Clermont's manhood, blowing as slang for oral sex seems not be a seventeenth century use. Raking Clermont out of his dung-hill sniffs of sodomy, however. The outraged 'Why do I love thee then?' has the same taint of self-deception which Joe Orton exposes in a twentieth century Monsieur, Ed in *Entertaining Mr Sloane*:

> No principles? Oh, you really have upset me now. Why am I interested in your welfare? Why did I give you a job? Why do thinking men everywhere show young boys the strait and narrow? Flash cheque-books when delinquency is mentioned? Support the Scout-movement? Principles, boy, bleeding principles. And don't you dare say otherwise or you'll land in serious trouble.

Ed inexpertly tries to conceal his real interests from Sloane and the audience, morality a sorry fig-leaf to hide his sexual motives. Monsieur, as a French aristocrat, requires no such self-deception: everything has its price in this decadent world.

Except, it seems, true masculine love, making a comeback even in the world of the saucy bon companions which Chapman creates in Henry's court (and reflects from James's). When Clermont is accused of treason, Guise eulogizes his friend to the king, and the play ends in a sequence of pathos-packed scenes to rival anything in *Damon and Pithias*. Henry is suspicious, calling Guise's appeals 'his saucy forcing of my hand'. The calculating, sexually manipulative language of the court is all he has to describe Guise and Clermont, yet their final scenes suggest something different. Guise praises Clermont's resistance of passion from men and women, in favour of a greater good:

> How strangely thou art loved of both the sexes;
> Yet thou lov'st neither, but the good of both.

They swear a masculine friendship, which Clermont describes as chaste, albeit with an image which begins like one of Monsieur's, hot with kindling, knowledge and spirit again:

> For when love kindles any knowing spirit,
> It ends in virtue and effects divine;
> And is in friendship chaste, and masculine.

Guise responds with more overt heat: his blood is up for the man he wants as his mistress:

> Thou shalt my mistresse be; me thinks my blood
> Is taken up to all love with thy virtues.

And howsoever other men despise
These paradoxes strange and too precise,
Since they hold on the right sway of our reason,
I could attend them ever . . .

Whatever other men think of us and our way of thinking, I will stay this way for ever, he promises. It is a touching declaration of love between men in a hostile world, and leaves nothing more for them to do except die nobly.

Guise dies begging someone to send Clermont his love:

GUISE Is there no friend here
    Will bear my love to him?

AUMAL I will my lord.

GUISE Thanks with my last breath: recommend me then
    To the most worthy of the race of men.

   Dies

In a climax more like *Romeo and Juliet* than *Edward II*, Clermont refuses to live without his dead friend:

   Shall I live, and he
Dead, that alone gave means of life to me?

For him, a friend cannot be amputated, for without him, no life is possible. There are no longer two bodies, but, as in marriage, one flesh:

But friendship is the sement [cement] of two mindes,
As of one man the soul and body is,
Of which one cannot sever, but the other
Suffers a needful separation

Cement was spelled with both s and c in the early seventeenth century. It also, as the rhythm of this line makes clear, tended to be stressed on the first syllable, making it just a touch of the tongue away from 'semen'.

This seepage of sexual meaning into even the purest of Clermont's declarations suggests how the language of romantic friendship is no longer as pure as it had been for Lyly's boys. However much Clermont and Guise set themselves apart from the sodomy and corruption of their surroundings, they are still French. Equally, Chapman cannot imagine in them an innocence on which a casual observer of his own court and theatre would choke. Even Clermont's penultimate word casts himself as a court puppet: a creature, albeit one of the man he loves. To come is to die, as we saw with Gaveston's opening speech. Clermont dies, in order to come:

I come my Lord, Clermont thy creature comes.

He kills himself

The equivalence of Clermont's passion for Guise and that of a woman for a man is recognized by the woman who loved him. 'It must be so, he lived but in the Guise / As I in him', says the Countess after his death. Thus *The Revenge of Bussy D'Ambois* begins the illustrious history of the gay suicide play, a genre still running in London nearly four hundred years later.

Guise and dolls

Chapman's portrait of the Duke of Guise suggests that the love between a nobleman and his creature need not be entirely base. This may simply reflect political expedience: in 1605 Chapman had been imprisoned with Jonson for satirizing the new King's Scottish cohorts in *Eastward Ho!* and he may have wanted to cover his back here. He gives Guise and Clermont pre-eminence in his plotting, however, rather than concentrating on the more conventional rascality of Monsieur. This suggests more interest in the conflicting natures of 'masculine love' and the manipulation of minions. What is certain, however, is that his Duke of Guise is hardly recognizable as the same character depicted in Marlowe's *The Massacre at Paris*, performed twenty years earlier.

Chapman completed *Hero and Leander* after Marlowe's death, and must have known his former colleague's most popular play. In part, it exploits anti-Catholicism, beginning with the massacre of French Protestants on St Bartholomew's Day 1572. Yet its portrait of Guise, who is both wicked and appealing, complicates the easy propaganda which dominates the play's surviving text. Guise is ambitious, manipulative and cynical in his use of religion to inflame lesser people's passions. He plots mass murder and political assassination, as well as the death of one of King Henry's minions, Mugeroun, who is having an affair with his Duchess.

Fast, furious and grimly funny, the play survives in such a mangled and reduced form, however, that it is hard to see what the great attraction of *The Massacre at Paris* can have been. Even in the confusion of the massacre itself, however, Marlowe plays with intriguing intellectual and sexual themes. One of the fragmentary scenes has Guise's men Gonzago and Retes breaking into the home of the philosopher Petrus Ramus. The poor scholar, who was in his late fifties at the time of the massacre, has no gold with which to bribe the soldiers as they demand. Guise arrives, engages him in a detailed argument about Aristotle, then has him stabbed.

Ramus' radical ideas, which challenged the obscurity of standard philosophical thinking, and encouraged translation of texts to increase their accessibility, were current in Cambridge during Marlowe's time at the University. This scene contrasts a poor, plain-speaking protestant old man with the verbally flashy catholic aristocrat Guise, who abuses Ramus as a declaiming peasant, then has him murdered by his thugs. It begins, however, with another complication. Talaeus, Ramus' friend, rushes in, panic-stricken:

TALAEUS Fly, Ramus, fly, if thou wilt save thy life!

RAMUS Tell me, Talaeus, wherefore should I fly?

TALAEUS The Guisians are
    Hard at thy door, and mean to murder us.
    Hark, hark, they come! I'll leap out at the window.

RAMUS Sweet Talaeus, stay.

Talaeus was another scholar, but the brief presentation of him which survives in *The Massacre at Paris* is quite different to that of Ramus. Both are frightened, but Ramus keeps his ground while Talaeus runs around desperate to get out any way he can. When the soldiers Gonzago and Retes do come in, they find him trying to escape.

GONZAGO Who goes there?

RETES 'Tis Talaeus, Ramus' bedfellow.

GONZAGO What art thou?

TALAEUS I am, as Ramus is, a Christian.

RETES O, let him go; he is a Catholic.

Exit Talaeus.

Because he is a Catholic, Talaeus escapes, and presumably lives to a great age. Given the mess in which the play survives, some questions about this scene are impossible to answer. Is Talaeus' answer to the soldiers a brave attempt to save Ramus, and stand for cross-religious friendship and against sectarian bigotry? If so, why does he immediately run off, or is there part of the text missing at this point? What, moreover, is the implication of 'bedfellow'? Is Retes accusing Talaeus of sleeping with the enemy? If so, why let him go? If not, why mention it at all?

In one of William Fulke's 1579 attacks on Catholics, he asks 'Have not some popish priests such servants and bedfellows also?' Bedfellow here has the hint of sodomy, just as it did in John Bale's vituperations against popery. This combines in Marlowe's scene with the idea of treachery explored in *Henry V*. There the King's former bedfellow has betrayed his country: political and sexual treachery are metaphors of each other. In Marlowe's play, what is the betrayal? Is it miscegenation: a Protestant sleeping with a Catholic, just as a traitor slept with England, in the shape of Prince Hal its heir? Or does Marlowe reject Puritan theological distinctions? Richard Baines's unsupported testimony claims he said 'that the first beginning of religion was to keep men in awe'. In this case, surely the bed-sharing of two Christians would not be the crime, but the desertion of a friend. Religion is nationality in the Anglo-French paranoia on which *The Massacre at Paris* plays. Is there a hint here of E. M. Forster?

> If I had to choose between betraying my country and betraying my friend, I hope I should have the guts to betray my country.

In *Henry V*, there is no difference between betraying your country and betraying your friend. Gay spies from Marlowe to Anthony Blunt have seen the matter differently.

Charles Ludlam's Duke of Guise play borrows cheerfully from Marlowe, and plumps for provoking the descendents of the Puritans who fled Jacobean England for America.

> In the play, Protestantism is a radical new sect as viewed by the Catholics. I thought it would be very good for the moral majority

to remember what it was like when they were considered the *im*moral minority. They were considered an extremely radical, dangerous, perverted group.

Up to the ears in Italian

Euroscepticism entered the dictionary only recently, but its essentials were in place well before. The French court may have been full of vice, but the source was elsewhere. The prolific Robert Greene expresses a common Elizabethan view, that the court had imported sodomy, among other vices, to England from Italy:

> And whereas thou sayest thou wert born in Italy and called hither by our courtiers, him may we curse that brought thee first into England, for thou camest not alone, but accompanied with multitude of abominable vices, hanging on thy bumbast nothing but infectious abuses, and vain glory, self love, sodomy and strange poisonings, wherewith thou hast infected this glorious island.

English travellers confirmed what was rumoured at home: the vice was rife. Roger Ascham, who travelled to continental Europe in the 1550s, wrote against visiting Italy. The traveller William Lithgow, in *The Total Discourse of the Rare Adventures and Painful Peregrinations of Long Nineteen Years*, makes various observations on the prevalence of unnatural vice abroad. He tells how the punishment Edward I had favoured for sodomy was carried out in Malta in 1616, where he saw 'a Spanish soldier and a Maltese boy burnt in ashes, for the public profession of sodomy; and long or [ere] night there were above a hundred bardassoes – whorish boys – that fled away to Sicily in a galleon for fear of fire'. Lithgow distinguishes these boys from 'bugeron', presumably a version of buggers: 'never one bugeron stirred, being few or none there free of it'. This raises various questions about the relations between the confident bugeron and the persecuted bardassoes, which Lithgow does not answer. He does, however, confirm that, as well as these imports to Sicily, Italy is a hotbed of vice. From Padua, he describes a similar picture of buggers and bardassi, apparently a nationwide phenomenon:

> for beastly Sodomy, it is rife here as in Rome, Naples, Florence, Bolgna, Venice, Ferrara, Genoa, Parma not being exempted, nor

yet the smallest village of Italy. A monstrous filthiness, and yet to
them a pleasant pastime, making songs and singing sonnets of the
beauty and pleasure of their bardassi or buggered boys.

Around the same time, Sir Simonds D'Ewes attributes buggery to
Francis Bacon, and seems equally confident of it as a prevailing taste
elsewhere: 'his unnatural crime, deserting the bed of his lady, which he
accounted, as the Italians and Turks do, a poor and mean pleasure in
respect of the other'.`Forty years on, Samuel Pepys notes in his diary a
view that could have come from comments on the Elizabethan court:
'Sir J Mennes and Mr Batten both say that buggery is now almost
grown as common among our gallants as in Italy'.

Meanwhile Edward Coke's codification of the laws of England
confirms the view of Edward III's Parliament, that sodomy is a foreign
import. He also affirms that buggery – verbally at least – is taken from
the Italian.

> *Bugeria* is an Italian word, and signifies so much, as is before
> described, *paederestes* or *paiderestes* is a Greek word, *amator
> puerorum*, which is a species of buggery, and it was complained of
> in parliament, that the Lumbards brought into the realm the
> shameful sin of sodomy, that is not to be named, as there it is said.

This general association of Italy and buggery is a comic gift for
playwrights. In Thomas Dekker and Thomas Middleton's *The Honest
Whore* (1604), Hippolito describes a sexually diverse female prostitute:

> A harlot is like Dunkirk, true to none,
> Swallows both English, Spanish, fulsome Dutch,
> Back-doored Italian, last of all the French . . .

The Italian is actually 'Blacke-doord' in the first printed text of the play,
but either phrase is a reference to heterosexual anal intercourse.
Similarly, in Middleton and John Fletcher's *The Nice Valour* (c. 1620), a
printing pun is made out of Italic type and anal sex ('backward blows'),
although in a more sexually ambiguous context: 'All in Italica, your
backward blows. All in Italica you hermophrodite.'

The sexually diverse entourage of Ben Jonson's *Volpone* includes a
hermaphrodite, a eunuch and a dwarf. In diverging from the physical
norms of Jacobean England – still powerfully in place today – they are

made spectacles of deviation. From Richard III to Captain Hook, dramatists have used characters' outer, physical deformity (or, rather, their difference from current definitions of normality) to embody inner, psychological deformity (or, rather, their difference from current definitions of normality). Thus a brief reference to another dwarf, in Dekker and Webster's *Northward Ho!*, combines Jacobean notions of physical and mental abnormality with those of sexual and national perversion.

Bellamont, the Chapman-inspired poet who boasted of his play's success at the French court, is lured to Bedlam, the famous hospital for those considered lunatics. There he meets a Musician, whom Full-Moon, keeper of Bedlam, claims fell mad 'For love of an Italian dwarf'. 'Has he been in Italy then?' asks Bellamont. 'Yes' replies the keeper, 'and speaks they say all manner of languages'. Love of a dwarf has made the Musician mad: the confusion of being physically disabled with mental illness is one which can still be difficult to shift. The sexual perversity implied in loving a dwarf is enhanced by giving this imaginary person no distinct gender, like the eunuch or hermaphrodite with whom he or she makes Volpone's trinity. On top of all this, the dwarf is Italian, suggesting that the languages spoken by the Musician are, like the swallowings of Hippolito's harlot, euphemisms for sexual variations.

Gaveston's musicians 'with touching of a string May draw the pliant king which way I please'. Wilde's Algernon in *The Importance of Being Earnest*, despite his lack of skill on the piano, is suspiciously 'musical', a euphemism for homosexual which lasted well into the twentieth century. In *Northward Ho!*, the plight of the Musician is an early example of the indignities heaped on those considered sexually abnormal by the institutions of madness. At least he does not have to suffer aversion therapy. Bellamont takes an interest in the love-lorn Musician, which provides his companions (and the dramatists) with opportunities for fun at his expense.

BELLAMONT What are you a doing my friend?

MUSICIAN Pricking, pricking.

BELLAMONT What do you mean by pricking?

Pricking is writing music: setting down the notes, or pricks. Bellamont's failure to understand does not prevent the bawdy pun, continued when he finds the Musician 'prouder' than other men. Bellamont's vanity leads him to claim that he is a musician too. At this the Musician decides he has found a fellow spirit, and informs Bellamont: 'We'll be sworn brothers then, look you sweet rogue'. Seeing this, Bellamont's companions decide it will be amusing to leave the two alone together.

After the Musician's song, the bawdiness turns to distinct flirtation. Bellamont is drawn away by the Musician, who claims that he needs to walk because his robe is too flimsy: 'Walk, I'm a cold, this white satin is too thin unless it be cut, for then the Sun enters.' This has the paradoxical logic of madness, but also of seduction, with a pun on Sun and son, both penetrating him. The Musician is playing the same game as Kath in *Entertaining Mr Sloane*:

> I haven't a stitch on . . . except my shoes . . . I'm in the rude under this dress. I tell you because you're bound to have noticed. . . . (Leans over him.) You can't see through this dress can you? I been worried for fear of embarrassing you.

Having drawn Bellamont's attention to his as yet unslit white satin, the Musician finds another point of contact. The final evidence that this is a man just like him is a shared tongue – Italian.

MUSICIAN Can you speak Italian too, Sapetè Italiano?

BELLAMONT Un poco.

Bellamont's desire to claim skills he may not have here lays him wide open. The Musician responds in a frenzy, improvising on the theme of Bellamont's little Italian:

> 'Sblood if it be in you, I'll poke it out of you. Un poco, come march, lie here with me but till the fall of the leaf, and if you have but poco Italiano in you, I'll fill you full of more poco. March.

If Bellamont has any ability in Italian, then the musician will poke it out of him, and fill him with more. Given this sustained metaphor for buggery, the image it surrounds seems a tame pun on autumn and genital revelation, both 'the fall of the leaf'. Bellamont responds to the command to march off and lie with the musician with no dismay. 'Come on', he says, and the two men go off together.

Bellamont's companions compound their attempt to humiliate him by pretending he is mad and asking the asylum keeper to keep him locked up. Like his earlier fantasy about being intoduced by the back door into the French court, Bellamont seems prone to placing himself in apparently accidental sodomitical situations with continentals. The poet returns, quite converted to Italian by his 'mad dialogue':

BELLAMONT Perdonate mi, si Io dimando del vostro nome. Oh, whether shrunk you? I have had such a mad dialogue here.

ALL We ha been with the other mad folks.

MAYBERRY And what says he and his prick-song?

BELLAMONT We were up to the ears in Italian i'faith.

ALL In Italian! O good master Bellamont, let's hear him.

In fact what they do is have him tied up and imprisoned, just as Falstaff is humiliated and punished in *The Merry Wives of Windsor* for his vanity and concupiscence. Mayberry's reference to 'prick-song' confirms that their joke on him has a sexual root, and Bellamont, inadvertent as ever, backs it up. The title of the play Joe Orton was planning when he died became that of his biography. *Prick Up Your Ears* is bold enough, but it is the final anagram which made him call it 'one of Kenneth Halliwell's most brilliant titles'. It would not be too hard for Bellamont's affected pronunciation to make 'ears' into 'arse', the other destination of the Musician's prick-song. This is a play written for teenage boys to perform.

Just one more Venetian

Rome was the spiritual centre of the sodomite world for John Bale and the anti-Catholics. Similarly, the cast list for Thomas Dekker's 1607 play *The Whore of Babylon* makes its allegorical point clear: 'Th'Empress of Babylon: under whom is figured Rome'. This Babylon is a place where churches are brothels, and sodomy a daily ocurrence. Proverbial Romish decadence is useful to Dekker's political allegory, but this is not as narrowly anti-Catholic in focus as Bale. Rome is listed by Lithgow in 1614 as one of the Italian cities where perversion is rife, but he does not single it out from the prevailing national dissipation.

If there is a capital city of vice for Elizabethan and Jacobean writers, it must be Venice. Thomas Nashe in his picaresque tale of a page in Europe, *The Unfortunate Traveller* (1594), calls the city 'The Sodom of Italy', making it the *ne plus ultra* of sexual deviation. The association has persevered, particularly as a venue for an awakening of visitors' homosexual desire. Frederick Rolfe, Baron Corvo's 1913 *The Desire and Pursuit of the Whole* is 'A Romance of Modern Venice' between an English man and an Italian boy. Thomas Mann's 1912 *Death in Venice* is the twentieth-century's most influential tale of gay desire. Ian McEwen's 1981 *The Comfort of Strangers* continues to develop this literary tradition of canal sexuality. Even Daphne du Maurier made the connection, worrying that she might be considered a lesbian: 'just one more Venetian wanting to make a pass'.

Shakespeare's titular Venetians tend to make disastrous sexual passes. His Merchant of Venice is Antonio, a sodomite. His Moor of Venice is closer to Antony, Ancient Rome's 'amorous surfeiter'. Othello famously recognizes his excess of passion (the 'more' of Venice) just before he kills himself, having been 'one that loved not wisely but too well'. The heterosexual dynamic of the plot is enhanced by crude racial stereotyping: Othello's blackness makes him more manly; Desdemona's whiteness makes her more of a woman. White supremacist anxiety around black male sexuality has surfaced persistently in discussion of the play. Tradition makes Desdemona the first 'real' woman on the English stage, in a 1660 production of *The Moor of Venice*:

> The woman plays today, mistake me not
> No man in gown, or page in petticoat

A satire on a contemporary Othello, Thomas Betterton, derides his supposed low birth, as well as his stiffness and muscularity. These characteristics are combined with Othello's race and notions of the sexually uncontrolled black man, in a portrait of vigorous heterosexual excess:

> Methinks I see him mounted, hear him roar,
> And foaming cry Odsblood, you little whore,
> Zounds, how I ——! I —— like any moor.

Othello dramatizes more harshly than *Much Ado About Nothing* what happens when men move from the masculine world of soldiering to the feminine terrain of passion. Both are set in Italy, at the gateway to what

Richard Burton would define as the 'sotadic zone', where sodomy was prevalent and unpunished. It is a border between East and West, and between Christianity and its competitor religions. *The Merchant of Venice* stages one religious confrontation in Italy. Another drives the offstage action in *Othello*. Othello has such status in Venice because he can defend them from other Moors: the Moslem Turks.

Francis Bacon is supposed to have preferred sodomy 'as the Italians and Turks do'. William Lithgow claims of the Turks:

> They are extremely inclined to all sorts of lascivious luxury; and generally addicted, beside all their sensual and incestuous lusts, unto sodomy, which they account as a dainty to digest all other libidinous pleasures.

Moving from Venice to Cyprus (well into the sotadic zone), the Moor of Venice successfully defends an island outpost of the Christian state against the Turks. A Moor on the outside, by colouring, he vanquishes those who are Moors on the inside, by religion. What he cannot vanquish is inside himself, preyed on by one who is secretly part of the opposition. Othello's trusted ensign is a closet Turk: a sodomite.

Othello's excess of passion is manipulated by Iago. Notable actresses have played the role, including Charlotte Cushman (see chapter eleven), whose offstage lesbianism interestingly enhances the possibilities in Iago's frustrated desire for Desdemona. Twentieth-century male Iagos have found homosexuality a means to explore his malignity, developing the popular notion of the sinister, vengeful deviant. Lawrence Mass, looking back on his own self-loathing as a gay man in the 1960s, discovered a review of the film in which Laurence Olivier played Othello, based on the 1964 National Theatre production. He comments that 'The malevolence of Frank Finlay's Iago was enhanced by a none too subtle hint of homosexuality'.

Iago's betrayal of Othello is based on a great lie: that Cassio has, impossibly, had sex with Desdemona. Sigmund Freud says all homosexuals are liars. Michel Foucault responds:

> during the Nineteenth Century, it was, to a certain degree, necessary to hide one's homosexuality. But to call homosexuals liars is equivalent to calling the resistors under a military occupation liars. It's like calling Jews 'money-lenders', when it was the only profession they were allowed to practise.

Iago's bogus reluctance to prove Desdemona's disloyalty is overcome by a combination of entering and pricking, caused, he claims, by love. He has started so he will finish.

> I do not like the office,
> But sith I am entered in this cause so far
> Pricked to't by foolish honesty and love,
> I will go on:

Iago's proof is another story of treachery and a shared bed. He claims that Desdemona has betrayed her bed-partner, and in doing so, betrays his own. He has shared Cassio's secrets while lying in bed with him. This intimacy does not bind him to Cassio, but gives his claims added conviction for Othello.

> IAGO I lay with Cassio lately,
> And being troubled with a raging tooth,
> I could not sleep. There are a kind of men
> So loose of soul, that in their sleeps
> Will mutter their affairs. One of this kind is Cassio.
> In sleep I heard him say 'Sweet Desdemona,
> Let us be wary, let us hide our loves',
> And then, sir, would he grip and wring my hand,
> Cry 'O, Sweet creature!' then kiss me hard,
> As if he plucked up kisses by the roots,
> That grew upon my lips, lay his leg o'er my thigh
> And sigh, and kiss, and then cry 'Cursèd fate
> That gave thee to the Moor!'

> OTHELLO O monstrous, monstrous!

> IAGO Nay, this was but his dream.

Iago cannot sleep because he has 'a raging tooth'. A raging hard-on is a pornographic cliché, and equally likely to cause insomnia for sexually frustrated men in bed together. Whatever it is of Iago's that is throbbing, it leads him into Cassio's dreams, an easy task with one so loose of soul.

It may be true, although it seems unlikely, that Cassio indeed harbours a subconscious longing for Desdemona. Only Iago has been awake during the scene he describes, so the question is unanswerable. Even Cassio may be unaware of what he has said, if he said it at all.

Is the scene entirely Iago's fantasy, or an embellishment of something which has taken place? It is certainly rich with the detail needed to convince Othello.

Words are not enough for Iago to dramatize Desdemona's sexual betrayal. He physically imagines himself as Desdemona, playing the part of the errant wife to Cassio's importunate lover. His passivity belies the fact that the whole story is created by him. He makes Cassio perform what he desires in order to convince Othello. His deliberately ineffectual 'Nay, this was but his dream' deftly throws his audience off the scent. We watch him implying that this was more than a dream of Cassio's. Yet it is not Cassio's dream at all, but his own.

The metre of the lines here is confused, and the first editions of the play vary in the tenses and lineation. One version puts the final sequence into the past tense: 'then [he] laid his leg Over my thigh, and sighed, and kissed . . . ' That given above changes tense after Iago reports what Cassio has spoken: 'And then sir, would he . . . lay his leg . . . '. Here Iago may be reporting a regular occurrence: 'and then he would do . . . ' . There is also, however, a sense of looking forward: 'and I wish he would do . . .'. Thanks to this textual uncertainty, the anatomical details of Iago's Cassio dream are obscure. They may always have been, of course. What is clear is that this is not a purely romantic fantasy, but a vigorous sexual one. Cassio does hold Iago/Desdemona's hand and talk of love, but even then he is gripping and wringing. He rapidly moves on to hard kissing, applying suction to the lips, where they root. A growing root is an erection, but what it is doing growing near Iago's lips can only be wondered at. Cassio ends with a sigh, a kiss, and a cry, and the monstrous job is done.

Where is Sodom?

Pizzles and Fops

The location of Sodom may have been definitely east of England in the Restoration, but its whereabouts on the sexual map of the time is far less clear. One confused guide to the area is Cosmo Manuche's play *The Loyal Lovers: A Tragi-Comedy* which was printed in 1652, before the theatres reopened. It is hard to imagine it ever being produced, given its general obscenity, and some of its stage directions would challenge any theatrical management. Even today it would be a brave company who staged what must be the only scene in English drama in which one man flogs another with the dismembered penis of a bull.

The play opens with a bookseller offering Adrastus 'A true, perfect and exact account of Justice Dapper and his clerk's sodomitical revenue, to the great disabling and impoverishing the active and well-affected females.' The monk Sodome, described as 'one of the synod', 'a zealous Brother' and 'an abuser of the Commonwealth' is watched by Adrastus' servant Mettle in pursuit of Riggle 'a common strumpet'. The monk and the prostitute make an assignation:

SODOME Pray name the place most convenient to you,
  And I'll not fail to attend you.

RIGGLE What think you of the Naked-boy in Flesh lane?

While Adrastus and his friends wait for Sodome to meet his appointment, an obscene play within the play is performed for them. Mettle plays Phanaticus, a fradulent priest, and Symphronia is Fly-Blow, a Butcher. It appears that Fly-Blow's wife has given Phanaticus money, which Fly-blow then demands at pizil and knife-point:

[SYMPHRONIUS AS] FLY-BLOW . . . I came not altogether unfurnished
    With what, I hope, shall (in some reasonable measure)
    Satisfy you.

FLY-BLOW *lays off his cloak and reveals a Bull's pizzle*

[METTLE AS] PHANATICUS Good Sir, I doubt it not.

FLY-BLOW You shall not need; behold this ell of mettle,

    Raises his pizzle

    'Tis a good one: the Bull it once belonged to
    Cost me eight pounds.
    Marry, I shall give nine for yours, if you waste it not
    Too much in the service of the Elect. . . .

FLY-BLOW *beats the priest egregiously with a bulls pizzle*

PHANATICUS O Sir! draw in your pizzle, (if you be a man) and
    spare me
    Till the next Lord's day is past, or I shall be unable
    To scatter the sanctified seed of Reformation into the bowel
    Of our dear Sister-hood.

This pantomime over, they return to the business of humiliating Sodome, getting him drunk and tossing him in a blanket, making him shit himself. They then pin him into the blanket with butcher's pricks and leave him to pay their bill.

In its zealous vilification of religious figures, *The Loyal Lovers* revels in various forms of sexual excess. Sodome's punishment has him smothered in faeces and pinned by pricks for his pursuit of a female whore. The brothel is called 'the Naked-Boy', however, and in 1652 Manuche would have written Riggle to be played by a boy. Judge Dapper and his clerk's 'sodomitical revenue' which is 'to the great disabling and impoverishing the active and well-affected females' is the semen spent in boys' arses which deprives female prostitutes of their income. This hostility of female whores to gay men for spoiling their trade is a feature of ballads and news reports of arrested sodomites up to Oscar Wilde's conviction. In the play within the play Phanaticus has conned a married woman out of money, with the implication that, like the nuns, Mrs Fly-Blow has had the sanctified seed of Reformation scattered into her bowels by him. Mr Fly-Blow's impressive pizzle can hardly be only a subconscious homoerotic focus, with the humour to be got out of 'what, I hope, shall (in some reasonable measure) Satisfy you' and 'O Sir! draw in your pizzle, (if you be a man)'.

Sexual incontinence with 'plump muddy whore, or prostitute boy' are both the sins of Sodome and his brothers, with no more than a hint that anal intercourse is the specific transgression. Confusions about placing the sin of Sodom linger into this century. Britain's 1967 Sexual Offences Act distinguished between the forms of sodomy in a more specific anatomical definition than Manuche's, with anal intercourse between a man and a woman left technically a crime, while the same act between men was, with limitations, decriminalized. In the United States more recently, the attorney general of Georgia, Michael J. Bowers fired one of his staff when she announced that she intended to marry another woman arguing that 'by admitting her marriage to another woman and making it public knowledge', she had violated the state's anti-sodomy law. For Bowers, sodomy appears to include *any* expression of lesbian or gay identity, whether or not it is specifically sexual.

The search for the exact theatrical location of Sodom takes in another dramatic piece not intended for performance, George Lesly's 1675 *Fire and Brimstone, or, The Destruction of Sodom*. Like Manuche, Lesly's God depicts Sodom as a place of generalized debauchery, not specific to sexual acts or the gender of participants.

> GOD Behold, how Sodom swaggers in its pride,
>   And lust, and gluttony! none is espied
>   That thoughts of heaven have; or bow a knee:
>   But one poor stranger, who adoreth me.
>   My servant Lot: whose holy soul they vex;
>   Because there's no distinction made of sex
>   Nor age, but all promiscuously do go,
>   Like goats and leopards that they all may know
>   Each other . . .

Nevertheless, the interest of the Sodomite is in buggering handsome men:

> SODOMITE Confounded dog, bring forth thy handsome guests
>   Or by our great god Priapus we swear,
>   That we thy body will in pieces tear.

LOT . . . Neighbours be ruled, this wickedness give o'er.
  And if your beastly lust cannot refrain,
  But that these strangers you with sin would stain,
  See here two maids of mine who virgins be,
  Use them at pleasure, and let them go free.

SODOMITE Rogue, runagate, slave, think not that thou must,
  Make such exchanges to restrain our Lust.
  Who made thee a judge? If we be ruled by thee,
  Then must we bid adieu to buggery.
  But hold, stand back, or we will break the door.

Buggery was an activity which even the worldly Samuel Pepys in 1663 claimed quite confused him: 'I do not to this day know what is the meaning of this sin, nor which is the agent nor which the patient'. He is presumably talking of sexual activity between two men, rather than a man with a woman or a boy when the conventional roles would be easy to guess, unless Pepys is affecting his innocence.

The last unperformable play on the subject is the most infamous, *Sodom or The Quintessence of Debauchery*, published at the same time as Lesly's piece and attributed to John Wilmot, Earl of Rochester. The King of Sodom, Bolloximian, is tired of sex with women, and switches to sex with men for a change, ordering that the rest of the population do likewise: 'I do proclaim, that buggery may be used O'er all the land, so cunt not be abused.' Borastus, Buggermaster-general, counsels the King in his choice of catamite:

I would advise you, sir, to make a pass
Once more at Pockenello's loyal arse.
Besides, sir, Pene has so soft a skin
'Twould tempt a saint to thrust his pintle in.

Even without *Sodom*, John Wilmot remains the most notorious pornographic writer in English. Rapacious in his desire for women, his poetry also celebrates sex with boys. His mother, who outlived his early death, burned his papers 'lest the example of his works should lead others to sin'. If he did write *Sodom*, he is supposed to have rejected it as fit only for the toilet:

There bugger wiping Porters while they shite
And so thy book itself turn Sodomite.

Restoration predation

A gruesome gay stereotype makes his first stage appearance in the sexually provocative comedies of the Restoration. Thomas Southerne's *Sir Anthony Love* includes an early example: Lucia is a boyish girl who has a pass made at her by a sodomitical homosexual Abbé. The predatory old queer became almost as regular a feature in the plays of the early eighteenth century as his opposite number, the fop. Although the two roles later converged, fops began as effeminate and heterosexual. John Vanbrugh's *The Relapse* (1696) opens the century with classic examples of both: Lord Foppington, first played by Charlotte Charke's father, Colley Cibber; and Coupler, a lascivious sodomite. Foppington's brother, Young Fashion, fends off repeated advances by Coupler, a matchmaker who is arranging Lord Foppington's wedding to an heiress.

> COUPLER Ha! You young lascivious rogue you. Let me put my
> hand in your bosom, sirrah.
>
> YOUNG FASHION Stand off, old Sodom.
>
> COUPLER Nay, prithee now, don't be so coy.
>
> YOUNG FASHION Keep your hands to yourself, you old dog you, or
> I'll wring your nose off.
>
> COUPLER Has thou been a year in Italy, and brought home a fool
> at last? By my conscience, the young fellows of this age profit
> no more by their going abroad, than they do by their going
> to church. Sirrah, sirrah, if you are not hanged before you
> come to my years, you'll know a cock from a hen.

Coupler follows the time's conventional wisdom that visiting Italy is quite enough to open a man's eyes to sex with other men. He also suggests that, even if continental travel fails, age brings all men an interest in cocks; quite the reverse of the psychiatric notion of homosexuality as a standard aberration of youth. Young Fashion was originally played by Mary Kent as a breeches role, which increases the erotic tension in the scene. An awareness of the female body within the male role gives Coupler's enthusiasm to feel Young Fashion's breast added ironies.

Without celebrating these characters, the early eighteenth century stage did use them to expand the possibilities of sexual representation. Pix's *The Adventures in Madrid* (1706) uses a setting nearly as sexually suspicious as an Italian city to introduce another version of the predator queen. Lisset, locked up for 'coming in at the Garden-Gate' bribes her way out and buys boys' clothes, only to be pursued by Gaylove who calls her his little Ganymede and fairy. This may be the first recorded use of 'gay' and 'fairy' in the context of male homosexuality. If so, it reverses the etymology of 'gay', usually described as a development from describing prostitutes as 'gay women', for which the earliest references are in the nineteenth century, over one hundred and twenty years after Pix's play was seen.

Priests of all descriptions were portrayed as lascivious sodomites. Always quick to pick up other's ideas, Colley Cibber uses the device in *Woman's Wit* and *The Schoolboy*, which have boys fending off Jesuit tutors. At the masquerade life again imitates theatre when a *Guardian* writer is approached by his Indian prince, a 'Presbyterian parson' who tells him he is a 'pretty fellow' and offers to meet him in Spring Gardens the next night. Once again, the same-sex implications are softened by the suggestion that the parson is also a woman in disguise.

Fop attraction

In Shakespeare's time, a fop was simply a fool, but by the time of George Etherege's *The Man of Mode* in 1676, his characteristics have become much more specific: he is vain, pretentious, absurdly overdressed and obsessed with his appearance. Although his adoration of all things French marks him out as suspicious to an English audience, the original Restoration fop avidly pursues women, the excessive pursuit of whom could be considered unmanly, as in John Donne's verse letter 'To Sir Henry Wotton':

> Thou call'st me effeminate, for I love women's joys;
> I call not thee manly, though thou follow boys

The changing manners of Restoration men were not universally approved. In *The Man of Mode*, for example, when one of the men greets Dorimant, a rake assumed to be modelled on Rochester, with 'my life, my joy, my darling sin; how dost thou?', the orange-woman who is pimping for Dorimant is disgusted: 'Lord what a filthy trick these men have got of kissing one another! (*She spits*).' The joke is not that Medley and Dorimant are gay, but that the bawdy gossip has such puritanical views. Rochester, as we have seen, was no stranger to buggery, and the fictional Medley delights in gossiping with the ladies, rather than seducing them. According to a letter written after the premiere of Etherege's play, 'the general opinion will have Sir Fopling to be Mr Villiers, Lord Grandison's eldest son'. Villiers was later suggested to be part of a gay circle around William III. The epilogue specifically, but perhaps disingenuously, rules out any single model for Sir Fopling: 'no one fop was hunted from the herd'. Nevertheless, it appears many in the audience thought he shared characteristics with Villiers. Presumably he was a flamboyant fop, but was he also rumoured to be a sodomite at that time? If so, he would be closer to contemporary notions of effeminate men than his supposed stage portrait. The need to streamline ideas about the ways sexuality reveals itself comes from the relatively recent solidification of desire into homo-, bi- and heterosexual blocks. It is no surprise, therefore, that three-hundred-year-old characters fail to fit them neatly. Modern revivals of *The Man of Mode* sometimes interpret Sir Fopling Flutter's affectations as synonymous with contemporary gay camp, although his function in the plot is purely as a lover of women, a determined rival to Dorimant in pursuit of the awesome Mrs Loveit. Despite his pageboy and Gallic ways, there is no reason to assume Etherege imagines Sir Fopling's interest in Loveit to be sexless.

In *The Relapse*, Coupler is one of those Restoration men who make passes at boys who are in fact girls who wear breeches. Lord Foppington is, like Sir Fopling and other fops, in pursuit of a woman. Both conventions may of course stem from a single nervousness: although Restoration plays lay unperformed for over two hundred years for their bawdiness, they are still tame compared with some of their contemporary poetry, like the unperformable Sodom dramas. Given the boundaries of sexual expression which the theatre still observed, maybe the boys who are 'really' girls, and the fops who are 'really' after women both allow the fact of sexual desire between men to be reflected on stage, but not viewed directly lest, like the sun's rays, it prove too blinding for its audience. This audience could still read printed accounts of widespread buggery, albeit with the coyness of the substituted dash, a piece of bizarre prudery which persists to a recent Gay Sweatshop tour of a play which some publicity had to title *F——ing Martin*, while the cover of the book from which it was adapted always displayed the extra three offending letters. Just as James I and his favourites affected the representation of love between kings and their minions during his reign, the activities of William III must have complicated decisions about how far same-sex relations could safely be staged. The most explicit portrayals of a sodomite are in plays about Titus Oates: Alexander Oldys' *The Fair Extravagant* and Tom Brown's *The Salamanca Wedding*. Oates' interest in other men is part of an anti-Catholic demonization of him, and therefore could be sanctioned as patriotism, rather than condemned as obscene.

It is during the reign of William III (1689–1702) that recognizable stereotypes of the effeminate homosexual start to appear on stage. Fops tended to be popular with the their audiences, and were portrayed affectionately, if ridiculed, while boy-pursuing lechers got harsher treatment. Maiden in Baker's *Tunbridge Wells* and Varish and Bardash in John Leigh's *Kensington Gardens* combine characteristics from both sets of roles. The fop influence dominated, indeed Colley Cibber's fop Sir Novelty Fashion in *Love's Last Shift* claims he invented the bardash.

Charlotte Charke's novel *The History of Henry Dumont* contains a sneering portrait of an effeminate gay man, but, although Cibber comes across as a dreadful father in her autobiography, she does not link him with sodomy. Others were more forthcoming about the most notorious actor, manager and playwright of his time, accusing him of seeming homosexual in the devotedness of the Dedication to Henry Pelham in his autobiography. The satire stops short, just like Lord Queensberry's goading card to Oscar Wilde, of criticizing him for being a sodomite, and just accuses him of posing as one. In the book, Cibber robustly condemns the effeminacy of boy actors:

> The characters of women on former theatres were performed by boys or young men of the most effeminate aspect. And what grace or master-strokes of action can we conceive such ungain hoydens to have been capable of? . . . The additional objects then, of real, beautiful women could not but draw a proportion of new admirers to the theatre.

This may be simply covering his back, or what he think his readers want to hear: both being more important than the truth when it comes to the writing of theatrical autobiography, then as now.

Just as it is dangerous to believe all the self-aggrandizing claims of theatrical memoirs, however shrouded in bogus modesty, there are snares in the vituperation of the scandal-mongers, from Restoration broadsheets to modern tabloids. It is hardly in the interests of publishers and their hacks that all leading entertainers be seen to lead spotless lives. A few must do so, but in order to enhance the contrast with the vicious depravity of their colleagues. Neither assertions of purity nor accusations of sin can ever be entirely believed therefore: imagine trying to describe Hollywood in the 1950s based on a few back copies of the *National Enquirer* and *Doris Day: Her Own Story*. The flawed evidence of hagiography and scandal sheet are, however, all we have with which to reconstruct backstage mores at the Restoration playhouse, called in Gould's 1686 satire, 'a nest of lechers worse than Sodom bore'.

A typical representation of a gay actor comes in this description of James Nokes:

> You smockfaced lads, secure your gentle bums
> For full of lust and fury see he comes!
> 'Tis bugger Nokes, whose damned unwieldy tarse
> Weeps to be buried in his foreman's arse
> Unnatural sinner, lecher without sense,
> To leave kind cunt, to dive in excrements.

Those who cross-dressed after the Restoration were particularly vulnerable: Nokes was noted as an early version of the pantomime dame, a role which still attracts its fair share of gay men. Edward Kynaston was a noted boy actor before the Civil War, 'the Adonis of his day' and thought to have been a lover of the man James I called 'wife and child': George Villiers, Duke of Buckingham. His cross-dressed career continued after the Restoration, Pepys thinking him very good in a revival of Ben Jonson's classic man/woman play, *Epicoene*, and playing Evadne in *The Maid's Tragedy* for James's grandson Charles II. One account places Kynaston in a class of his own:

Mr. Kynaston, being then very young, made a complete female stage beauty, performing his parts so well . . . that it has since been disputable among the judicious, whether any woman that succeeded him so sensibly touched the audience as he.

Players of fops were vulnerable to sodomitical whispers, which supports the notion of the heterosexualization of their roles. Nokes and Cibber were noted fops, as was William Mountfort, accused in the same satire as Nokes. Politics larger than backstage spite linked the actor Joe Haines with Titus Oates, who was satirized in pictures and verse. Tom Brown, whose *The Salamanca Wedding* is one of the Oates plays, writes verse purporting to be Haines defending himself:

> . . . don't despise me now because I've lived
> Where . . . boys claim your prerogative.
> No sisters; no –
> I ne'er turned heretic in love at least;
> Twas decent whoring kept my thoughts still chaste

Although the rumour denied is standard muck-raking practice – "'I'M NOT GAY" SAYS [fill in celebrity]' – the verse does make a clear moral distinction between decent whoring and having sex with boys. Another playwright who accuses Haines is John Dryden, supposed to have written both the most scabrous satirical portraits of London actors and the Preface to *A Dialogue Concerning Women, Being a Defence of the Sex*, which contains arguments in favour of classical homosexuality. Shadwell, in 'The Medal', has Dryden saying: 'Let's bugger one another now, by God' and an anti-sodomy broadsheet, which was distributed as Edward Rigby stood in the pillory in 1698, has female prostitutes involving him in their 'Complaint to Venus': that sex between men ruins their trade:

> The beaus too, who most we relied on
> At night make a punk
> Of him that's first drunk
> Though unfit for the sport as John Dryden.

Fop and lover of men, Lord Hervey was the subject of Mary Wortley Montagu's observation that: 'The world consists of men, women and Hervey's' and Pope's comment in the Heroic Epistle from Bounce to Fop on

The motley race of Hervey queenies
And courtly vices, beastly venyes.

Hervey inspired pamphlet dramas which cast him in homosexualized versions of *The Recruiting Officer* and *Othello*, while two ballad operas put gossip about his life onto the stage: *The Intriguing Courtier* and *Humours of the Court*.

With all this going on behind the scenes with the actors and playwrights, it is hardly surprising that sodomy occurred between the patrons, as Susanna Centlivre's comment about 'false calves, bardash and favourites' suggests. Although separated by over sixty years, John Dennis's *The Usefulness of the Stage*, and Charles Churchill's *The Times* are both satires which list the theatre as a meeting place for male lovers. Two of those whose love-letters have survived, the Earl of Sunderland and Edward Wilson, record meeting to go to a show and having an argument afterwards. By 1783 the boxes at Drury Lane Theatre were 'a nest for prostitutes of both sexes'. In the nineteenth century, an anti-gay pamphlet published to coincide with the trial of Percy Jocelyn, Bishop of Clogher, stated that not only the theatres, but also the roads leading to them, were filled with predatory homosexuals.

Dressing for sex

Masquerades were at their height in the eighteenth century, and offered participants the chance to enact the sexual possibilities presented in the theatre of the time. The inversions were not only of gender, but also of class, and occasionally of both, as in Ogle's description of 'a nobleman like a cinder-wench' in Benjamin Griffin's *The Masquerade*. Such events were condemned by the pamphleteers: the unknown author of *Short Remarks upon the Original and Pernicious Consequences of Masquerades* (1721) claims cross-dressing leads to sexual 'abomination': 'Heliogabalus, Sporus, Sardanapulus, Caligula all began their careers in vice . . . by dressing as women', and have been 'justly branded in history as monsters of nature, the scum and scandal, and Shame of Mankind. . . . These sallies of gallantry, I fear, will soon metamorphose the kingdom into a Sodom for lewdness.'

This attractive account presumably overstates the licentiousness of masquerades, but other sources confirm their reputation as gay meeting places. In John Cleland's novel *Fanny Hill* (1748), Emily is at a masquerade dressed as a shepherd and gets picked up by a man who nearly fucks her arse, but converts his aim to her vagina once corrected. Spy of the *Weekly Journal* goes to Heidegger's masquerade at the Haymarket 'to view the follies of the place' dressed as a 'female Quaker . . . padded out to the size of Sir John Falstaff' and accompanied by a small male gallant in harlequin costume. On the way, there is a foretaste of the sexual innuendo to come: 'feeling about the sides of my petticoat . . . [my companion] met with a slit, thro' which he crept into my pocket, which it seems was designedly made capacious enough to receive him'. At a private party before the masquerade itself, as a 'matter of mirth . . . I drew my lover out of my pocket, and we danced a minuet to the no small diversion of the company'. Another benefit of Spy's capacious underneath is that his friend can sneak into the Haymarket under his skirts without paying. Once inside, 'the little Fox' creeps out of 'his Hole' and Spy meets a 'forward young puppy' who thinks him 'a German woman of quality'. The two men go into a corner and 'I was never so near being ravished in my whole Life' until Spy's mask falls off, revealing a beard and the young man runs off 'as if he apprehended correction'.

Spy is clearly having fun at the expense of Quakers, Germans and women, but the account suggests his own enjoyment of the confusion, as well as that of his two paramours. Both his audiences, the company at the private party, and the readers of the *Weekly Journal*, are also presumably entertained by this salacious account of all-male sexual adventure.

The flight of Spy's 'forward young puppy' keeps the anecdote just this side of ravishment. A report later in the century gives one possible reason for his alarm, as masquerades seem to have become covers for a more sinister version of importuning, involving blackmail:

On 12 June 1790 the Honourable Mr Cuffe and his friend Lord John Netterville were importuned in Covent Garden by a thug named Charles Jones, a well-known sodomitical prostitute who had followed them shouting and ranting and accusing them of committing an indecent offence and demanding money from them as blackmail. The two men, horrified, hurried home, pursued by a mob. They complained to the Bow Street magistrate, when it was disclosed that Frank Vaughan alias Charles Jones alias Fat Phyllis was known to the officers as a frequenter of Masquerades always in female attire and is extremely effeminate and much painted . . . as also are his companions.

Another regular masquerader, Robert Jones, popular not as a transvestite character but as Mr. Punch, was sentenced to death in 1772 for sodomy with the thirteen-year-old Francis Henry Hay. His popularity seems to have earned him his pardon, however, and he survived to be later reported 'living with a lovely Ganymede' in Lyons.

Horace Walpole, whose Strawberry Hill estate was a lesbian enclave (see chapter eleven), enjoyed dressing up as an old woman at masquerades, and reports how the opera singer Theresa Cornelys made Carlyle House, Soho Square 'a fairy palace, for balls, concerts and masquerades' between 1760 and 1772. In 1770, a Captain Walters attended one of these dressed as Adam, in a flesh-coloured body stocking embroidered with fig leaves. Such excesses are sadly uncommemorated in contemporary Soho Square, despite its location within London's new gay commercial village. London's gay scene always seems to have had its own private performances, from the days of the molly houses, where mock births and weddings were enacted in the eighteenth century, events which inspired John Russell's 1992 play *Mother Clap's Molly House*.

Gay Ladies of the Stage

Notorious Whores and Leading Lesbians

Following the reopening of the theatres at the Restoration, sexual life in London became rather more liberated. There were the first stirrings of London's gay scene: a network of meeting places which was to persist, despite raids, undercover infiltration and press exposure, into the twentieth century. Women took powerful roles on and off stage, as performers, playwrights and even as theatre managers. Among the women who transformed the Restoration and eighteenth-century stage were, inevitably, the theatre's first leading lesbians.

The first actresses

The puritans hated women performing. One vigorous pamphleteer, William Prynne, called Queen Henrietta and some of her ladies 'notorious whores', for taking part in a rehearsal at court in 1632. Prynne's encyclopedic attack on the stage *Histriomastix, The Players Scourge* (1633) condemns everything from mixed dancing to Christmas-keeping, alongside stage plays, as wicked, unchristian pastimes. He was, however, even more opposed to the sexual disruption involved in boys playing women, it being far worse for 'a boy to put on woman's apparel, person and behaviour, to act a feminine part: which the scripture expressly prohibits, as an abomination to the lord our God'. He was ruthlessly punished by Charles I for his theatre criticism, having his ears cut off in the pillory.

The idea of women on stage did not catch on, however, until Charles II reopened the theatres after the Commonwealth in 1660. Two years later, he decreed that all women's parts be played by women so that roles considered offensive when performed by a cross-dressed boy 'may by such reformation be esteemed not only harmless delight, but useful and instructive representations of human life'.

This did not please all theatregoers, judging from the character of Snarl in Thomas Shadwell's *The Virtuoso*, who says he 'can never endure to see plays since women came on the stage; boys are better by half'. Since his sexual tastes turn out to consist of being beaten by a schoolmistress, it appears that opposition to women on stage was not confined to disgruntled pederasts.

Women were, as the theatre managers could see, a draw for their audience members, male and female, whatever the noble words of the king's patent. Marketing this new sex appeal led them to calculate that if one woman was good for the box office then twenty would be marvellous, and they occasionally went as far as they could, producing plays with entirely female casts. These often had sexual plots which were heightened by such presentation. According to Pepys, Thomas Killigrew's *The Parson's Wedding* was a bawdy and loose play, whose licentiousness must have been enhanced by an all-woman version. The plot of Beaumont and Fletcher's Jacobean romance *Philaster* turns on whether the page Bellario – who is in fact a woman – had sex with the princess Arethusa. In a production with actresses, the homoerotics of the situation are inverted from those of the original all-boy cast. Women dressed as men could legitimately be watched wooing women: offering the English stage's first taste of lesbian fantasy.

Some idea of the opportunities cross-dressed women offered for titillation can be seen in Aphra Behn's play *The Younger Brother* in which Prince Frederick accuses a page, who is in fact a woman, of having amorous designs on his beloved Mirtilla. In response to this:

MIRTILLA (*opens Olivia's bosom, shows her Breasts*) Ha.

PRINCE By heaven, a woman!

Women disguised as boys soon became a popular feature of Restoration plays. Many of those in the audience were old enough to remember the easy gender-bending conventions of the pre-Civil War all-male stage. Disguised female pages appear not just for laughs in comedies like William Wycherley's *The Country Wife* and *The Plain Dealer*, but also in tragedies of the period including Thomas Otway's version of Romeo and Juliet, *The History and Fall of Caius Marius*. George Granville's *The She-Gallants* praises women playing boys. Playwrights began to introduce breeches parts, male roles deliberately written for women to play, in which one woman could now both woo and wed another, costumed in tighter, shorter, more revealing clothes as a man than she could wear as a woman. In such roles women got the chance to enact taking the sexual initiative on stage. Such cross-dressed and sexualized wooing of one woman by another occurs in many Restoration plays, from Behn to George Farquhar.

The major actresses of the time performed in male clothing, and some were particularly noted for their successes in it. Cross-dressing was not confined to actresses, however, becoming a popular sport for ladies attending costume parties. Ogle in Benjamin Griffin's 1717 play *The Masquerade, or, An Evening's Intrigue* says you might catch 'a lady of quality in Dutch trousers' at such an event. Harriet attends as 'a kind of hermaphroditical mixture; half man, half woman; coat, wig, hat and feather, with all the ornaments requisite'. With the pun on ornaments as testicles, Harriet's hermaphrodite costume heightens her sexual representation.

The debate over such costuming surfaces in descriptions of perform-ances. Among the most famous roles of the celebrated early eighteenth-century actress Peg Woffington were Sir Harry Wildair in Farquhar's *The Constant Couple* and Lothario in Nicholas Rowe's *The Fair Penitent*. According to one of her biographers, she 'always conferred a favour upon the managers when she changed her sex, and filled their houses' and was capable of arousing passion in both men and women, depending on what costume she wore:

> When first in petticoats you trod the stage
> Our sex with love you fired, your own with rage!
> In breeches next, so well you played the cheat,
> The pretty fellow and the rake complete –
> Each sex were then with different passions moved.
> The men grew envious, and the women loved.

The same sexual appeal repulsed her entire audience, according to another commentator: 'Mrs Woffington pleases in Sir Harry Wildair in every part, except where she makes love; but there no one of the audience ever saw her without disgust; it is insipid, or it is worse; it conveys no ideas at all, or very hateful ones; and either the insensibility, or the disgust we conceive, quite break in upon the delusion'. The objection makes explicit the hateful lesbian implications of women's cross-dressed wooing, particularly when playing these rakish, predatory men in pursuit.

These same-sex amours were performed not just for men. Restoration women went to the theatre: orange-sellers and whores; citizen's wives and widows; the ladies of the court. They were part of an audience experiencing a far greater sexual frankness in plays of contemporary life than had been seen before, many of them written by women. Unconventional sexuality, until this point the stuff of either monstrous tragedy or low comedy, became part of the topical representation of morals and manners. From Behn's 1681 play *The False Count* it is clear that lesbianism is something of which her audience is aware, Francisco warning: 'I have known as much danger under a petticoat, as a pair of breeches. I have heard of two women that married each other – oh abominable, as if there were so prodigious a scarcity of Christian man's flesh.' Contemporary satires tell tales of affairs between Whitehall Maids of Honour, describing dildo-use 'a deux' and Lady Harvey's 'long-cunted muscle', presumably an enlarged clitoris. These smack of heterosexual male fantasy, but confirm that the existence of sex between women was public knowledge in the seventeenth century.

By the beginning of the eighteenth century, groups of lesbian performers are being identified, at least by the gossip of the time. Pre-eminent scandal pieces of the period are the playwright Mary Delarivière Manley's books *The New Atlantis* and *Memoirs of Europe*. Manley was arrested for her thinly disguised portraits of contemporary figures. Her lesbian Cabal includes a tale of a noblewoman's pursuit of an actress, thought to be Laetitia Cross, and she portrays the singer Catharine Tofts as a lover of Lucy Wharton. The Italian opera is given as a cause of sexual perversion in the 1749 pamphlet *Plain Reasons for the Growth of Sodomy* which provides various continental figures for lesbian speculation. The singer Faustina Bordoni Hasse was in 1727 the subject of the anonymously written poem *An Epistle from Signora F. to a Lady*, about her love for an unidentified woman, which includes a reference to another singer Margherita Durastanti, as a previous lover.

This is mild stuff compared to France, where rumours of lesbianism reached as far as Marie Antoinette, although political spite may well have inspired such reports. Madeleine Maupin d'Aubigny, who often played male roles at the Paris Opéra, ran off with the daughter of a wealthy family, and was the inspiration, more than a century later, for Gautier's novel *Mademoiselle de Maupin*. A 1736 poem about a dancer at the Paris Opéra runs:

> The critic is perplexed about Salle:
> > Some believe that she has made many happy;
> Others claim that she prefers her own sex.
> A third party replies that she tries both.
> But it's an injustice that everyone debases her.
> As for me, I'm certain of her virtue;
> Resnel [her supposed male lover] tells us that she's a tribade,
> Gronet [another female dancer who accompanied her on a trip to
> > England] tells us she's not a w[hore]

That lesbianism continued to be an issue in English theatrical circles into the late eighteenth century is confirmed by the virulently anti-gay Hester Thrale, who claims that the sister of star actress Sarah Siddons 'was in personal danger once from a female fiend of this sort'. Meanwhile the actress Mary Ann Yates, running the Haymarket opera house with the writer Frances Brooke was accused of being president of an Anandrinic Society, or lesbian club.

The centre of attention on eighteenth century lesbians became a village in West London. The gay scare broadsheet *Satan's Harvest Home* had claimed in 1749 that Sappho 'teaches the female world a new sort of sin, called the flats [after the rubbing together of female genitals], that . . . is practised frequently in Turkey, as well as Twickenham at this day'. Strawberry Hill, Twickenham, was the home of Horace Walpole, and later of Anne Damer, daughter of Walpole's great love, his cousin Henry Seymour Conway. Although Damer had only just been born at the time of *Satan's Harvest Home*, she was as an adult part of a Twickenham lesbian set. A sculptor, she enjoyed amateur dramatics, and was romantically linked with the editor of Walpole's works, Mary Berry, and the actress Elizabeth Farren. In the political satire *The Whig Club, or a Sketch of Modern Patriotism* Farren is described as 'superior to the influence of men, she is supposed to feel more exquisite delight from the touch of the cheek of Mrs D[ame]r than the fancy of any novelties which the wedding night can promise'. Damer, who liked to dress in men's clothes, became another target for the acidic Thrale: "Tis now grown common to suspect impossibilities – (such I think 'em) – whenever two ladies live too much together; the Queen of France was all along accused, so was Raucoux the famous actress of the Paris stage: and 'tis a joke in London now to say such a one visits Mrs Damer.'

Another actress taking part in the Strawberry Hill theatricals was Catherine 'Kitty' Clive, implicated with Damer in *A Sapphic Epistle, from Jack Cavendish to the Honourable and most beautiful Mrs D.*

Strawberry-hill at once doth prove,
Taste, elegance and Sapphic love,
In gentle Kitty [Clive]

Clive, seventy years old at the time of this satire, was a grande dame, who made her reputation as a singer and comic. Although legend has her first appearance on stage as a page 'in boy's clothes', she is actually first recorded in female roles. She was a notable Celia, Shakespeare's betrayed lesbian (see chapter five) for twenty-three years. Unlike Woffington, with whom her backstage fights were famous, Clive wore trousers rarely and without theatrical success: one failure was a comic Portia in a version of *The Merchant of Venice*. Her temper was part of her popularity: in a 1737 ballad about her row with Susannah Cibber over the role of Polly in John Gay's *The Beggar's Opera*, she is called 'fierce Amazonian dame'. How much of her early career is remembered in the light of her later reputation is hard to judge, but she was a figure who inspired gossip, as the highest paid woman on the London stage. Briefly married in her twenties to a man who later ended up a domestic companion to a Mr Ince, Clive retired at fifty-seven, having moved to Strawberry Hill some years earlier. Her longtime friend and protégée was Jane Pope, the original Mrs Candour in Sheridan's *The School for Scandal*, who took over many of Clive's roles and placed the monument to her in St Mary's Church, Twickenham.

It is clear from autobiographies by late eighteenth-century actresses that many had passionate attachments to women. George Ann Bellamy was brought up by nuns, one of whom 'perfectly idolized me. When I took my leave of her, my feelings were such as I am not able to describe. Their pungency was far beyond what a girl my age could be supposed to experience.' A later friendship with Miss Butler she describes 'as if it had been cemented by ties of blood', and the bond between her and her patron she compares to that of Achilles and Patroclus. The devoted friendship of the actresses Sophia Baddeley and Elizabeth Steele is documented in *The Memoirs of Mrs Sophia Baddeley*, written by Steele. These accounts are heavily fictionalized, and not surprisingly avoid references to sexual contact between them and other women. As accounts of love between women, they are part of lesbian and gay history despite the impossibility of proving whether or not sexual contact took place.

The most notorious autobiography of an actress of this period is *A Narrative of the Life of Charlotte Charke* (1755). It opens with an account of her tomboyish childhood; she was a well-educated girl who enjoyed hunting and a brief spell as a mountebank physician, stating 'I have, through the whole course of my life, acted in contradiction to all points of regularity'. Having started cross-dressing at four years old, disguising herself as her father, the actor-manager Colley Cibber, she briefly married at seventeen. Charke then went on stage, playing male as well as female roles, choosing Roderigo in *Othello* as her benefit performance in 1734. She played Falstaff and Pistol in Shakespeare adaptations, and Macheath in *The Beggar's Opera*. Her male range seems to have gone beyond the traditional youths and rakes: like Woffington she was Lothario in *The Fair Penitent*, but she was also seen as the effeminate Lord Foppington, a role made famous by her father and also played by her brother Theophilus. Her female roles included the gender-bending Pope Joan in Elkanah Settle's *The Female Prelate*.

The mysteries in Charke's account of her life begin when, in about 1741, she is arrested for debt while in male clothing, her man's hat being the way she is distinguished by the bailiff. Her book persistently says she wore men's clothes 'for some substantial reasons' but cannot reveal why, and indeed never does. Kept at the officer's house, she is within half an hour 'surrounded by all the ladies who kept coffee houses in and around the garden [Covent Garden], each offering money for my ransom . . . the relief of poor Sir Charles, as they were pleased to style me'.

Remaining in semi-disguise, presumably to elude her creditors, Charke appears as Mr Brown in a theatre near London where she became 'the unhappy object of love in a young lady'. Courted by a rich orphan heiress, 'with money in the Bank and effects in the Indies', she goes to visit the young woman, although still dressed as a man. The meeting, claims Charke, is to 'kill or cure her hopes of me for ever' but she finds everything set up for a quick, private marriage. Left alone with the heiress, Charke reveals her true identity, but is still not believed, the girl assuming she had disappointed 'Mr Brown' as too easy a conquest. As Charke puts it: 'a most horrible disappointment on both sides; the lady of the husband and I of the money'. It all sounds rather like the plot from a play, and the situation is, Charke says, repeated when she later works in a tavern, the mechanism on both occasions being a mischievous maid. Things are made worse the second time when, on hearing it suggested that the object of her affections is actually female, the woman says 'I should hardly be enamoured with one of my own sect', at which 'Mr Brown' laughs, upsetting her even more.

Less than eight of Charlotte Charke's forty-seven years were spent married or in the relationships with men described in her *Life*. During the rest of her adult life, estranged from her father and others in her family, she was supported, through poverty and illness, by a series of loyal, devoted women friends, like the coffee house keepers of Covent Garden, whom she thanks fulsomely. Most are anonymous, but one actress companion becomes known as Mrs Brown to Charke's Mr Brown as they tour the country together. Mrs Brown nurses her through three years' illness, and at one point literally gives Charke the clothes off her back, 'the only decent gown she had', to pay debts. The two women survive, sharing Mrs Brown's uncle's 'genteel' legacy, acting various engagements along the way until they settle together in Bath. According to Thrale some years later, the town was a hotbed of lesbianism: 'a cage of these unclean birds'.

Charke denies the rumour that she had to leave Bath for having been on the streets in men's clothing, claiming it was because of 'an absolute abhorrence to the office I was in' (that of prompter). Once again, accusations of cross-dressing pursue her, yet she still declines to explain. She sets off from Bath with Mrs Brown, who disappears from her story just before Charke's return to London in 1754, having spent at least five years with her, for richer for poorer, in sickness and in health. Was she the woman still living with Charke soon after the return to London in a 'wretched thatched hovel' near Clerkenwell Prison? Samuel Whyte describes that woman as:

a tall, meagre, ragged figure, with a blue apron, indicating, what otherwise was doubtful, that it was a female before us; a perfect model for the Copper Captain's tattered landlady, that deplorable exhibition of the fair sex in the comedy *Rule a Wife and Have A Wife*.

With her 'torpid voice and hungry smile', what the man calls Charke's 'squalid handmaiden' has clearly suffered, as Mrs Brown must certainly have done in sharing the real version of Charke's life. This episode gives a more gloomy end to the story, although Whyte, arriving to pay Charke for a manuscript, may have his own reasons for exaggerating her misery. It is a shame that the novel Charke sold him, *The History of Henry Dumont*, is so vicious to its gay character, Loveman, claiming 'no punishment was sufficiently severe for such unnatural monsters'. This lack of solidarity with her gay brothers has been cited as proof against Charke's lesbianism, which is pretty flimsy. What does seem clear is that, whether or not Mr Brown had sex with women, there were several women who fell for her.

From this account, it seems that actresses who cross-dressed offstage were quite able to pass as men in eighteenth-century Britain. Masquerades, like that attended by Benjamin Griffin's Harriet, offered great scope for such confusion. At one, the actress and playwright Elizabeth Inchbald, whose roles included the female boy Bellario in *Philaster*, is supposed to have experienced in real life a situation familiar from the stage. After attending the party in male dress, she was 'charged with having captivated the affections of sundry witless admirers of her own sex'. Inchbald's response draws attention to the theatricality of the situation, likening it to 'the beautiful equivoque on the character of Viola' in *Twelfth Night*. If it was like something in Shakespeare, then surely there could be nothing untoward in attracting one's own sex.

Hannah Snell was not an actress, but still ended up on stage in men's clothing. During five years in the British Army as 'James Gray', Snell enjoyed numerous romances with women along the way, in part, it was claimed, to put off her fellow soldiers, who were keen to have sex with the boy they called Molly. On leaving the army she became a celebrity, exhibiting her military techniques 'in her regimentals' to a keen public.

In the United States, the most celebrated actress of the nineteenth century was the lesbian Charlotte Cushman, whom Walt Whitman called 'the greatest performer on the stage "in any hemisphere"' and who President Lincoln's assassin John Wilkes Booth claimed scarred him for life, when she played Lady Macbeth opposite him. The biography of Cushman by one of her lovers records the actress claiming 'I was born a tomboy', following the familiar pattern of such reminiscences. Cushman was to be notable for a wide range of male roles, classical and modern, including nearly twenty years as Romeo, and ending up with Hamlet. Offstage, her romances involved women on both sides of the Atlantic: first the Philadelphia writer Annie Brewster, later the crop-haired British poet Eliza Cook, who became her companion in London. Other literary fans, but not lovers, included Manchester feminist Geraldine Jewsbury, whose novel *The Half Sisters* contains a character based on Cushman, and Louisa May Alcott, who turned her into Miss Cameron in *Jo's Boys*.

Cushman toured extensively, arriving in Edinburgh in 1845, where some who saw her as Romeo 'objected strongly to Charlotte's "masculine" demeanour as Romeo, her straight limbs as "strident as those of a youth," her amorous advances towards her sister so erotic "that no man would have dared indulge in them" publicly'. This led one of her hosts, George Combe, founder of the Phrenological Society, to write to his relative the actress Fanny Kemble, inquiring about Cushman's 'private virtue'. Kemble wondered: 'Why the deuce doesn't he look for it in her skull?' Some of the scandal about Cushman and her sister Susan, who played Juliet, was spread by rival US actor Edwin Forrest whose tour followed them into town. Despite all this, Charlotte not only returned, but went sightseeing there in men's clothes.

Her next Juliet was a lover both sides of the footlights. Matilda Hays knocked on Cushman's door in 1849 and set off with her as a partner in theatre and life. Elizabeth Barrett, poet and friend of Cushman's, described their relationship as a 'female marriage . . . she and Miss Hays have made vows of celibacy and of eternal attachment to each other – they live together, dress alike'. This comment leads Cushman's modern biographer to observe that the relationship 'could scarcely offer the intimate rewards of marriage', a misconception which colours what is otherwise a thorough account of her life. After four years, things began to strain between the two women, and Hays finally left in 1856, when Cushman was in Rome, to write for *The English Women's Journal* back in London.

Cushman was in Rome with another love, one in a line of visual artists that had began with another relation of Kemble's, the painter Rosalie Kemble Sully. The young sculptor Harriet Hosmer was a friend of Kemble's, but in 1851, aged twenty, she met Cushman at the point of her first retirement from the stage – there were to be many more over the next eighteen years. That year, the unmarried Cushman also adopted her sister's son Ned and decided to lead a party of 'jolly female bachelors' to Europe, including Hays and the writer Sara Jane Clarke. Hosmer followed them to Rome, where she set up a studio and stayed.

In Rome, Cushman met another sculptor, Emma Stebbins, with whom she returned to the United States in 1857, then moved back and forth, living for a while with both Stebbins and Hosmer until Hosmer moved out in 1864. Stebbins and Cushman stayed together for twenty years, until Cushman's death in 1876. At the funeral, according to Stebbins's biography, the Reverend Henry W. Foote praised Cushman for having shown that a pure spirit could go stainless in the theatre.

Women writing: out of closet drama

Although women playwrights came to prominence only at the same time as women appeared on stage after the Restoration, they were not the first. These early women's sense of pioneering or their unusual classical education may have given them a wider perspective on sexual matters (the first translation of Greek tragedy into English was by Joanna Lumley in the sixteenth century) since those few women who did write plays before 1660 seem interested in stories of love between men. Elizabeth Cary's 1613 play *Mariam* is the first full-length original play by an English woman. She is also thought to have written a prose *Life of Edward II*, published some years after Marlowe's play, which characterized the King's love for Piers Gaveston, 'his ganymede', as the first relationship of its kind. She presumably wrote with an eye on her own King James and his notorious male favourites. Similarly, Mary Wroth, one of those women who so infuriated William Prynne by their acting, and whose play *Love's Victory* is sceptical about the delights of marriage, wrote her 1621 romance *Urania* about a duke 'besotted on a young man', claiming 'all delights and pastimes were to me tedious and loathsome, if not liking, or begun by him'.

The first of many women to be called The English Sappho is better known for her passionate love poems addressed to woman than for her translation of Corneille's play *La Mort de Pompée*. In the character of Orinda, Katherine Philips addresses her love poetry to other pseudonymous women in her 'Society of Friendship': Rosania (Mary Aubrey), Lucasia (Anne Owen), and Pastora, among others. She clearly loved women, but disputes about the injunctions against eroticism in her writing have led some critics to insist she be excluded from the lesbian canon. Since there is no way to prove what she did in bed The English Sappho is at least a contender for the title of first lesbian playwright, even if the plays are versions of the work of men. The first lesbian play, however, must surely be *The Convent of Pleasure*, published in 1668, written by another of Queen Henrietta's former ladies, Margaret Cavendish. Unperformed, it remains a 'closet drama' despite, or perhaps because of, its tale of a lavish, women-only sanctuary, where Lady Happy falls in love with a visiting princess.

After the Restoration, women who were not nobility began to write plays and those who could live by their writing were able, if they wished, to be independent of men. The London theatre's 'new Scots Sappho' was the young marvel Catherine Trotter, whose playwriting career began at the age of sixteen with the tragedy *Agnes de Castro*, about a woman torn between love for a man and a woman. Its epilogue 'Spoke by Mrs. Verbruggen in men's clothes' is a chance for cross-dressed flirtation with the audience. Trotter's comedy *Love at a Loss* features the heiress Lesbia, and her *The Unhappy Penitent* also features another devoted female friendship. *The Fatal Friendship* is dedicated to Princess, later Queen, Anne, who was at the time under pressure to end her own devoted friendship with Sarah Churchill. All this is no evidence of what Catherine Trotter did in her own life, although as Daphne in Manley's *The New Atlantis* she is implicated in a love affair with James II's mistress Catherine Colyear. She gave up playwriting after her marriage in 1708.

Jane Wiseman's play *Antiochus the Great* features maids devoted beyond death to their mistresses, and earned the playwright enough to keep her out of the domestic service in which she had started. As one of the only options for women's economic independence, the eighteenth-century theatre provides numerous examples of life partnerships built on love rather than economics. Romantic friendship was not only a feature of many early plays by women, it was also a fact of many of those playwrights' lives. The pious Hannah More lived with Eva Garrick, widow of the man who produced her plays at Drury Lane. As we have seen, Frances Brooke, editor of the weekly *The Old Maid*, ran the Haymarket in partnership with the supposed lesbian club proprietor Mary Ann Yates. Thus, over a century before Henry James wrote his novel *The Bostonians* about 'those friendships between women which are so common in New England', Boston marriages were familiar in British theatre circles.

Romantic friendship was of course not defined in sexual terms. Indeed, pure same-sex love was often raised morally above the tawdry physicalities of heterosexual passion. The theme of an agonizing choice between a spouse and a friend is also a theme in plays about men in the Restoration and after. Thomas Otway's *Venice Preserv'd* has Jaffeir fatally betraying his friend Pierre to save his wife Belvedira. Nathaniel Lee's comedy *The Princess of Cleve* explores similar territory. Lee is one of those Restoration theatre figures embroiled in rumours about his sexual relations with men.

Women and men mixed more freely in the theatre than outside, and relationships between them seem to have been less conventional than their contemporaries. Another of Restoration theatre's Sapphos was Aphra Behn, whose *The False Count* is quoted above as an example of contemporary lesbian awareness and who, like Katherine Philips, wrote love poetry addressed to women. She had a long relationship with John Hoyle, who was also known for his affairs with men. The actress and playwright Susanna Centlivre, who lived for a time disguised as boy with the poet Anthony Hammond, talks in the epilogue to her play *The Platonic Lady*, of gay men's 'false calves, bardash and favourites'. The developing worlds of lesbian and gay male theatre were not in isolation from each other.

Mary Pix wrote two plays about royal women devoted to female friends during Princess Anne's troubles over her love for Sarah Churchill. In theatres where part of the fun on some nights was recognizing variously disguised public figures in the plays, and which were regularly attended by members of the royal family, such a choice of theme is bound to be topical. Pix's comedies were better loved than her tragedies, although both featured a robust sense of sexual innuendo. Her first play, *Ibrahim, the Thirteenth Emperor of the Turks*, provides *Agnes de Castro*'s cross-dressed epiloguist Susan Verbruggen with the role of Chief Eunuch. That it fails to provide anything other than a grotesque caricature of Oriental decadence is unsurprising. Even the title is wrong: as Pix apologizes in a later preface, Ibrahim was actually the twelfth emperor. When Mrs Verbruggen's Achmet introduces music 'prepared by the Italian Masters' to cheer the emperor, it is actually a pretty crude piece of testicular humour, a 'dialogue song supposed to be between an eunuch Boy and a virgin' by Thomas D'Urfey, beginning:

HE Why do'st thou hate me, Ah confess:
   Thou sweet disposer of my joys?

SHE The reason is, I only guess,
   By something in thy face and voice,
   That thou art not made like other boys.

That there was humour to be got out of the sexual ambivalence of castrati is clear from the 1736 satire *An Epistle to John James Heidegger, on the Report of Signor Farinelli's Being with Child*. Heidegger was the major impresario of eighteenth-century masquerades. Another dressed-up masquerade encounter shows how the East was linked with sexual adventure at the time, when a male writer for *The Guardian* reports meeting an Indian King: 'a tall, slender youth dressed up in a most beautiful party-coloured plumage'. The writer is attracted: 'my heart leaped as soon as he touched me, and was still in greater disorder, upon hearing his voice': it is actually his fiancée Leonora, playing a trick.

The Prevailing Dissipations of the Time

The Trials of the Georgian Stage

A theatre could stage a lively repertoire from the works of gay playwrights imprisoned by the English courts. Comic writers have always fared worse than tragedians: a defining moment in the history of homosexuality in this country is the transfer of Oscar Wilde from the West End to cell C33 of Reading Gaol. More than three hundred years earlier, in 1541, Nicholas Udall was sentenced to the Marshalsea Prison. As recently as 1962 Joe Orton and his lover Kenneth Halliwell got six months at Old Street Magistrates Court. The charge was defacing library books, but the prison sentence was, said Orton, 'because we were queers'.

In the years between Udall and Wilde, many other lives were ruined by the state's anti-gay persecutions. Scores were executed; still more physically or mentally destroyed. Most are forgotten, although explorations in lesbian and gay history have recently begun to tell the stories behind sodomy's legal statistics. Among those statistics are some leading theatrical figures, whose careers were interrupted or destroyed by accusations of same-sex activity. Even where these did not end up in court, the newspapers (and in some cases, their professional rivals) did their worst to Samuel Foote, Isaac Bickerstaffe, Charlotte Charke and Lord Byron. Even David Garrick, the first 'respectable' actor in England, found himself implicated in the disreputable business of sodomy.

David Garrick's Friends

Garrick was the most significant figure on the eighteenth-century British stage as actor, playwright and theatre manager. He might have been the first man to achieve an unassailable social position through the theatre, a century before Henry Irving got its first knighthood. He was, however, embroiled in gay sex scandals throughout his career. He may never have deserved the implication of sexual unorthodoxy, and escaped all the innuendo with his own reputation intact, but had to ditch colleagues along the way in a manner which reflects far worse on him today than any amount of sodomy.

Unsurprisingly, some of the Garrick accusations came from his theatrical rivals the Cibber family. Like Colley and his son Theophilus Cibber, Garrick was popular in drag roles, although Vanbrugh's *The Provok'd Wife* provides more plot justification than most for Sir John Brute's appearance in a dress. Garrick was also a writer and performer of fops: Daffodil in *The Male Coquette* and Fribble in *Miss in Her Teens*, but he wrote a satire against effeminacy *The Fribbleriad* in 1761. This may have been prompted by attacks from Theophilus Cibber, who mocked Garrick's lack of manliness in his 'To David Garrick Esquire' in 1759.

All this is unexceptional in the context of eighteenth-century theatrical squabbling, but a legal case involving Garrick's friend and theatrical partner Isaac Bickerstaffe was far more troubling. Bickerstaffe was involved in a sex scandal in 1772, when, in attempting to avoid blackmail by a guardsman, he gave the young man his watch and other distinctive jewellery. Once the press got hold of descriptions, Bickerstaffe's identity was discovered, and innuendo forced him to flee to France. William Kenrick's satire *Love in the Suds* cashed in on the affair, pretending to be a lament by Garrick for his lost lover, Bickerstaffe. Garrick sued Kenrick for libel and the two fought publicly for years. Meanwhile Garrick deserted his old friend, ignoring the letters which came across the Channel for him. As Wilde would do a hundred years later, Bickerstaffe died in France, driven out of the country, reviled by those he had once entertained.

Another collaborator with Bickerstaffe persecuted for homosexuality was the popular comedian Samuel Foote, called The English Aristophanes, on whose death Samuel Johnson asked: 'Will genius change his sex to weep?' Foote and Bickerstaffe wrote the 1769 *Dr Last in his Chariot* together, a version of Molière's *Malade Imaginaire*. It was a disaster, and could not even be finished at the first performance, so noisy were the audience's objections to the play. Foote was an entrepreneur and rival manager to Garrick, and as such features as an annoyance of Nyky, the Garrick character in *Love in the Suds*, but is not implicated in the Bickerstaffe sex scandal.

One of Foote's biographers, William Cooke, says that, 'incapable of the ordering restraints of life . . . he dashed into all the prevailing dissipations of the time', although does not indicate whether sodomy was one such prevailing dissipation. Born in 1720, he married Mary Hickes when about twenty-one years old, and Cooke says Foote mistreated and soon deserted her. The two sons Foote mentions in his will seem to have been illegitimate children with one of his servants.

Foote initially played fops, but found a more effective role as a mimic in his own satiric farces, which he produced and promoted himself, ingeniously working around the limitations of London theatre licensing, and sailing close to the tightening censorship of the new Lord Chamberlain's office. His drag roles included the character of Lady Pentweazle, in his own play *Taste*, although the first to play the role was another actor, Jemmy Worsdale. The very successful play *The Minor* was a satire on Methodism, in which Foote played Mother Cole, a character said to be based on the procuress Jennie Douglas.

From the beginning of his career to the final messy libels, he made many enemies with his abuse: the Archbishop of Canterbury complained about *The Minor*, and another victim, Henry Fielding, sentences Foote to be pissed on as punishment in a counter-satire. He quarrelled vehemently even with his friends, who included the older actor Macklin, the younger actor Thomas Weston, and writers Arthur Murphy, John Cleland and Laurence Sterne.

With Jemmy Worsdale and another friend, Francis Blake Delaval, he was involved in a ludicrous plot involving a bogus fortune-teller, all to persuade a wealthy woman who had fallen for Foote to marry Delaval instead. Delaval was present when Foote broke his leg falling from a horse in 1766, an injury which led to amputation. When Delaval died five years later, Foote 'burst into a flood of tears, retired to his room, and saw no company for three days' according to Cooke. He then paid off all the debts of Delaval's illegitimate sons.

The first person to hint at the accusations which would destroy Foote was David Garrick, in a prologue to a 1753 revival of Foote's own play *The Englishman in Paris*. Foote's trips to the continent were well known. Garrick plays on the rumour that Foote had been condemned for an unnamed crime near Bordeaux:

I thought that fool had done his devil's dance;
Was he not hanged some months ago in France

Arthur Murphy was more friendly to Foote than Garrick, but in a parody of *Hamlet* which attacks Garrick, he also includes innuendo about Foote:

Foote's an unweeded garden,
That grows to seed; things rank, and gross in nature
Possess him merely

Foote was determined to be a major player in the London theatre, and, after his amputation, obtained a licence to run the Haymarket during the summer, when other theatres were closed. He bought the theatre and moved in. William Jewel was his treasurer there, and remained with Foote all his life, despite a brief separation when Jewel secretly married a singer in the company.

Foote satirized scores of figures, one of whom was his undoing: Elizabeth Chudleigh, Duchess of Kingston. Chudleigh was being tried for bigamy when Foote wrote *The Trip to Calais*, in which she appears as Kitty Crocodile. Chudleigh pressured the Lord Chamberlain to censor it, which he did, despite Foote's protests. When stories about Foote began to appear in *The Public Ledger*, edited by the former parson William Jackson, and other papers, he offered a truce. Chudleigh's reply, which she sent to the newspapers, continued the implications about his sex life:

A member of your privy council can never hope to be of a Lady's cabinet . . . [a man] of private reputation . . . I am writing to the descendant of a Merry Andrew, and prostitute the term of manhood by applying it to Mr Foote . . . I will keep the pity you send, until the morning you are turned off: when I will return it by a Cupid with a box of lip-salve; and a choir of choristers shall chaunt a stave to your requiem.

With no chance of putting the play on in the 1775 season, Foote waited for the following year. His friend, the alcoholic actor Thomas Weston died penniless in January 1776, praising Foote in his will. In April Chudleigh was found guilty of bigamy, although as a Countess she was spared being branded on the hand for the crime. Jackson and his newspaper continued to accuse Foote, and the affair became widely discussed. Boswell reports George Steevens, the man who said of Shakespeare's twentieth sonnet, 'It is impossible to read this fulsome panegyrick, addressed to a male object, without an equal mixture of disgust and indignation', on the case:

> [Steevens said] he would rather have the character of a Sodomite than an infidel. I said I would not. Samuel Johnson: 'Yes. An infidel would be it if he inclined.'

Foote opened his 1776 season in May with a satire on the press, *The Bankrupt*, and prefaced it with an address protesting his innocence which was loudly applauded. George III attended that season four times, at one of which performances Foote gave his Lady Pentweazle in a spectacular new headdress. Notable defenders included Joshua Reynolds and Edmund Burke, who would himself be abused for his softness on sodomites when he complained of a pillorying in 1780. Despite this support, however, Jackson had found one of Foote's former servants, John Sangster, to charge the playwright with attempted sodomy. Foote evaded the humiliation of arrest during a performance only with the help of friends. A rewritten version of *The Trip to Calais*, *The Capuchin*, attacked Jackson, but at the end of the season Foote gave up his lease of the Haymarket to George Colman. A pamphlet by 'Humphrey Nettle', who was presumably Jackson, called *Sodom and Onan*, accused Foote along with Bickerstaffe, Jewel and others, and called for his plays to be watched by 'male whores of quality'. Jackson's efforts collapsed at the December trial, however, when Sangster's account of Foote's whereabouts at the time of the allegation was heavily contradicted. Foote was found not guilty.

The following summer Foote appeared at the Haymarket again, now under Colman's ownership. Looking ill, he was generally applauded, but some of the audience hissed him. Setting off to spend the winter in France, he died in Dover on the way. He was buried at night, by torchlight, in the west cloister of Westminster Abbey. His only memorial is in St Martin's Church, Cannon Street, Dover, set up by Jewel, who in the inscription calls himself 'his affectionate friend'. According to Garrick, however, Foote's death was 'very little regretted even by his nearest acquaintance'.

The grim nineteenth century

The ambivalence of London crowds is peculiarly demonstrated by the simultaneous popularity of two quasi-homosexual experiences in the early nineteenth century. One involved crowds pelting men accused of sodomy locked in the pillory; the other led members of those same crowds to mob the streets, the theatres and, if they could afford it, the dressing rooms, of a boy actor whose cult status stemmed from being both a curiosity and a sexual object.

William Henry West Betty was a child star, who arrived in London after a highly publicized tour of Ireland and Great Britain, to play leading roles, including Hamlet, aged only thirteen. His appearances provoked massive public hysteria, and inspired a wave of adolescent imitators. His father and manager worked him hard during his period of celebrity, inspiring an anonymous letter of complaint about his mistreatment to the Lord Chancellor. A lucky few were even charged to see the boy changing after the performance, as the painter James Northcote records in his diary:

> His dressing room was crowded as full as it could contain of all the
> court of England and happy were those who could get in at the
> time his father was rubbing his naked body from the perspiration.

Madame Vestris describes these visitors as 'offensively amusing', and detects sexual undertones to the display: 'had his person been as feminine as his name, [Betty] could not have had more fervent male adorers, some of whom were almost impious in their enthusiasms'. A contemporary print shows actor and Covent Garden manager John Kemble riding behind Betty on 'The Theatrical Pegasus'; their positions and captions playing on implications of buggery.

KEMBLE If I don't take great care he will certainly have me off. He
　　has got me onto the crupper [buttocks] already.

BETTY Never fear sir – we shall agree very well – but when two
　　ride on a horse, one must ride behind, you know.

This pederastic sideshow was the hit of the London theatre season during a period of vicious purges against the city's mollies. *The Times* makes a clear connection between the boy wonder and contemporary homosexuals:

Master Betty's success is very naturally the cause of much envy and heartbreak among the Master Polly's and Master Jenny's of Bond Street and Cheapside, who in all their attempt to distinguish their pretty persons and effeminate airs, have only miscarried.

While William Betty was the toast of London, the Master Polly's and Master Jenny's of Bond Street and Cheapside found themselves part of a different spectacle at the very same time: that of the public pillory. Convicted sodomites were locked on display, and pelted by the London public with mud, potatoes, rotten eggs, blood, offal, animal corpses and dung. Some of those people were presumably among the throngs around Drury Lane and Covent Garden, desperate for a glimpse of the Young Roscius. One hundred years before, satire about actors and their sexual habits had been part of the general back-biting and competitiveness of the business. There was now a crucial division between the social policing of a legitimate activity – gazing on the naked sweating body of a thirteen-year-old boy – and the illegitimate sexual activity between men punishable by torture and death. The closet became essential, perhaps an ironic contribution to the new era in gay subjectivity which would, one hundred and fifty years later, breed gay liberation.

That it became imperative at this point for men to distinguish the carnal and the spiritual in their appreciation of each other is clear from the works of Shelley. He can appreciate Greek statuary with the zeal of the backstage Betty watchers, saying it is 'difficult to conceive anything more delicately beautiful than the Ganymede', yet he distances himself from physical feelings, even when describing boyhood loves. Such friendship was:

> a profound and sentimental attachment to one of the same sex, wholly divested of the smallest alloy of sensual intermixture . . . It rejects, with disdain, all thoughts but those of an elevated and imaginative character . . . I remember forming an attachment of this kind at school . . .

Later writers would stretch this even further, claiming that the sensual was unthinkable in such a context, but for the young Shelley the road to Sodom is a clearly available route: one to be rejected and disdained. The desires of the mind and the body must be separated. The adult Shelley was infamous for his sexual freedom with young women, and his notion that youthful homosexual attachments give way with maturity to opposite-sex sensuality prefigures the psychiatric model popular a century later. Radical in so many other ways, Shelley is on the side of the reactionaries as far as gay sex is concerned. In the preface to his play *The Cenci*, he joins the judgement of the English courts in describing Count Cenci's homosexual acts as 'capital crimes of the most enormous and unspeakable kind'.

Classic romance

Given the penalties for love between men which took physical expression, it is hardly surprising that homosexual feelings are submerged in sentimentality in the late eighteenth and early nineteenth centuries. The early sentimentalist Richard Cumberland nevertheless found himself accused by Hester Thrale of effeminacy, and being over fond of young men in his plays. In poetry, Tennyson's *In Memoriam A. H. H.* would be the most famous testament of friendship by one man for another, despite some doubts over the seemliness of the expression. His play *The Promise of May* was assaulted by Oscar Wilde's nemesis, the Marquess of Queensberry, who, having been told that it featured an unflattering portrait of an agnostic, flung vegetables at the cast and made a speech defending atheism. It is a strange contradiction that, with the church being so much to blame for many of the horrors heaped on lesbians and gay men in Britain, the notorious man who persecuted Wilde should have been a vehement atheist, while a vicar, Stewart Headlam, stood by the dramatist at his lowest point.

Romantic friendship had been a staple of drama by and about women since the beginning of the eighteenth century. Towards the end of the century sentimental neoclassical dramas, which are never now revived, provided one of the few literary forms in which love between men could safely be explored. Not only were the interactions stripped of carnality and idealized into pure friendship in Shelley's sense, they were also legitimized by an ancient setting. At the same time, investigations into the lives of the Greeks and Romans were prompting discreet discussions of homosexuality and its treatment in contemporary society, in the works of Jeremy Bentham and Edward Gibbon as well as Shelley – Bentham the only one to favour law reform.

The limits on dramatic expression constricted: opinion was turned against the bawdiness of Restoration drama, and only a few scholars knew about Renaissance works which suggested a different perspective on love. Among those nineteenth-century theatre historians were Richard Heber, a major collector of early English drama, who fled the country after an 1826 scandal, and John Addington Symonds. The tubercular Symonds wrote *Shakespere's Predecessors in the English Drama*, and collaborated with Havelock Ellis on *Sexual Inversion*. His privately printed 1883 book *A Problem in Greek Ethics* is among the first defences of potential sensuality in 'platonic love'.

On the public stage, however, nineteenth-century platonics were resolutely non-physical. There were versions of the classic male friendship story *Damon and Pythias* by R. L. Sheil and John Banim in 1821, and by Buckshe in 1831. Thomas Noon Talfourd wrote the Greek tale *Ion* in which Charlotte Cushman performed, and his *The Athenian Captive* is a good example of the period's submerged homoerotics. Written for Macready, whom Talfourd called 'the most romantic of actors' as Thaos, it also featured the young actor Edmund Glover as the king's son Hyllus. Hyllus has been wounded in battle against the Athenians, but his life was nobly spared on the battlefield by the now captive Thaos. Forced to punish his saviour, Hyllus strips Thaos in a scene of Greek Love which was presumably as far as anyone dared go at the time.

There is an early fragment of a neoclassical tragedy *Agrippina* by Thomas Gray, but his exposure to the Mediterranean came on the Grand Tour with his romantic friend (at least for a while), Horace Walpole. Walpole's own contributions to the theatre, in addition to his drag masquerading, are in another long neglected dramatic form, however: the Gothic. Same-sex enthusiasts were prime movers in the Gothic, in fiction, drama and even architecture. Walpole and William Beckford each built themselves their own high concept castles: one bequeathed his estate to what was reputedly a lesbian salon; the other retreated behind his faux-medieval walls, his reputation but not his fortune destroyed by rumours about his friendship with the young William Courtenay. Hester Thrale was happy to link him with a playwright gone into exile ten years before: 'Our Beckfords and Bickerstaffes too run away from the original Theatre of their crimes'.

Like these fantasy dwellings, the settings of Gothic fiction can be seen as concrete manifestations of characters' hidden desires: their land-scapes are outward expressions of the torture within the soul. This allowed Gothic theatre to excel as an opportunity for extravagant stage settings, whatever its shortcomings as playwriting. Almost all of the plays feature a secret mine: a place of terror, but also the route which must be taken to discover what curses the characters. At one extreme, such gloomy, damp and muddy passages are the anal excursions of the beleaguered sodomites who created the genre: the black holes of medieval devilry. While the plays which idealize same-sex friendship are set in pagan times but cleansed by neoclassicism, the Gothic plays have the imagined sensuality of closer non-Protestant worlds, particularly the Islamic East and the Catholic Mediterranean. Both would be toured extensively by nineteenth-century Britons, leaving the country either by choice or necessity, and reporting back their findings of the love not to be named among Christians. The medievalism of the Gothic movement in architecture is less significant in the literature, although it too thrills in a world before the Reformation. It is no surprise that the other vigorous exponents of such excessive dramas were in Germany, Schiller's *The Robbers* being published in English in 1792.

Early Gothic heroes are weak, disempowered figures, their weapons broken or mislaid. They face tortured villains; punished and agonized figures guilty of murder or, more sensationally, sexual crimes. These villains are the star roles in Gothic drama: the heirs of Faust, once transfigured by Romanticism, become the forebears of our own century's tortured lesbian and gay heroes and heroines. Wilde would choose the name Sebastian Melmoth for his post-prison life: a combination of the iconic gay saint and the wicked, wandering central character in his great-uncle Charles Maturin's Gothic novel *Melmoth the Wanderer*. Gothic sexual villainies are, however, always between men and women, for the horrors of homosexuality could not possibly be explicit at the time. Nevertheless, Walpole and Beckford are joined by another lover of young men, Matthew Lewis, author of *The Monk* as a gay trinity attracted to the fictional opportunities of the Gothic genre.

Just as Walpole's Strawberry Hill was the first Gothic home, and his 1764 *The Castle of Otranto* the first Gothic novel, so *The Mysterious Mother*, privately printed in 1768, was the first Gothic drama. It has all the necessary elements, chiefly a terrible sexual secret which casts its shadow over the characters. Martin, a friar, wonders at it:

What is this secret sin, this untold tale,
That art cannot extract, nor penance cleanse?

The play was never acted, Walpole says, because he thought the plot, of revealed incest between mother and son, too horrid for the stage. He was attracted to it, however, as a way to show 'a contrast of virtue and vice in the same character'. In the twentieth-century West End, Noel Coward in *The Vortex* and Terence Rattigan in *The Deep Blue Sea* would balk at representing either incest or homosexuality: sexual transgression between a woman and a younger man was scandalous enough: a route to the further depravities of drug addiction or a room in Ladbroke Grove. The grim excesses of the Gothic castles with their princes and duchesses would translate into the more modest torments of drawing-room drama. Horror at losing the comforts of middle-class life through sexual excess would be a theme in the dramas of middle-class homosexuals, just as their aristocratic ancestors pondered the issue in their Gothic stately homes.

Matthew Lewis was more important as a gothic dramatist than Walpole, with a campy relish for theatrical spectacle. His work was more controversial: the Gothic novel *The Monk* was censored for immorality, and appeared on stage in heavily bowdlerized forms, as James Boaden's *Aurelio and Miranda* and Farley's ballet *Don Raymond*. Byron would disparage Lewis's taste in middle age for Albany dinner parties with young men, but Byron's unfinished drama *The Deformed Transformed* owes its origins to Lewis' *The Wood Demon*. In that play, Lewis writes about a deformed peasant who must murder a boy in order to retain his beauty and invulnerability.

William Dimond's *The Foundling of the Forest* includes a gothic dramatization of an intimate relationship between two men: Longueville and his creature Bertrand. Bertrand eventually sees the light and reforms, turning against his master. Censorship required that all dramas of the time had such moral endings to show that the good ended happily and the bad unhappily. These were gratuitous concessions from a writer like Lewis, but women like Hannah More, who lived with Garrick's wife after his death, and Joanna Baillie wrote deliberately moral plays to show the dangers of unchecked passion. Where women and men had explored the same territory in much the same forms in Restoration drama, this separation by gender at the end of the eighteenth century is one instance of feminism on one side, and conservatism on the other, leading some women dramatists to an assessment of sexual villainy different from that in the plays of male Gothicists. A cult of libertinism and free sexual expression for men might attract gay men, but it represents serious dangers for women. Particularly at a time when public acknowledgement of one woman's sexual desire for another was impossible, there was no reason for nineteenth-century lesbians to take the same sensational route. Once sexual double standards were addressed, with the New Woman plays of the late nineteenth century, feminists and male sexual subversives would begin to share an agenda.

Gorgeous George

The other major gothic dramatist was Wilde's ancestor, Charles Maturin, whose first play *Bertram* was chosen for performance at Drury Lane by George Gordon, Lord Byron, whose dramatic work shows the influences of the Gothic. A friend of Lewis and a lover of both women and boys, Byron joined the sexual exodus in 1816, leaving Britain amid rumours of incest and sodomy. 'I was advised not to go to the theatres, lest I should be hissed', he writes of the period preceding his departure. 'However, I was not deterred by these counsels from seeing Kean in his best characters'. On this and later trips, he would live out the life only fantasized in Gothic literature, watching boy dancers in Constantinople, flirting with Ali Pasha, ruler of Albania, and dying in Greece, in love with the fifteen-year-old Lukas Chalandritsanos.

Byron's plays were written for readers rather than performance: their poetry is not the stuff of the nineteenth-century stage. *Manfred*, which he wrote in his first sexual exile, is inspired by passages from Goethe's *Faust*, which Lewis had translated for him. Manfred is that classic gothic figure: a man with an unexplained torment which he never reveals. The assumption, based on Byron's own life and the events of the play, is that this crime, like that in Walpole's play, is male-female incest. The crime which dare not be spoken of is there too, if only as metaphor. If an account of Byron's conversation recorded eighty years after his death is to be believed, this was the writer's deliberate choice:

> I expected a while ago to write a drama on Greek Love – not less –
> modernizing the atmosphere – glooming it over – to throw the

whole subject back into nature, where it belongs now as always – to paint the struggle of the finer moral mind against it – or rather remorse for it, when it seems to be chastized . . . But I made up my mind that British philosophy is not far enough on for swallowing such a thing neat. So I turned much of it into *Manfred*.

Whether Byron ever said those words, or anything like them is impossible to know. His characters can still speak, however, just as they did one hundred and eighty years ago. The voices may be distorted a little, but they can still be made clear. Even Garcio of Wakefield lives on, half a millenium after his birth, in a performance of an old play. The theatre creates worlds which tantalize us: imaginary places conjured out of a past which can never be visited.

There is no lesbian or gay theatre. There is just theatre. Yet a theatre which excludes erotic and romantic activity between men and between women is impossible. The evidence is not hard to uncover, simply because of its abundance. Throughout the period covered by this book, the love that dare not speak its name is persistently visible on stage, even where it has been left unrecorded. Even where it has been recorded it has been ignored, disguised, and sometimes perverted, in order to stop it being recognized. Why staging love is so dangerous that it has to be prevented is a question beyond the scope of this book: but the one which makes it worth writing.

Notes

Chapter one: A Queer Business

2   'OF AGRICULTURAL WORSHIP': Edmund K. Chambers, *The Medieval Stage* (Oxford, 1903), vol. I, p. 262.

3   'BESSEY . . . MADGY PEG': Edmund K. Chambers, *The English Folk Play* (Oxford, 1933), p. 125.

3   'COMPANION OF A TOMMY': Alan Brody, *The English Mummers and Their Plays* (London, 1981), p. 90; has a picture of Bessey and Tommy.

3   'TO MEET CLYM YEOBRIGHT': Thomas Hardy, *The Return of the Native*, Book Two, Chapters 4–6.

3   'GEORGE-A'-GREEN, PINNER OF WAKEFIELD': Robert Greene (?), *George-a'-Green, Pinner of Wakefield* (London, 1595).

4   'KNOWN AS MADGE WILDFIRE': Natalie Zemon Davies, *Society and Culture in Early Modern France* (Cambridge, 1987), pp. 148–9.

5   'A RINGLEADER IN EARLIER RIOTS': Charlotte Charke and Fidelis Morgan, *The Well-Known Troublemaker: A Life of Charlotte Charke* (London, 1988), pp. 199–200.

5   'STONEWALL': Martin Bauml Duberman, *Stonewall* (New York, 1993); Nigel Finch, *Stonewall* (1995).

5   'AS TIME GOES BY': Noel Greig and Drew Griffiths, *As Time Goes By*, in *Two Gay Sweatshop Plays* (London, 1981).

6   'STREET THEATER': Doric Wilson, *Street Theater*, in *Out Front: Contemporary Gay and Lesbian Plays*, ed. Don Shewey (New York, 1988).

6   'THE BOYS IN THE BAND': Mart Crowley, *The Boys in the Band* (London, 1969).

6   'AN ACTUAL PIECE OF STREET THEATRE': Phil Willmott, *Pink Paper,* 17 June 1994.

6   '"JUDY WHO?" THE WOMAN REPLIES': Guy Trebay, 'Notes from Stonewall 25: If happy little bluebirds fly', *Village Voice* vol. 39, issue 27 (1994), pp. 22–23.

7   'WHAT? THIS DIVE?': Jeremiah Norton, 'Streetbeat',*Village Voice* vol. 39, issue 27 (1994), p. 13.

7   'THEY'RE DESTROYING PROPERTY?': Wilson, 'Street Theater', p. 73, Act II.

7   'HIGH QUALITY PRODUCTS': Greg Dalton, 'Firms target gays in more open ads', *The Times Picayune (New Orleans),* 17 October 1994 pp. C1–C3, C1, quoting Dick Martin, vice–president of advertising at AT&T. This is not as new as it seems; a radio campaign advertised Chesterfield cigarettes using Fire Island imagery in the 1970s, with the slogan 'the best fags in the world'.

9   'TO THE BEST OF MY ABILITY': Roswitha, *The Plays of Roswitha*, trans. Christopher St John (Christabel Marshall), (London, 1923).

9   'A WITNESS OF HIS END': Roswitha, *The Plays of Roswitha.*

9   'CORRUPTED BY THE VICE OF THE SODOMITES': Roswitha, 'Passio sancti Pelagi', in *Hrotsvithae Opera*, ed. H. Homeyer Paderborn (1970), line 205: 'Corruptum

vitiis cognoscebant Sodomitis'.

9   'IDIOT CLAY GODS': 'Passio sancti Pelagi', lines 243–9: 'Non decet ergo virum
     Christi baptismate lotum/ Sobria barbarico complexu subdere colla,/ Sed nec
     christicolam sacrato crismate tinctum/ Daemonis oscillum spurci captare
     famelli./ Ergo corde viros licito complectere stultos,/ Qui tecum fatuos
     placantur caespite divos;/ Sintque tibi socii, servi qui sunt imulacri.'

9   'AS JOHN BOSWELL POINTS OUT': John Boswell, *Christianity, Social Tolerance
     and Homosexuality* (Chicago, 1981), p. 199.

10   'STICK TO YOUR OWN KIND': Stephen Sondheim (lyrics), Leonard Bernstein
     (music), and Arthur Laurents (book), *West Side Story* (1957).

11   'ENTIRELY ABOUT PERVERTS': John Johnston, *The Lord Chamberlain's Blue
     Pencil* (London, 1990), p. 175.

11   'NIGHT AFTER NIGHT': Neil Bartlett and Nicolas Bloomfield, *Night After
     Night* (London, 1993).

11   'SOME VERY PLEASANT PEOPLE': Peter M. Nardi, David Sanders and Judd
     Marmor, *Growing Up Before Stonewall: Life Stories of Some Gay Men*
     (London, 1994), p. 19.

12   'BROADWAY AGENT CONFIDED': Martin Bauml Duberman, '1956: The gay
     "stranglehold" on theater', in *About Time: Exploring the Gay Past* (New
     York, 1991), p. 222.

13   'STRICTLY FOR THE BOYS': Duberman '1956: The gay "stranglehold" on theater',
     p. 222.

Chapter two: Bum Boys

17   'TILL HIS TETHE BLEDE': anonymous, *The Killing of Abel [Mactacio Abel]*', in
     The Towneley Plays (Early English Text Society Extra Series LXXI), ed.
     George England (London, 1897), lines 6–9.

18   'THE NATIVITY': Tony Harrison, *The Nativity*, in *The Mysteries* (London,
     1985).

18   'KISS MY ASS!': anonymous, *The Wakefield Mysteries*, adapted by Adrian Henri
     (London, 1991), p. 14.

18   'SUITABLE DIALOGUE CHANGES': Henri, 'Introduction', *The Wakefield Mysteries* ,
     p. vi.

18   'THE WIVES OF THE TOWN': Glynne Wickham, *The Medieval Theatre*
     (Cambridge, 1987), p. 93; David M Bevington, *From Mankind to Marlowe*
     (1962), p. 79: 'women were paid for appearing in a London Lord Mayor's
     Show in 1523'.

19   'BOTTOM TO THE AUDIENCE': Henri, *The Wakefield Mysteries*, p. 97.

19   'PISS-ELEGANT KOOZE': Mart Crowley, *The Boys in the Band* (London, 1969), p.
     88, Act II.

20   'THAT SHALL BI THI FALS CHEKIS': *The Killing of Abel*, lines 44–48.

20   'FOR THAT IS THE MOSTE LEFE': *The Killing of Abel*, lines 59–65.

20   'TOO OFFENSIVE TO BE REPRODUCED': Joseph Quincy Adams, *Chief
     Pre-Shakespearian Dramas* (Cambridge, Mass., 1952), p. 95.

20   'ANUS AND THE DEVIL': *The Killing of Abel*: 'Yei, kys the dwills ars behynde'
     (line 266); 'Com kys the dwill right in the ars' (line 287).

20   'FIRST SHEPHERD'S PLAY': anonymous, First Shepherd's Play [Prima Pastorum],
     in *The Towneley Plays (Early English Text Society Extra Series LXXI)*, ed.
     George England.

22   'FART PRICK IN CULE': Henry Medwall, *Fulgens and Lucrece* (London, 1516), line 1169.

22   'TROUBLE US IN ALL': *Fulgens and Lucrece,* lines 1181–2.

22   'TAKEN UP BEHIND': *Fulgens and Lucrece,* lines 1216–7.

22   'NOR BEHIND NEITHER': anonymous, *Revesby Sword Play*, lines 404–6.

23   'I LOVE THEE': Thomas Dekker, *Satiromastix*, in *Dramatic Works*. ed. Fredson Bowers (Cambridge, 1962), vol. I. Act III, scene ii, lines 199–200.

23   'DEVIL THOU MEANST!': 'Mr S.', *Gammer Gurton's Needle* (abbreviated *GGN* below), in *Three Sixteenth Century Comedies,* ed. Charles Walters Whitworth (London, 1984). Act II, scene i, lines 42–5.

24   'HE KISSETH DICCON'S BREECH': *GGN*, Act II, scene ii, lines 67–76.

25   'THOU WITHERED WITCH!': *GGN*, Act III, scene iii, lines 46–7.

26   'CREEP IN FOR NEED?': *GGN*, Act IV, scene iv, lines 31–2.

26   'STANDS NOT HEREABOUT?': *GGN*, Act IV, scene iv, line 35.

26   'BRAINS KNOCKED OUT': *GGN*, Act V, scene i, lines 29–30.

26   'MINIONS': *GGN*, Act V, scene ii, line 13.

26   'TO FIND YOU OUT': *GGN*, Act V, scene ii, lines 186–9.

26   'BY COCK'S BONES!': *GGN*, Act V, scene ii, line 211.

27   'HODGE'S LEATHER BREECH': *GGN*, Act V, scene ii, lines 268–71.

27   'INTO THE BUTTOCK': *GGN*, Act V, scene ii, line 293.

27   'CHAM I NOT?': *GGN*, Act V, scene ii, lines 306–9.

27   'LET US HAVE A PLAUDITE!': *GGN*, Act V, scene ii, lines 328–33.

28   'THE NATION'S HERITAGE': Joe Orton, *What the Butler Saw*, in *The Complete Plays* (London, 1976), pp. 446–8, Act II.

29   'A DIRTY PLAY': Stanley Baxter quoted in John Lahr, *Prick Up Your Ears* (Harmondsworth, 1980), p. 332.

29   'PAY THEM TO DO THAT': Joe Orton, 27 July 1967, *The Orton Diaries* ed. John Lahr (London, 1986), p. 256.

29   'LIKE PHRYGIAN GANYMEDE': John Marston, *The Scourge of Villainie*, sigs c5.

30   'ALL THAT HE CAN': Nicholas Udall (?), *Jack Juggler*, in *Three Tudor Classical Interludes*, ed. Marie Axton (Cambridge, 1982), lines 124–5.

30   'HIS SHORT COAT': Udall, *Jack Juggler*, line 137.

30   'VALUE THAN THE CROWN': Christopher Marlowe, *Edward II*, in *The Complete Plays*, ed. J. B. Steane (Harmondsworth, 1969). Act I, scene iv, lines 414–17.

30   'MASTER BOUNGRACE' PAGE': Udall, *Jack Juggler*, lines 574–9.

30   'WITHOUT ANY FAIL': Udall, *Jack Juggler*, lines 580–1.

31   'STAND UPON HIS FEET': Desiderius Erasmus, *Apophthegms,* trans. Nicholas Udall (1542), p. 81.

31   'PLUMP-THIGHED CATAMITE': Michael Drayton, *The Moon-Calf*, in *Works*, ed. J. William Hebel (1961), pp. 173–4, lines 283–8, 315–16.

32   'PLACE OF AN INGLE': Thomas Middleton, *The Black Book*, in *Works* , vol. VIII, p. 21.

32   'OTHER HOUSEHOLD SERVANTS': Sir Simonds D'Ewes, 'The Fall and Great Vices of Sir Francis Bacon', in *Historia Vitae et Regni Ricardi II; Prince Charles's Journey into Spain*, ed. Thomas Hearne (London, 1729), pp. 387–8.

32   'THEIR MASTERS FOR IT': Samuel Pepys, 1 July 1663, *Diaries*.

32   'WORTH FORTY WENCHES': John Wilmot, Earl of Rochester, 'Love a woman! Y'are an ass!', in *Complete Poems and Plays*, ed. Paddy Lyons (London, 1993), p. 45.

33   'TRANSFORMED HIM APE': William Shakespeare, *2 Henry IV*, in *The Complete Works*, ed. Stanley Wells, Gary Taylor *et al.* (Oxford, 1988). Act II, scene ii, lines 63–5.

33   'HOLE FOR A NEED': Nicholas Udall, *Ralph Roister Doister* (abbreviated *RRD* below), in *Three Sixteenth Century Comedies,* ed. Charles Walters Whitworth (London, 1984). Act I, scene i, lines 55–6.

33   'AT THE TAIL': Nicholas Udall, *Flowers for Latin Speaking* (Menston, 1972), p. 67r–v.

34   'WHAT ANSWER TO MAKE': *RRD*, Act I, scene ii, lines 114–7.

35   'DESPISE HER AGAIN': *RRD*, Act III, scene iv, lines 86–90.

35   'THOU DOST THE TRUTH TELL': *RRD*, Act III, scene iv, lines 91–100.

36   'FOR YOUR SAKE': *RRD*, Act III, scene iv, lines 101–4.

36   'THOU WOULDEST TO ME SEEK': *RRD*, Act III, scene iv, lines 105–10.

37   'SIR, BUT YE BE': *RRD*, Act III, scene iv, lines 111–4.

37   'SEE YOU NOW HERE': *RRD*, Act III, scene iv, lines 115–18.

37   'WILL YE PLAY A WISE PART?': *RRD*, Act III, scene iv, lines 119–20.

38   'THE CURRENT VIEWS IN SOCIETY': Tony Higton quoted by Catherine Bennett in the *Guardian*, 14 January 1994, Section 2, p. 5.

39   'OF HIM WHO LOVES YOU': Desiderius Erasmus, letter to Servatius Roger c. 1490, in *Collected Works of Erasmus,* ed. Wallace K Ferguson, R. A. B. Mynors and D. F. S. Thomson (Toronto, 1974), vol. I.

39   'COMMITTED TO THE MARSHALSEA': *Acts of the Privy Council,* ed. Sir H. Nicolas, vol. VII, p. 153.

40   'OONS BY THE ROOTS EXTIRPED': *Original Letters of Eminent Literary Men*, ed. Henry Ellis (London, 1843), pp. 2, 2–3, 4.

40   'ADMITTED TO HIS CLERGY': Edward Coke, *An Exact Abridgement of the Two Last Volumes of Reports, entitled the Twelfth and Thirteenth Parts* (London, 1670), pp. 36–7.

40   'LOSE HIS CLERGY': Coke, *Twelfth and Thirteenth Parts,* pp. 36–7.

41   'A HEINOUS OFFENCE': Udall, *Ralph Roister Doister* (London, 1847).

Chapter three: The Freaks' Roll Call

43   'PERISHED ON YOUR GIBBETS': Louis Crompton, *Byron and Greek Love: Homophobia in 19th-Century England* (Berkeley, 1985), p. 39.

44   'GRAVE SOCRATES WILD ALCIBIADES': Christopher Marlowe, *Edward II*, in *The Complete Plays*, ed. J. B. Steane (Harmondsworth, 1969), Act I, scene iv, lines 390–9.

44   'THEMSELVES TO USE UNNATURALLY': John Bale, *Three Laws of Nature, Moses and Christ, Corrupted by the Sodomites, Pharisees and Papists Most Wicked*, in *The Complete Plays* ed. Peter Happé (Cambridge, 1986), vol. II, lines 611–14.

45   'A PRINCE FOR THAT PURPOSE': *An Account of the Proceedings Against Captain Edward Rigby*, in *Old Bailey Sessions* 7 December 1698.

45   'NOT INVISIBLE MEN': Larry Kramer, *The Normal Heart* (London, 1986), p. 41, Act II, scene xiii.

45   'A PERFECT FIT': Charles McNulty, 'The Queer as Drama Critic', *Theater* , vol. 24, issue 2 (1993), p. 13.

46   'THE PRISONERS OF WAR': J. R. Ackerley, *The Prisoners of War*, in *Gay Plays:*

Three, ed. Michael Wilcox (London, 1988).

47 'LAND THAT NEEDS HEROES': Bertolt Brecht, *Life of Galileo*, trans. John Willett, ed. John Willett and Ralph Manheim (London, 1980), p. 98, scene 13.

47 'SO LONG AS HE ENDURE': Bale, *Three Laws*, lines 627–30.

47 'STINKING SODOMETRY': *Three Laws*, lines 22–3.

48 'TO GIVE MANKIND A FALL': R. Wever, *Lusty Juventus* (Oxford, 1971), lines 406–8.

49 'YOUR TONGUE SHALL IT UNLOCK': Bale, *Three Laws*, lines 216 –17.

49 'THE DEVIL OF HELLS': *Three Laws*, lines 357–72.

50 'AND COME OUT OF THE DARK': *Three Laws*, lines 389–94.

50 'SIR AMBO': George Chapman, *Bussy D'Ambois*, ed. John H. Smith, in *The Plays of George Chapman; The Tragedies with Sir Gyles Goosecappe* (Cambridge, 1987), Act I.

51 'HOLY ORDER'S SAKE': Bale, *Three Laws*, lines 395–8.

51 'A PRETTY MINION': *Three Laws*, line 406.

51 'A GOOD MIDWIFE PERDY': *Three Laws*, lines 425–7.

52 'I SAY, YET NOT TOO BOLD': *Three Laws*, lines 475–82.

52 'BLESSED ROD OF KENT': *Three Laws*, lines 483–95.

54 'TO ABUSE MOST MONSTROUSLY': *Three Laws*, lines 555–618.

56 'FROM THE CARDINAL OF NANTES': *Three Laws*, lines 619–50.

57 'THOUGHT IT NO REBUKE': *Three Laws*, lines 1476–80.

57 'MIXED THEM WITH BUGGERAGE': *Three Laws*, lines 673–4.

57 'IN THEIR OLD BUGGERAGE': *Three Laws*, line 1386.

57 'PURSE OR ARSE?': *Three Laws*, line 1437.

58 'THIS IS JUST': *Three Laws*, lines 728–39.

58 'SIN OF SODOMY': Pisanus Fraxi (Henry Spencer Ashbee), *The Fraud of Romish Monks and Priests (1691)*, in *Bibliography of Prohibited Books* (London/New York, 1962 [1869], vol. II, p. 125.

59 'MASSAGING . . . OH STOP IT': Jill Posener, *Any Woman Can*, in *Lesbian Plays*, ed. Jill Davis (London, 1987), p. 15.

60 'MUST BE ACKNOWLEDGED': Roger Baker, 'Introduction' to *Mister X* (London, 1985).

61 'NOT PRETENDING ANYMORE': Roger Baker and Drew Griffiths, *Mister X* (London, 1985).

64 'MINNESOTA HEALTH AUTHORITIES': Frank Rich, 'The gay card', *New York Times*, 26 June 1994, Section 4, p. 17.

64 'JERK SCUM FINLEY': C. Carr, 'Washed in the blood', *Village Voice*, vol. 39, issue 27, 5 July 1994, p. 16.

64 'NO DIALOGUE TO BE HAD': Carr, 'Washed in the blood', p. 16.

Chapter four: Boys R Us

67 'WHOM VICE NEVER DEFAMED': Richard Edwards, *Damon and Pithias, The Excellent Comedy of Two the Most Faithfullest Friends* (abbreviated *D&P* below) (Oxford, 1957), scene v, lines 12–16.

68 'THE APE OF EUPHUES': Gabriel Harvey, *Four Letters* (London, 1592),.

68 'ONE HEART BETWEEN THEM': Edwards, *D&P*, scene v, lines 25–32.

68 'ALL MEN COUNTED COMMENDABLE': John Lyly, *Euphues*, in *The Complete Works*, ed. R. W. Bond (Oxford, 1902), vol. I p. 199.

69 'DAMON MY FRIEND MUST DIE': Edwards, *D&P*, scene x, lines 54–61.

69 'WITH SHEARS HIS THREAD OF SILK': William Shakespeare, *A Midsummer Night's Dream*, in *The Complete Works*, ed. Stanley Wells, Gary Taylor *et al.* (Oxford, 1988), Act V, scene i, lines 331–6.

70 'YEA, THAT I WILL': Edwards, *D&P*, scene xii, lines 162–5.

70 'WHERESOEVER THOU BE': *D&P*, scene xii, lines 170–6.

71 'ABOVE THE HEAVENS SHALL FLY': *D&P*, scene xii, lines 181–3.

71 'GREAT PLAYER OF PLAYS': Hollyband, *The French Schoolmaster* (1573), in *The Elizabethan Home*, ed. M. St. Clare Byrne (London, 1949), p. 33.

71 'BANIM AND SHEIL': John Banim (revised and altered by Richard Lalor Sheil), *Damon and Pythias or the Tyrant of Syracuse* revived Victoria Theatre 1841 and in March at Princess's Theatre with Edwin Forrest as Damon; J. B. Buckstone, *Damon and Pythias* Grecian Theatre 1841.

71 'DANGEROUS AND INFECTIOUS BEAST': John Lyly, *The Complete Works*, ed. R.W. Bond, vol. I, p. 280.

72 'THOU THY PITHYASSE': Dekker, *Satiromastix*, in *Dramatic Works*, ed. Fredson Bowers (Cambridge, 1962), Act I, scene ii, line 332.

72 'AND TUCCA THESEUS': Dekker, *Satiromastix*, Act IV, scene ii, lines 92–4.

72 'THE DUCHESS OF MALFI': John Webster, *The Duchess of Malfi*, ed. Elizabeth M. Brennan (London, 1993), Act I, scene ii, lines 413–414.

72 'THE TWO NOBLE KINSMEN': John Fletcher and William Shakespeare, *The Two Noble Kinsmen*, in *The Complete Works*, ed. Wells, Taylor *et al.*, Act I, scene iii, line 59.

73 'COMPROMISED, EVEN NEGATED?': Joanna Coles, 'Estranged bedfellows', *Guardian,* 20 December 1995, Section 2, pp. 2–3.

74 'PAEDERASTES AMATOR PUERORUM': Edward Coke, *An Exact Abridgement of the Two Last Volumes of Reports, entitled the Twelfth and Thirteenth Parts* (London, 1670), pp. 36–7.

75 'BE DISTINGUISHED FROM IT': Alan Bray, 'Homosexuality and the Signs of Male Friendship in Elizabethan England', in *Queering the Renaissance*, ed. Jonathan Goldberg (Durham, 1994), pp. 56–7.

76 'IN MARLOWE'S PLAY': Christopher Marlowe, *Edward II*, in *The Complete Plays*, ed. J. B. Steane, Act I, scene iv, line 394: 'Great Alexander lov'd Hephaestion'.

76 'VICEMASTER OF PAUL'S': Gabriel Harvey quoted in *John Lyly: The Humanist as Courtier,* ed. G. K. Hunter (London, 1962), pp. 75–6: 'he hath not payed the Vicemaster of Paul's and the Foolmaster of the Theatre for naughts'.

77 'NOT A CHAMBER': John Lyly, *Campaspe*, ed. G. K. Hunter, in *Campaspe and Sapho and Phaon* (Manchester, 1991), Act II, scene ii, line 70.

77 'ASSAULTS OF WAR': *Campaspe*, Act II, scene ii, line 72.

78 'THAT SHE IS A WOMAN': *Campaspe*, Act V, scene iv, lines 71–4.

78 'COME IN AT HIS BACK': *Campaspe*, Act III, scene iii, lines 63–7.

79 'A TESTAMENT OF NOBLE-ENDING LOVE': William Shakespeare, *Henry V*, in *The Complete Works*, ed. Wells, Taylor *et al.*, Act IV, scene vi, lines 11–19, 24–27.

80 'POETRY OF THE FIRST WORLD WAR': Martin Taylor, *Lads: Love Poetry of the Trenches* (London, 1989) is an interesting anthology.

Chapter five: Lesbian Double Cherries

81   'WOULD ANOTHER WED': William Shakespeare, *The Passionate Pilgrim*, in *The Complete Works*, ed. Stanley Wells, Gary Taylor *et al.* (Oxford, 1988), lines 47–8.

82   'LESBIAN LOVE ELEGY IN ENGLISH': James Holstun, *'Will You Rent Our Ancient Love Asunder?': Lesbian Elegy in Donne, Marvell and Milton*, in *ELH* vol. 54 (1987), pp. 835–67, p. 838.

82   'OF LESBIAN SAPPHO': Helen Gardner, *John Donne: The Elegies and the Songs and Sonnets* (Oxford, 1965), p. xlvi, cited James Holstun, *'Will You Rent Our Ancient Love Asunder?'*, pp. 835–67, p. 837.

83   'YET NEVER LOVED': John Lyly, *Sapho and Phaon*, ed. David Bevington, in *Campaspe and Sapho and Phaon* (Manchester, 1991), Act I, scene i, lines 37–8.

83   'WHAT ELSE CUPID?': Lyly, *Sapho and Phaon*, Act V, scene ii, lines 14–15.

84   'FLATTERING QUEEN ELIZABETH': David Bevington, *Campaspe and Sapho and Phaon*, p. 153.

84   'ONLY FOR LADIES': Lyly, *Sapho and Phaon*, Act V, scene iii, lines 103–5.

85   'TO HOLLOW THOUGHTS?': John Lyly, *Gallathea*, in *The Plays of John Lyly*, ed. Carter A. Daniel (Lewisburg, 1988), p. 129. Act III, scene iv.

86   'SLUIC'D IN'S ABSENCE': Shakespeare, *The Winter's Tale*, in *The Complete Works*, Act I, scene ii, lines 192–4.

86   'SEEM AS BEASTS': Lyly, *Gallathea*, Act I, scene i.

86   'BLUSHING AT EVERYTHING': *Gallathea*, Act I, scene i.

87   'A SOUR DECEIT': *Gallathea*, Act V, scene iii.

87   'BY HER WORDS': *Gallathea*, Act V, scene iii.

88   'IF THY LOVE BE NOT SO': *Gallathea*, Act V, scene iii.

88   'SO I MAY ENJOY PHYLLIDA': *Gallathea*, Act V, scene iii.

89   'I BEGAT YOU, A DAUGHTER': *Gallathea*, Act V, scene iii.

90   'THERE IS NOTHING LOST': *Gallathea*, Act V, scene iii.

90   'BEARDS THAT PLEASED ME': Shakespeare, *As You Like It*, in *The Complete Works*, Epilogue, lines 16–18.

91   'EXCESSIVE CONTRIBUTION OF THE MALE': Eric Partridge, *Shakespeare's Bawdy* (London, 1990), pp. 13–14.

91   'POTENTIAL LESBIAN CONTAMINATION': Ferdinand Lundberg and Marynia Farnham, *Modern Woman: The Lost Sex* (New York, 1947), pp. 365–6, cited in: Lillian Faderman, *Surpassing the Love of Men: Romantic Friendship and Love between Women from the Renaissance to the Present* (London, 1985), p. 340.

91   'SENSIBLE, IF SIMPLISTIC': Stanley Wells, Foreword, in Eric Partridge, *Shakespeare's Bawdy* (London, 1990), p. viii.

92   'AS MINE IS TO THEE': William Shakespeare, *As You Like It*, Act I, scene ii, lines 7–13.

93   'SEEK ANOTHER HEIR': Shakespeare, *As You Like It*, Act I, scene iii, lines 93–8.

93   'PILADES AND ORESTES': Thomas Lodge, *Rosalynde*, in *The Complete Works* (London, 1883), vol. II pp. 34–5.

94   'WHAT SHALL BE OUR SPORT THEN?': Shakespeare, *As You Like It*, Act I, scene ii, line 29.

94   'OVERTHROW LOVE AND FAITH': Lyly, *Gallathea*, Act V, scene iii.

94   'HER GIFTS TO WOMEN': Shakespeare, *As You Like It*, Act I, scene ii, lines 34–5.

95 'WILL YOU GO COZ?': Shakespeare, *As You Like It*, Act I, scene ii, line 245.

95 'IS A ROSE,': Gertrude Stein, *Sacred Emily* (1913), p. 187.

95 'LOVE'S PRICK AND ROSALIND': Shakespeare, *As You Like It*, Act III, scene ii, lines 109–10.

95 'AND LEAVES HIM TO BASE BRIERS': John Fletcher and William Shakespeare, *The Two Noble Kinsmen*, in *The Complete Works*, Act II, scene ii, lines 137–43.

95 'MORE THAN IN SEX DIVIDUAL': Fletcher and Shakespeare, *The Two Noble Kinsmen*, Act I, scene iii, lines 81–2.

96 'TO TAKE EXAMPLE BY HER': Fletcher and Shakespeare, *The Two Noble Kinsmen*, Act II, scene ii, lines 143–7.

96 'TO PRAY TO DIANA TO HELP HER': *The Two Noble Kinsmen*, Act V, scene iii.

96 'LEARN'D, PLAY'D, EAT TOGETHER': Shakespeare, *As You Like It*, Act I, scene iii, lines 71–3.

97 'WHEN SHE IS GONE': *As You Like It*, Act I, scene iii, lines 79–81.

97 'NO LONGER CELIA, BUT ALIENA': *As You Like It*, Act I, scene iii, lines 126–7.

97 'THEN OPEN NOT THY LIPS': *As You Like It*, Act I, scene iii, line 81.

98 'A BETTER LEER THAN YOU': *As You Like It*, Act IV, scene i, lines 62–3.

98 'TO HER OWN NEST': *As You Like It*, Act IV, scene i, lines 191–4. 'Is it not a foul bird defiles its own nest', *Rosalynde*, 35.

99 'YOU POUR AFFECTION IN, IT RUNS OUT': *As You Like It*, Act IV, scene i, lines 195–200.

100 'THE FIGHT OF TWO RAMS': *As You Like It*, Act V, scene ii, lines 28–30.

100 'TO LEAVE MY WIFE': *As You Like It*, Act III, scene iii, lines 82–4.

100 'AND AS I LOVE NO WOMAN, I'LL MEET': *As You Like It*, Act V, scene ii, line 114.

100 'OR HAVE A WOMAN TO YOUR LORD': *As You Like It*, Act V, scene iv, lines 131–2.

101 'WAS EACH ELEVEN': Fletcher and Shakespeare, *The Two Noble Kinsmen*, Act I, scene iii, lines 49–54.

101 'IN MORTAL BOSOMS': *The Two Noble Kinsmen*, Act V, scene ii, lines 62–3.

102 'DID SO TO ONE ANOTHER': *The Two Noble Kinsmen*, Act I, scene iii, lines 59–64.

102 'NO MORE ARRAIGNMENT': *The Two Noble Kinsmen*, Act I, scene iii, lines 64–6.

102 'THEY DIED IN PERFUME': *The Two Noble Kinsmen*, Act I, scene iii, lines 66–71.

103 'HAD BEEN INCORPORATE': Shakespeare, *A Midsummer Night's Dream*, in *The Complete Works,* Act III, scene ii, lines 204–9.

103 'AND SING IT IN HER SLUMBERS': Fletcher and Shakespeare, *The Two Noble Kinsmen*, Act I, scene iii, lines 66–71.

103 'AND CROWNED WITH ONE CREST': Shakespeare, *A Midsummer Night's Dream*, Act III, scene ii, lines 209–15.

103 'OR BIRDS IN AIR': John Donne, *Sapho to Philaenis*, in *Poetical Works*, ed. Herbert J. C. Grierson (Oxford, 1933), p. 111, lines 39–42.

104 'ALL SEEMS DONE TO THEE': Donne, *Sapho to Philaenis*, p. 111, lines 45–52.

104 'FITTER FOR GIRLS AND SCHOOLBOYS': Fletcher and Shakespeare, *The Two Noble Kinsmen*, Act III, scene vi, lines 33–4.

104 'A BOY OR WOMAN': *The Two Noble Kinsmen*, Act IV, scene i, lines 58–9.

105 'THOUGH I ALONE DO FEEL THE INJURY': Shakespeare, *A Midsummer Night's Dream*, Act III, scene ii, lines 216–20.

105 'MY HALF, MY ALL, MY MORE': Donne, *Sapho to Philaenis*, p. 111, lines 57–8.

105 'TO THY SEX CAPTIVE': Fletcher and Shakespeare, *The Two Noble Kinsmen*, Act I, scene i, lines 80–81.

105 'I AM SURE I SHALL NOT': *The Two Noble Kinsmen*, Act I, scene iii, lines 84–6.

106 'THAT LOATHES EVEN AS IT LONGS': *The Two Noble Kinsmen*, Act I, scene iii, lines 87–91.

106 'THE ALL-NOBLE THESEUS': *The Two Noble Kinsmen*, Act I, scene iii, lines 91–4.

106 'YET I CONTINUE MINE': *The Two Noble Kinsmen*, Act I, scene iii, lines 94–8.

107 'THE MISADVENTURE OF THEIR OWN EYES': *The Two Noble Kinsmen*, Act III, scene vi, line 190.

107 'TOO EXCELLENT FOR ME': *The Two Noble Kinsmen*, Act III, scene vi, lines 285–6.

107 'THE SCORN OF WOMEN': *The Two Noble Kinsmen*, Act III, scene vi, lines 245–50.

107 'THAN MINISTER TO SUCH HARM': *The Two Noble Kinsmen*, Act V, scene iii, lines 65–6.

108 'THAN ALL WOMEN': *The Two Noble Kinsmen*, Act V, scene iii, lines 141–3.

108 'TO LIE WITH A WOMAN': Thomas Dekker, *Satiromastix*, in *Dramatic Works,* ed. Fredson Bowers (Cambridge, 1962), vol. I, Act I, scene i, lines 17–20.

109 'AND ONLY FOR FREE WOMAN': Thomas Heywood, *The Golden Age*, in *Works* (London, 1874), vol. III, p. 17, Act I.

109 'TO BLIND THE EYES OF MAN': Heywood, *The Golden Age*, p. 17, Act I.

109 'KILLED HER MALE CONSORT': Robert Graves, *The Greek Myths* (Harmondsworth, 1960), vol. I, p. 42.

109 'SICK WITH PASSION?': Heywood, *The Golden Age*, vol. III, p. 24, Act II.

110 'FROM ALL OFFENSIVE DANGER': *The Golden Age*, p. 24, Act II.

110 'GO CALL THE KING MY FATHER': *The Golden Age*, p. 24, Act II.

111 'WE CAN SPARE YOU BEST': *The Golden Age*, p. 25, Act II.

111 'AND PROFESSED MAID MAY LIVE': *The Golden Age*, p. 25, Act II.

111 'AND FROM OTHERS PLEASURE': *The Golden Age*, p. 25, Act II.

111 'HAVE ALL THINGS THAT SHE HAD': *The Golden Age*, p. 26, Act II.

112 'IN YOUR FAIR ISSUE?': *The Golden Age*, p. 26, Act II.

112 'HIS UNIVERSAL GRAVE': *The Golden Age*, p. 6, Act I.

112 'NOT WORTHY YOUR RESPECT': *The Golden Age*, p. 26, Act II.

112 'OR THE OTHER WAY AROUND': James Holstun, *'Will You Rent Our Ancient Love Asunder?'*, pp. 835–67, 850.

112 'I WILL NEXT PURSUE': *The Golden Age*, p. 26, Act II.

113 'BETOOK HER TO THE FORESTS': *The Golden Age*, p. 27, Act II.

113 'THEIR QUEEN AND EMPRESS': *The Golden Age*, p. 27, Act II.

113 'AND DWELL IN PEACE': *The Golden Age*, p. 28, Act II.

114 'WHERE WOMEN COULD STAY': Lisa Power, *No Bath But Plenty of Bubbles: An Oral History of the Gay Liberation Front 1970–73* (London, 1995), p. 235.

114 'IS ALL OUR PRACTICE': Heywood, *The Golden Age*, p. 28, Act II.

114 'VOWED SACRED VIRGINITY': *The Golden Age*, pp. 28–9, Act II.

114 'THAT FOR NOTHING CARE': *The Golden Age*, p. 29, Act II.

115 'TO CHANGE HER BEDFELLOW': *The Golden Age*, p. 29, Act II.

115 'SO 'TIS LOTTED': *The Golden Age*, p. 29, Act II.

115 'HAVE TO TALK ABOUT IT ALL NIGHT': Power, *No Bath But Plenty of Bubbles,* pp. 235, 237.

115 'LONG-TERM RELATIONSHIPS': Kaye Wellings, Julia Field, Anne M. Johnson and

Jane Wadswoth with Sally Bradshaw, *Sexual Behaviour in Britain: The National Survey of Sexual Attitudes and Lifestyles* (London, 1994), p. 213.

116 'MEN'S SUBTLE TREACHERIES': Thomas Heywood, *The Golden Age*, p. 30, Act II.

116 'TO ALL OUR WRONGED LADIES': *The Golden Age*, pp. 30–31, Act II.

116 'AND HER TRAIN I'LL STAND': *The Golden Age*, p. 31, Act II.

116 'THAT'S MORE THAN I CAN PROMISE': *The Golden Age*, p. 31, Act II.

117 'BY ALL THE GODS TO KEEP': *The Golden Age*, p. 31, Act II.

117 'A WOMAN SHALL HAVE MINE': *The Golden Age*, p. 31, Act II.

117 'YOUR BED-FELLOW SHALL BE': *The Golden Age*, p. 31, Act II.

118 'SO HOT PURSUED': *The Golden Age*, p. 32, Act II.

118 'OR ME INTO A MAN': *The Golden Age*, p. 33, Act II.

119 'BY BOTH ARMS AND COURTESY': *The Golden Age*, p. 76, Act V.

120 'WRITTEN ON THE TOILET WALL': Power, *No Bath But Plenty of Bubbles*, p. 237.

120 'FORSAKES THE PLACE': Heywood, *The Golden Age* p. 35. Act III,

121 'SHE CHILDS A VALIANT SON': *The Golden Age*, p. 35, Act III.

121 'MANY OUT-RAGES': *The Golden Age*, p. 36, Act III.

122 'THEIR PRICK POWER': Power, *No Bath But Plenty of Bubbles*, pp. 244–5.

123 'AND USURP THY NAME': Heywood, *The Golden Age*, p. 46, Act III.

123 'A FEMALE-ORIENTED EROTICISM': Valerie Traub, 'The (In)Significance of "Lesbian" Desire in Early Modern England', in *Queering the Renaissance,* ed. Jonathan Goldberg (Durham, 1994), pp. 62–83.

Chapter six: Shakespeare's Sodomite Stage

125 'TO POISON THE VERY GODLY': A. L. Rowse, *Homosexuals in History* (London, 1977), p. 44.

125 'BOYS ABLE TO RAVISH A MAN': Thomas Middleton, *Father Hubbard's Tales*, in *Works,* ed. A. H. Bullen (London, 1885).

125 'PLAY THE SODOMITES, OR WORSE': Philip Stubbes, *The Anatomie of Abuses*, ed. Arthur Freeman (New York, 1973), N8r–v.

126 'THE PROFANEST CONDITION': I. G. (John Greene?), *A Refutation of the Apology for Actors* (London, 1615), p. 4.

126 'HIS FIRST OVERTHROW': Francis Lenton, *The Young Gallants Whirligig* (London, 1629).

127 'AS NERO SHOWED IN SPORUS': John Rainolds, *Th'Overthrow of Stage-Playes* (London, 1599).

127 'SCHOOL OF ABUSE': Stephen Gosson, *The School of Abuse* (London, 1579).

127 'AN INGLE FOR PLAYERS?': Ben Jonson, *Poetaster*, in *Works,* ed. C. H. Herford and P. and E. Simpson (Oxford, 1925), Act I, scene ii.

127 'HE MAY QUIT THE STAGE': Francis Bacon, 'On Friendship', in *A Harmony of the Essays etc. of Francis Bacon,* ed. Edward Arber (London, 1871), p. 40.

127 'NO LESS THAN THEY DO MY EXPERIENCE': Rictor Norton, *Mother Clap's Molly House: The Gay Subculture in England 1700–1830* (London, 1992), p. 22.

128 'THE PORTRAIT OF MR. W. H.': Oscar Wilde, *The Portrait of Mr. W. H.*, in *Works* (Glasgow, 1994), pp. 302–50.

129 'COMPLEMENT OF HORMONES': Eric Partridge, *Shakespeare's Bawdy* (London, 1990), p. 13.

129 'QUITE A HOMOSEXUAL THING': Matthew Hodson, *Angels at the National*, in *Gay Times*, November 1993, pp. 32–3.

130 'LINED WITH DULL RED': Oscar Wilde, *The Picture of Dorian Gray*, in *Works*, p. 65.

130 'BETTER SPEAK FIRST': William Shakespeare, *As You Like It*, in *The Complete Works* ed. Stanley Wells, Gary Taylor *et al.* (Oxford, 1988), Act IV, scene i, lines 64–8.

132 'HIS ALIAS IN FRANCE': Richard Ellmann, *Oscar Wilde* (London, 1987), p. 68n.

132 'I'TH' POSTURE OF A WHORE': Shakespeare, *Antony and Cleopatra*, in *The Complete Works*, Act V, scene ii, lines 218–20.

133 'CONTRARY TO "NATURE"': John Boswell, *Christianity, Social Tolerance and Homosexuality* (Chicago, 1981), p. 330.

133 'CALLED USURERS BUGGERS': Boswell, *Christianity, Social Tolerance and Homosexuality*, p. 290, n62.

134 'AND SO LET ME': Shakespeare, *The Merchant of Venice*, in *The Complete Works*, Act IV, scene i, lines 113–5.

134 'TO HEAR YOU MAKE THE OFFER': *The Merchant of Venice*, Act IV, scene i, lines 285–6.

134 'YOU SHALL BE HIS SURETY': *The Merchant of Venice*, Act V, scene i, lines 249–54.

135 'OR A WHORE'S OATH': Shakespeare, *The History of King Lear*, in *The Complete Works*, Act III, scene vi, lines 14–15.

135 'IN THY WOMAN'S WEEDS': Shakespeare, *Twelfth Night*, Act V, scene i, lines 270–1.

135 'AND HIS FANCY'S QUEEN': Shakespeare, *Twelfth Night*, Act V, scene i, lines 381–4.

136 'ESSAY BY STEPHEN ORGEL': Stephen Orgel, 'Nobody's Perfect: Or Why Did the English Stage Take Boys for Women?', in *Displacing Homophobia: Gay Male Perspectives in Literature and Culture*, ed. Ronald R Butters, John M. Clum and Michael Moon (Durham, North Carolina, 1989), pp. 7–30.

137 'MAY BE OUTWORN, NEVER OUTDONE': John Fletcher and William Shakespeare, *The Two Noble Kinsmen*, in Shakespeare, *The Complete Works,* Act I, scene iii, lines 41–4. Colin Gray pointed out the implications of this scene to me.

137 'INTERTANGLED ROOTS OF LOVE': *The Two Noble Kinsmen*, Act I, scene iii, lines 56–9.

138 'BUT LIFE AND WEAKNESS': *The Two Noble Kinsmen*, Act I, scene ii, lines 1–12.

138 'WILL NEVER SINK': *The Two Noble Kinsmen*, Act II, scene ii, lines 55–67.

139 'TILL OUR DEATHS IT CANNOT': *The Two Noble Kinsmen*, Act II, scene ii, lines 79–115.

140 'WERE THERE NOT MAIDS ENOUGH?': *The Two Noble Kinsmen*, Act II, scene ii, lines 118–121.

141 'HE SHALL ENJOY HER': *The Two Noble Kinsmen*, Act III, scene vi, lines 294–6.

141 'BECOMES THE RIDER'S LOAD': *The Two Noble Kinsmen*, Act V, scene vi, lines 74–82.

141 'BUT LOSS OF DEAR LOVE!': *The Two Noble Kinsmen*, Act V, scene vi, lines 109–112.

142 'A THOUSAND POUND ERE A BE CURED': Shakespeare, *Much Ado About Nothing*, in *The Complete Works,* Act I, scene i, lines 68–78.

143 'I HAVE A BEARD COMING': Shakespeare, *A Midsummer Night's Dream*, in *The Complete Works,* Act I, scene ii, lines 43–4.

143 'NOT UNSYMPATHETICALLY LAUGHED AT': William Shakespeare, *A Midsummer*

Night's Dream, ed. Harold F. Brooks (London, 1983), p. 22n.

143 'IS BUT THE SHARPNESS OF THE WEATHER': John Fletcher, *Monsieur Thomas,* in *Works,* ed. A. Glover and A. R. Waller (London, 1905), Act I, scene ii.

143 'HIS DAUGHTER, AND HIS DUCATS!': Shakespeare, *The Merchant of Venice,* in *The Complete Works,* Act II, scene viii, lines 23–4.

144 'HAIR KNIT UP IN THEE':Shakespeare, *A Midsummer Night's Dream,* in *The Complete Works,* Act V, scene i, lines 189–90. Some of the double-meanings in this sequence were uncovered during work on the play with students at Drama Centre, London in 1994.

145 'IN A NOOK MERELY MONASTIC': Shakespeare, *As You Like It,* Act III, scene ii, lines 394–405.

145 'CAN POSSIBLY DEVISE': Shakespeare, *Love's Labour's Lost,* in *The Complete Works,* Act I, scene i, lines 119–130.

146 'THUS DALLY WITH MY EXCREMENT': *Love's Labour's Lost,* Act V, scene i, lines 96–9.

146 'A SPANIARD'S RAPIER': *Love's Labour's Lost,* Act I, scene ii, lines 167–9.

146 'JACK HATH NOT JILL': *Love's Labour's Lost,* Act V, scene ii, lines 860–1.

147 'YOU, THAT WAY; WE THIS WAY': *Love's Labour's Lost,* Act V, scene ii, lines 913–4.

147 'COACH COMPANION AND BED COMPANION': Alan Bray, 'Homosexuality and the Signs of Male Friendship in Elizabethan England', in *Queering the Renaissance,* ed. Jonathan Goldberg (Durham, 1994), p. 43, quoting Gustav Ungerer, *A Spaniard in Elizabethan England: The Correspondence of Antonio Peréz's Exile* (London: 1974 and 1976), vol. I, p. 219.

Chapter seven: Wearing the Trousers

148 'LEAD HIS APES INTO HELL': William Shakespeare, *Much Ado About Nothing,* in *The Complete Works,* ed. Stanley Wells, Gary Taylor *et al.* (Oxford, 1988), Act II, scene i, lines 34–6.

150 'YOU STRAIGHT SLIP INTO HELL': Thomas Dekker, Henry Chettle and William Haughton, *Patient Grissil,* in Dekker, *Works,* ed. Fredson Bowers (Cambridge, 1962), vol. I, Act II, scene i, lines 252–83.

150 'IF YOU FROWN I'LL BEND MY FIST': Dekker, Chettle and Haughton, *Patient Grissil,* Act IV, scene iii, lines 216–21.

151 'AND BE CONTINUALLY IN HELL': *Patient Grissil,* Act V, scene ii, lines 275–83.

152 'REVEALED TO ME': Philip Massinger, *The Bondman,* in *Works,* ed. William Gifford (London, 1805), Act II, scene ii.

153 'TO THE TENDING OF CHILDREN': anonymous, *The Life and Death of Mrs. Mary Frith. Commonly Called Mal Cutpurse* (London, 1662), pp. 6, 13. The biography conforms to a still-widespread theory that childhood behaviour inappropriate to biological gender predicts later subversion of sex roles: indeed it may have invented or embroidered the accounts of Frith's childhood to support it. Charlotte Charke (see chapter eleven), makes similar claims about her own childhood in her autobiography.

154 'TO BECKON HER TO YOU': Thomas Middleton and Thomas Dekker, *The Roaring Girl,* ed. Paul A. Mulholland (Manchester, 1987), Epilogue, lines 31–8.

155 'WITH WINGS MORE LOFTY': Middleton and Dekker, *The Roaring Girl,* Prologue, lines 13–26.

155 'I DOTE UPON THIS ROARING GIRL': Thomas Middleton and Thomas Dekker, *The Roaring Girl*, Act I, scene i, lines 93–9.

155 'MAN MORE THAN WOMAN': *The Roaring Girl*, Act I, scene ii, lines 127–31.

157 'AND CAN CONCEIVE': Nathan Field, *Amends For Ladies*, in *Plays*, ed. William Perry (Austin, 1950), Act II, scene i.

157 'LONG MEG AND MARY UMBREE': Thomas Dekker, *Satiromastix*, in *Works*, ed. Fredson Bowers (Cambridge, 1962), vol. I, Act III, scene i, lines 174, 232.

158 'AS MUCH FOR THE WIFE': Middleton and Dekker, *The Roaring Girl*, Act II, scene i, lines 191–212.

160 'I WARRANT YOU': *The Roaring Girl*, Act II, scene ii, lines 77–90.

160 'GOOD MASTER LAXTON': *The Roaring Girl*, Act I, scene ii, lines 55–6.

160 'SIR BEAUTEOUS GANYMEDE': Stephen Orgel, 'The Subtexts of the Roaring Girl', in *Erotic Politics: Desire on the Renaissance Stage*, ed. Susan Zimmerman (London, 1992), p. 24. Paul Mulholland, in his edition of *The Roaring Girl* (Manchester 1987), suggests that Sir Beauteous Ganymede may be a comment on James I's lover Robert Carr (pp. 61–2 n104). See chapter eight for more on Carr and Ganymedes.

160 'PROSTITUTE A MAN TO ME!': Middleton and Dekker, *The Roaring Girl*, Act III, scene i, lines 111–12.

161 'TASTES WELL IN A DOUBLET': Middleton and Dekker, *The Roaring Girl*, Act IV, scene i, lines 45–7.

162 'NAMED IT AFTER ME': Carrie Fisher, 'True Confessions: The "Rolling Stone" Interview with Madonna', in *Rolling Stone*, issue 606, 13 June 1991, pp. 120, 36–9.

162 'EITHER OF THOSE IMPUTATIONS': *Consistory of London Correction Book*, folios 19–20, cited in Middleton and Dekker, *The Roaring Girl*, ed. Paul A. Mulholland, p. 262.

162 'RATHER TO HEAR MOLL CUTPURSE THAN HIM': John Chamberlain, *Letters*, ed. N. E. McLure (Philadelphia, 1939), vol. I, p. 334, cited in Stephen Orgel, 'The Subtexts of the Roaring Girl', pp. 21–2.

Chapter eight: King's Favourite

164 'LOVED NOT AT FIRST SIGHT?': William Shakespeare, *As You Like It*, in *The Complete Works*, ed. Stanley Wells, Gary Taylor *et al.* (Oxford, 1988), Act III, scene v, lines 82–3.

164 'TERRIFIED OF WHO YOU ARE': Larry Kramer, *The Normal Heart* (London, 1986), p. 42. Act II, scene xiii.

165 'NO EVIDENCE AT ALL': J. B. Steane, Introduction, in Christopher Marlowe, *The Complete Plays*, ed. J. B. Steane (Harmondsworth, 1969), p. 15.

165 'CLEAR SOCIETY FROM A STAIN': *The Trials of Oscar Wilde*, ed. H. Montgomery Hyde (London, 1948), pp. 211, 220, 251, 250.

166 'FIRED MY IMAGINATION': Noel Greig, Introduction, in Edward Carpenter, *Selected Writings*, ed. Noel Greig (London, 1984), vol. I, p. 16.

167 'THE WITNESS SHALL BE PRODUCED': British Museum Harl. 6848 fol 185, in *Marlowe: The Critical Heritage 1588–1896*, ed. Millar Maclure (London, 1979), pp. 36–8.

168 'AND BE MY LOVE': Christopher Marlowe, 'The Passionate Shepherd to His Love', in *The Complete Poems and Translations*, ed. Stephen Orgel (Harmondsworth, 1979), lines 21–4.

169 'DOING IN MY BEDROOM?': Michael Hardwick, in *Long Road to Freedom: The Advocate History of the Gay and Lesbian Movement*, ed. Mark Thompson (New York, 1994), p. 290.

169 'THE CRIMINAL LAW OF THE UNITED STATES': Janet E. Halley, 'Bowers v. Hardwick in the Renaissance', in *Queering the Renaissance*, ed. Jonathan Goldberg (Durham, 1994), p. 15, quoting *Hardwick, 478 U.S. at 196–97* (1986).

170 'THE LITTLE ATHEIST': Thomas Dekker, *Satiromastix*, in *Works*, ed. Fredson Bowers (Cambridge, 1962), vol. I, Act III, scene i, lines 255–6.

170 'HERETICS SHALL BE BURNED': Edward Coke, *25 Henry VIII c. 6*, in *An Exact Abridgement of the Two Last Volumes of Reports, entitled the Twelfth and Thirteenth Parts* (London, 1670), pp. 36–7.

170 'MORE NOW THAN EVER': Thomas Dekker, *If This be not a Good Play, the Devil is in It*, in *Works*, vol. II. Act I, scene i, lines 61–5.

171 'THE DIFFICULTIES OF BEING GAY': Stephen Holden, 'A Gay Festival Banishes Silence,' in the *New York Times*, 17 June 1994, 'Weekend', p. C27. Modern productions of *Edward II* have often involved gay male theatre practitioners. Nicholas Hytner revived it at Manchester's Royal Exchange Theatre a few years before Gerard Murphy directed Simon Russell Beale for the RSC in 1990; although Derek Jacobi rejected the Prospect pairing of Edward with Richard for a West End season.

172 'A SODOMITICAL RELATIONSHIP': Alan Bray, 'Homosexuality and the Signs of Male Friendship in Elizabethan England', in *Queering the Renaissance*, ed. Jonathan Goldberg (Durham, 1994), p. 48–9; discussion continues pp. 59–60n.

173 'THE ONLY MESSAGE THIS PLAY HAS': Derek Jarman, *Queer Edward II*, ed. Malcolm Sutherland and Keith Collins (London, 1991), p. iv.

173 'SAFETY OF A SCEPTRE': E. F., *The History of the Life, Reign and Death of Edward II, King of England and Lord of Ireland, with the Rise and Fall of his great Favourites, Gaveston and the Spencers* (London, 1680), p. 155.

174 'BUT NOT ENCHANT IT': E. F., *The History of the Life, Reign and Death of Edward II*, p. 137.

174 'TO PERPETUAL EXILE': E. F., *The History of the Life, Reign and Death of Edward II*, p. 4.

175 'ALTER THEM HE CANNOT': E. F., *The History of the Life, Reign and Death of Edward II*, pp. 28–9.

175 'UPON WHOSE BOSOM LET ME DIE': Christopher Marlowe, *Edward II*, in *The Complete Plays*, Act I, scene i, lines 6–14.

176 'CONFINES OF THIS KINGDOM': E. F., *The History of the Life, Reign and Death of Edward II*, p. 4.

176 'ALL THAT MEN DESIRE': Marlowe, *Hero and Leander*, in *The Complete Poems and Translations*, I, lines 84–5.

176 'AND TALK OF LOVE': Marlowe, *Hero and Leander*, II, lines 153–91.

177 'WOULD STEAL HIM THENCE': *Hero and Leander*, II, lines 193–210.

177 'PERSUADING ORATORY FAILS': *Hero and Leander*, II, lines 226–7.

178 'BEST PLEASE HIS MAJESTY': Marlowe, *Edward II*, Act I, scene i, lines 50–71.

180 'THAT MAKES ME IMPATIENT': *Edward II*, Act I, scene iv, lines 404–21.

181 'AND GLORIETH IN EVIL': John Marston, *The Scourge of Villainie*, E6v–E7r, cited in Gregory W. Bredbeck, *Sodomy and Interpretation: Marlowe to Milton*

(Ithaca, 1991), p. 12. Marston's 1599 gallant is an avant-garde dresser: the earliest reference to herring bone stitch recorded by the *Oxford English Dictionary* is in 1659.

182 'GREAT ALEXANDER LOV'D HEPHAESTION': Christopher Marlowe, *Edward II*, in *The Complete Plays*, ed. J. B. Steane (Harmondsworth, 1969), Act I, scene iv, lines 394–5.

182 'AND SMILES AT THOSE THAT PASS': *Edward II*, Act I, scene ii, lines 20–24.

182 'SEEING I HAVE GAVESTON': *Edward II*, Act I, scene ii, lines 49–55.

183 'AND SHOW OF MODESTY': Thomas Howard, Viscount of Bindon, *Letter to Sir John Harington (1611)*, in *Nugae Antiquae* (1779), vol. II, p. 271–7.

183 'HE WAS ENTICED BY ME': Michael Drayton, *Peirs Gaveston*, in *Works*, ed. J William Hebel (1961), vol. I, p. 94.

183 'ON CURSED GAVESTON': Marlowe, *Edward II*, Act I, scene iv, lines 181–2.

184 'THE GREATEST KINGS OF THE WORLD': Benvenuto Cellini, *Autobiography*, trans. George Bull (Harmondsworth, 1956), pp. 335–8, cited in James M. Saslow, *Ganymede in the Renaissance: Homosexuality in Art and Society* (New Haven, 1986), pp. 149–50.

185 'AND HOW HIS GANYMEDE MOVED': Ben Jonson, *Sir Voluptuous Beast*, in *Works*, ed. C. H. Herford and P. and E. Simpson (Oxford, 1925), vol. VIII, p. 34.

185 'AUGEAN OXSTALL FROM FOUL SIN': John Marston, *The Scourge of Villainie*, c5.

186 'AS HIS DERIDED FONDNESS TO DISGUISE': John Marston, *The Metamorphosis of Pygmalion's Image and Certain Satires*, pp. 51–2.

186 'AS THEY ARE GOING A MILKING': Thomas Dekker, *The Honest Whore Part Two*, in *Works*, vol. II, Act I, scene i, lines 7–9.

186 'ARMS SHALL CIRCLE THEE': Thomas Dekker, *Old Fortunatus*, in *Works*, vol. I, Act I, scene i, lines 239–43.

187 'FROM HER SHREWISH BLOWS!': Christopher Marlowe, *Dido, Queen of Carthage*, in *The Complete Plays*, Act I, scene i, lines 1–4.

187 'BRIGHT JEWELS FIT FOR CARR'S EARS': Thomas Howard, Viscount of Bindon, *Letter to Sir John Harington (1611)*, pp. 271–7.

187 'IF THOU WILT BE MY LOVE': Christopher Marlowe, *Dido, Queen of Carthage*, Act I, scene i, lines 42–5.

188 'ÆNEAS WANDERS ON THE SEAS': *Dido, Queen of Carthage*, Act I, scene i, lines 50–52.

189 'I AM NOT FOR HIM': Shakespeare, *Much Ado About Nothing*, in *The Complete Works*, Act I, scene iii, lines 26–34.

190 'MY GRIEF AND INNOCENCY': Marlowe, *Edward II*, Act V, scene vi, lines 99–102.

190 'IF SWIFT PUNISHMENT BE NOT ORDAINED': Edward Coke, *The Third Part of the Institutes of the Laws of England* (London, 1797), p. 58.

Chapter nine: Strange Bedfellows

192 'COCKING AN ELEGANT LEG OVER THE THRONE': Ian McKellen, *Acting Shakespeare (programme)*, (London, 1988), p. 6. McKellen's worldwide Shakespeare success after coming out has been as the traditionally monstrous Richard III, a role he played at the National Theatre in 1990 and then made into a film. Sexual deviance and disability are discussed later in the chapter, but they also feature in the preparations of McKellen's famous predecesor as a

celluloid Richard III – Laurence Olivier. Marjorie Garber quotes Michael Billington on Olivier's 'sinister amalgam of male power-hunger and female seductiveness' (Michael Billington, 'Lasciviously Pleasing' in Garry O'Connor, *Olivier: In Celebration* [New York, 1987], p. 73, quoted in Marjorie Garber, *Vested Interests: Cross–Dressing and Cultural Anxiety* [London, 1992], p. 33), but surely errs when she calls him 'arguably the most rampantly heterosexual Shakespearean actor of his generation' given recent biographical claims. Whatever the off-stage facts, in 1933 Olivier certainly played two sexually ambivalent roles, in Keith Winter's *The Rats of Norway* (Playhouse Theatre, London), and Mourdaint Shairp's *The Green Bay Tree* (Cort Theatre, New York). Despite rave reviews in the latter, 'He did not like himself in the part, largely because he felt uncomfortable playing a homosexual', according to one biographer (Anthony Holden, *Olivier* [London, 1989], p. 94). He got something from the experience, nevertheless: despite 'his young unease at finding himself in the part of a limp-wristed, submissive homosexual' (Holden, p. 95), Olivier's dislike of the director, Jed Harris, gave him a model of hatefulness he was to use as a model for his own Richard III.

192 'NOT TO COME NEAR OUR PERSON BY TEN MILE': William Shakespeare, *2 Henry IV*, in *The Complete Works*, ed. Stanley Wells, Gary Taylor *et al.* (Oxford, 1988), Act V, scene ii, lines 63–5.

192 'DESIRING HAL': Jonathan Goldberg, *Sodometries: Renaissance Texts, Modern Sexualities* (Stanford, 1992), pp. 145–75.

193 'PRACTIS'D ON ME FOR THY USE': Goldberg, *Sodometries*, p. 175. A key unlocking treasure is also the opening image of Shakespeare's Sonnet 52, a sustained play on the idea of sex between the poet and the youth he addresses. Goldberg cites William Empson's identification in *Some Versions of Pastoral* of the sonnet's young man with Hal (p. 152).

193 'AN EXORBITANT "BED-PRESSER"': Goldberg, *Sodometries*, pp. 162–3.

193 'HAL'S ASSOCIATION WITH FALSTAFF': P. H. Davison, Commentary, in *Henry IV, Part 1* (Harmondsworth, 1968), pp. 158–9n.

194 'MINIONS OF THE MOON': William Shakespeare, *1 Henry IV*, in *The Complete Works* ed. Stanley Wells, Gary Taylor *et al.* (Oxford, 1988), Act I, scene ii, lines 16, 23–6.

194 'THE BEST-GOVERNED NATION': Shakespeare, *1 Henry IV*, Act V, scene ii, lines 134–6.

195 'ESPOUSED TO DEATH': Shakespeare, *Henry V*, in *The Complete Works*, Act IV, scene vi, line 26.

195 'THE KING HAS KILLED HIS HEART': Shakespeare, *Henry V*, Act II, scene i, line 84.

195 'AND ABYSM OF FOLK-CUSTOM': John Dover Wilson, *The Fortunes of Falstaff* (Cambridge, 1943), p. 40.

196 'AN OLD, COZENING QUEAN': Shakespeare, *The Merry Wives of Windsor*, in *The Complete Works*, Act IV, scene ii, line 158.

196 'PADDED OUT TO THE SIZE OF SIR JOHN FALSTAFF': 'Spy', *The Weekly Journal*, 18 April 1724, cited in Terry Castle, *Masquerade and Civilisation: The Carnivalesque in Eighteenth-Century English Culture and Fiction* (Stanford, 1986), p. 48.

196 'I WOULD NOT HAVE HAD HIM': Shakespeare, *The Merry Wives of Windsor*, Act V, scene v, lines 188–90.

196 'AY BE GAR, AND 'TIS A BOY': Shakespeare, *The Merry Wives of Windsor*, Act V,

scene v, lines 203–4.

197 'NONE OF THEM EVER LIVED PAST THIRTY': Charles Ludlam, 'Confessions of a Farceur', in *Ridiculous Theatre: Scourge of Human Folly,* ed. Steven Samuels (New York, 1992), p. 60. Ludlum also records that 'A most unusual offer to write the book for a Broadway musical about Catherine de' Medici added *The Isle of the Hermaphrodites, or The Murdered Minion* to the growing corpus, although it was never produced.' (Steven Samuels, 'Charles Ludlam: A Brief Life', in *The Complete Plays of Charles Ludlam* [New York, 1989], p. xv.)

198 'TWO SEVERAL MARRIAGES': Thomas Dekker and John Webster, *Northward Ho,* in *Dramatic Works of Thomas Dekker,* ed. Fredson Bowers (Cambridge, 1955), vol. II, Act IV, scene i, lines 48–51.

198 'BEHIND YOUR BACK TO YOUR FACE?': Dekker and Webster, *Northward Ho*, Act IV, scene i, lines 52–62.

195 'HE'LL PUT HIS PLOW INTO ME, PLOW ME UP': George Chapman, *Bussy D'Ambois*, ed. John H. Smith, in *The Plays of George Chapman; The Tragedies with Sir Gyles Goosecappe* (Cambridge, 1987), Act I, scene i, lines 122–23.

199 'LIKE TO HIS JEWEL': George Chapman, *The Revenge of Bussy D'Ambois*, ed. Robert J. Lardi, in *The Plays of George Chapman*, Act I, scene i, lines 152–3.

200 'T'UNCLASP THY BOSOM': Chapman, *The Revenge of Bussy D'Ambois*, Act I, scene i, lines 184–93.

200 'NOTHING TO THIS BUBBLE?': Chapman, *The Revenge of Bussy D'Ambois*, Act I, scene i, lines 262–6.

201 'LAND IN SERIOUS TROUBLE': Joe Orton, *Entertaining Mr Sloane*, in *The Complete Plays* (London, 1976), pp. 134–5, Act III.

201 'BUT THE GOOD OF BOTH': Chapman, *The Revenge of Bussy D'Ambois*, Act V, scene i, lines 154–5.

202 'I COULD ATTEND THEM EVER': *The Revenge of Bussy D'Ambois*, Act V, scene i, lines 186–94.

202 'TO THE MOST WORTHY OF THE RACE OF MEN': *The Revenge of Bussy D'Ambois*, Act V, scene iv, lines 68–72.

202 'GAVE MEANS OF LIFE TO ME?': *The Revenge of Bussy D'Ambois*, Act V, scene v, lines 149–50.

202 'SUFFERS A NEEDFUL SEPARATION': *The Revenge of Bussy D'Ambois*, Act V, scene v, line 157–60.

203 'CLERMONT THY CREATURE COMES': Chapman, *The Revenge of Bussy D'Ambois*, Act V, scene v, line 194.

205 'O, LET HIM GO; HE IS A CATHOLIC': Christopher Marlowe, *The Massacre at Paris*, in *The Complete Plays*, ed. J. B. Steane (Harmondsworth, 1969), scene vii, lines 1–15.

205 'THE GUTS TO BETRAY MY COUNTRY': E. M. Forster, 'What I Believe', in *Two Cheers For Democracy* (Harmondsworth, 1976), p. 82.

206 'DANGEROUS, PERVERTED GROUP': Charles Ludlam, 'Confessions of a Farceur', in *Ridiculous Theatre: Scourge of Human Folly,* ed. Steven Samuels (New York, 1992), p. 61.

206 'INFECTED THIS GLORIOUS ISLAND': Robert Greene, *A Quip for an Upstart Courtier* (1592), cited in Rictor Norton, *Mother Clap's Molly House: The Gay Subculture in England 1700–1830* (London, 1992), p. 253.

207 'THEIR BARDASSI OR BUGGERED BOYS': William Lithgow, *The Total Discourse of the Rare Adventures and Painful Peregrinations of Long Nineteen Years'*

Travel From Scotland, ed. Gilbert Phelps (London, 1974), p. 43, cited in Rictor Norton, *Mother Clap's Molly House,* p. 252.

207 'AS THERE IT IS SAID': Edward Coke, *The Third Part of the Institutes of the Laws of England* (London, 1797), p. 58.

207 'LAST OF ALL THE FRENCH': Thomas Dekker and Thomas Middleton, *The Honest Whore, Part One,* in *Dramatic Works of Thomas Dekker,* vol. II, Act II, scene i, lines 353–5.

207 'ALL IN ITALICA YOU HERMOPHRODITE': John Fletcher and Thomas Middleton, *The Nice Valour,* in *Works,* ed. A. Glover and A. R. Waller (London, 1905), Act IV.

208 'ALL MANNER OF LANGUAGES': Thomas Dekker and John Webster, *Northward Ho,* in *Dramatic Works of Thomas Dekker,* vol. II, Act IV, scene iii, lines 45–8.

209 'FOR FEAR OF EMBARRASSING YOU': Joe Orton, *Entertaining Mr Sloane,* p. 78. Act I.

209 'I'LL FILL YOU FULL OF MORE POCO. MARCH': Dekker and Webster, *Northward Ho,* Act IV, scene iii, lines 103–126.

210 'O GOOD MASTER BELLAMONT, LET'S HEAR HIM': *Northward Ho,* Act IV, scene iii, lines 157–62.

210 'ONE OF KENNETH HALLIWELL'S MOST BRILLIANT TITLES': Joe Orton, 16 July 1967, in *The Orton Diaries,* ed. John Lahr (London, 1986), p. 242.

210 'UNDER WHOM IS FIGURED ROME': Thomas Dekker, *The Whore of Babylon,* in *Dramatic Works,* vol. II, *Dramatis Personae,* line 16.

211 'JUST ONE MORE VENETIAN WANTING TO MAKE A PASS': Daphne du Maurier, letter to Ellen Doubleday, 15 July 1948, quoted in Margaret Forster, *Daphne du Maurier* (London, 1993), p. 231.

211 'NO MAN IN GOWN, OR PAGE IN PETTICOAT': Thomas Jordan, *A Prologue to Introduce the first Woman that came to Act on the Stage in the Tragedy, Called The Moor of Venice,* in *A Royal Arbor of Loyal Poesie* (London, 1664), p. 21.

211 'LIKE ANY MOOR': anonymous, *Satyr on the Players,* in *Roscius Anglicanus,* ed. Montague Summers (New York, 1968), p. 55.

212 'ALL OTHER LIBIDINOUS PLEASURES': William Lithgow, *The Total Discourse of the Rare Adventures and Painful Peregrinations,* p. 57, cited in Rictor Norton, *Mother Clap's Molly House,* p. 252. Amid Captain Tucca's thesaurus of gay-baiting invective against Horace in Dekker's *Satiromastix* is the complaint that 'thy title's longer a reading than the style a the big Turks' (Thomas Dekker, *Satiromastix,* in *Works,* vol. I, Act I, scene ii, lines 312–13). He later calls Horace's lover, Asinius Bubo, 'Turk-a-ten-pence' (Act IV, scene ii, line 32).

212 'A NONE TOO SUBTLE HINT OF HOMOSEXUALITY': Lawrence D. Mass, *Confessions of a Jewish Wagnerite: Being Gay and Jewish in America* (London, 1994), p. 43.

212 'THE ONLY PROFESSION THEY WERE ALLOWED TO PRACTISE': Michel Foucault, 'Sexual Choice, Sexual Act: An Interview...', in *Salmagundi,* issue 58–59 (1982–3), pp. 10–24, 15.

213 'I WILL GO ON': Shakespeare, *Othello,* in *The Complete Works,* Act III, scene iii, lines 415–8.

213 'NAY, THIS WAS BUT HIS DREAM': *Othello,* Act III, scene iii, lines 418–32.

Chapter ten: Where is Sodom?

215 'THE NAKED-BOY IN FLESH LANE?': Cosmo Manuche, *The Loyal Lovers: A Tragi-Comedy* (London, 1652), p. 6. Although the play is supposed to be set in Amsterdam, this is surely a more local reference.

216 'OF OUR DEAR SISTERHOOD': Manuche, *The Loyal Lovers,* pp. 17, 19.

216 'ACTIVE AND WELL-AFFECTED FEMALES': Manuche, *The Loyal Lovers,* p. 1, Act I. I am grateful to Rictor Norton for clarifying the nature of Dapper's 'sodomitical revenue'.

217 'PLUMP MUDDY WHORE, OR PROSTITUTE BOY': John Donne, *Satyre 1,* in *Poetical Works,* ed. Herbert J. C. Grierson (Oxford, 1933), p. 130, lines 37–41: 'Why should'st thou (that dost not only approve, / But in rank itchy lust, desire, and love / The nakedness and barenness to enjoy, / Of thy plump muddy whore, or prostitute boy), / Hate virtue, though she be naked and bare?'

217 'VIOLATED THE STATE'S ANTI-SODOMY LAW': Janet E. Halley, 'Bowers v. Hardwick in the Renaissance', in *Queering the Renaissance,* ed. Jonathan Goldberg (Durham, 1994), p. 31n, citing 'Court Allows Lesbian Lawyer to Proceed with Suit over Withdrawal of Job Offer', *49 BNA Daily Labor Report A-7* (March 12, 1992). Making it public knowledge is as much part of the crime as the thing itself, as President Clinton's 'Don't Ask, Don't Tell' climb-down on lesbians and gay men in the US military conceded.

218 'OR WE WILL BREAK THE DOOR': George Lesly, *Fire and Brimstone, or, The Destruction of Sodom,* in *Divine Dialogues* (London, 1684), pp. 33–4, cited in Gregory W. Bredbeck, *Sodomy and Interpretation: Marlowe to Milton* (Ithaca, 1991), pp. 218–19.

218 'WHICH IS THE AGENT NOR WHICH THE PATIENT': Samuel Pepys, 1 July 1663, in *Diary,* ed. Robert Latham and William Matthews (London, 1971), vol. IV, pp. 209–10.

218 'TWOULD TEMPT A SAINT TO THRUST HIS PINTLE IN': John Wilmot, Earl of Rochester, *Sodom, or The Quintessence of Debauchery,* in *Complete Poems and Plays,* ed. Paddy Lyons (London, 1993), p. 130. Act I, scene i, lines 42–5. Parts of *Sodom* were finally staged as part of Stephen Jeffreys' 1994 play about Rochester: *The Libertine* (London, 1994), pp. 48–57, scene viii.

218 'AND SO THY BOOK ITSELF TURN SODOMITE': quoted in Pisanus Fraxi (Henry Spencer Ashbee), *Bibliography of Prohibited Books* (London and New York, 1962 [1869]).

219 'YOU'LL KNOW A COCK FROM A HEN': John Vanbrugh, *The Relapse,* in *Restoration Comedy,* ed. A. Norman Jeffares (London, 1974), p. 461, Act I, scene iii. I was lucky that Andrew McLeod taught me *The Relapse* for English A-level in the days before Clause 28 (although Coupler could hardly be reckoned to promote homosexuality).

220 'FIRST RECORDED USE OF "GAY"': Mary Pix, *The Adventures in Madrid,* in *The Plays of Mary Pix and Catherine Trotter,* ed. Edna L. Steeves (New York, 1982), p. 47, Act III; p. 22, Act II.

220 'THOUGH THOU FOLLOW BOYS': John Donne, *To Sir Henry Wotton,* in *The Satires, Epigrams and Verse Letters,* ed. W. Milgate (Oxford, 1967), p. 52.

222 'NEW ADMIRERS TO THE THEATRE': Colley Cibber, *An Apology for the Life of Colley Cibber* (London, 1740), vol. II, p. 222.

223 'TO LEAVE KIND CUNT, TO DIVE IN EXCREMENTS': anonymous, *Satyr on the Players*, in *Roscius Anglicanus,* ed. Montague Summers (New York, 1968), p. 56.

224 'SO SENSIBLY TOUCHED THE AUDIENCE AS HE': John Downes, *Roscius Anglicanus, or an Historical Review of the Stage,* ed. Montague Summers (New York, 1968), p. 19.

224 'TWAS DECENT WHORING KEPT MY THOUGHTS STILL CHASTE': Tom Brown, *Amusements, Serious and Comical and Other Works,* ed. Arthur L. Heywood (London, 1927), vol. II, pp. 213–14, cited in Kristina Straub, *Sexual Suspects: Eighteenth Century Players and Sexual Ideology* (Princeton, 1992), p. 49.

224 'THOUGH UNFIT FOR THE SPORT AS JOHN DRYDEN': anonymous, *The Women's Complaint to Venus* (London, 1698), quoted in Rictor Norton, *Mother Clap's Molly House: The Gay Subculture in England 1700–1830* (London, 1992), p. 47.

225 'AND COURTLY VICES, BEASTLY VENYES': Alexander Pope, *Bounce to Fop: An Heroick Epistle From a Dog at Twickenham to a Dog at Court,* in *Poems* ed. John Butt (London, 1968), p. 824, lines 39–40.

225 'A SODOM FOR LEWDNESS': anonymous, *Short Remarks upon the Original and Pernicious Consequences of Masquerades,* in *The Conduct of the Stage Consider'd* (London, 1721), quoted in Terry Castle, *Masquerade and Civilisation: The Carnivalesque in Eighteenth-Century English Culture and Fiction* (Stanford, 1986), p. 46.

227 'AS ALSO ARE HIS COMPANIONS': quoted in E. J. Burford, *Wits, Wenchers and Wantons: London's Low Life: Covent Garden in the Eighteenth Century* (London, 1986), pp. 206–8.

Chapter eleven: Gay Ladies of the Stage

228 'AN ABOMINATION TO THE LORD OUR GOD': William Prynne, *Histriomastix: The Players Scourge or Actors Tragedy* (London, 1633).

229 'BY HEAVEN, A WOMAN!': Aphra Behn, *The Younger Brother* (London, 1696).

230 'THE MEN GREW ENVIOUS, AND THE WOMEN LOVED': Benjamin Victor, *The History of the Theatres of London and Dublin from the Year 1730 to the Present Time* (London, 1761), vol. III, pp. 4–5, cited in Kristina Straub, *Sexual Suspects: Eighteenth Century Players and Sexual Ideology* (Princeton, 1992), p. 129.

232 'GRONET TELLS US SHE'S NOT A W[HORE]': *Chansonnier historique du XVIIIe siecle,* ed. Emile Raunié (Paris, 1879), vol. V, pp. 163–4, trans. and quoted in Lillian Faderman, *Surpassing the Love of Men: Romantic Friendship and Love Between Women from the Renaissance to the Present* (London, 1985), p. 420n.

232 'A FEMALE FIEND OF THIS SORT': Hester Lynch Thrale, 9 December 1795, *Thraliana* (Oxford, 1951).

233 'IN GENTLE KITTY [CLIVE]': anonymous, *A Sapphic Epistle from Jack Cavendish to the Honourable and Most Beautiful Mrs D——* (London, 1782).

233 'COULD BE SUPPOSED TO EXPERIENCE': George Ann Bellamy, *An Apology for the Life of George Ann Bellamy* (London, 1785), vol. I, pp. 27–8, cited in Kristina Straub, *Sexual Suspects,* pp. 114–15.

234 'ALL POINTS OF REGULARITY': Charlotte Charke and Fidelis Morgan, *The Well-Known Troublemaker: A Life of Charlotte Charke* (London, 1988), p. 188.

234 'AS THEY WERE PLEASED TO STYLE ME': Charke and Morgan, *The Well–Known Troublemaker,* p. 68.

236 'RULE A WIFE AND HAVE A WIFE': Samuel Whyte, *The Monthly Mirror* (1760), cited in Charke and Morgan, *The Well-Known Troublemaker*, p. 181. John Fletcher's comedy *Rule A Wife and Have a Wife* (1624) tells how the Spanish Margarita plans a cynical marriage, in which her husband will be 'a shadow, an umbrella, To keep the scorching world's opinion' from finding her secret pleasures. In 1733, while appearing in the play, Catherine (Kitty) Raftor married barrister (and shadow), George Clive. His name stuck, but not the marriage, which dissolved within a year.

236 'SUNDRY WITLESS ADMIRERS OF HER OWN SEX': James Boaden, *Life of Elizabeth Inchbald,* cited in Terry Castle, *Masquerade and Civilisation: The Carnivalesque in Eighteenth-Century English Culture and Fiction* (Stanford, 1986), p. 47.

237 'THEY LIVE TOGETHER, DRESS ALIKE': Elizabeth Barrett Browning, letter to sister Arabel, 22 October 1852, cited in Joseph Leach, *Bright Particular Star: The Life and Times of Charlotte Cushman* (New Haven, 1970), p. 210.

238 'STEBBINS'S BIOGRAPHY': Emma Stebbins, *Charlotte Cushman: Her Letters and Memories of Her Life* (1878), p. 291.

241 'THAT THOU ART NOT MADE LIKE OTHER BOYS': Mary Pix, *Ibrahim, the Thirteenth Emperor of the Turks*, in *The Plays of Mary Pix and Catherine Trotter,* ed. Edna L. Steeves (New York, 1982), vol. I, pp. 16–17.

Chapter twelve: Prevailing Dissipations

243 'TO DAVID GARRICK ESQUIRE': Theophilus Cibber, *Theophilus Cibber to David Garrick, Esq.; with Dissertations on Theatrical Subjects* (London, 1759). This was not a new ploy. Ten years earlier, Cibber had published mockery of Dublin theatre rival Thomas Sheridan as effeminate (*Dublin Miscellany*, 1743, pp. 64–5).

243 'WILL GENIUS CHANGE HIS SEX TO WEEP?': Samuel Johnson, *Letters* vol. II, p. 561, cited in Simon Trefman, *Sam. Foote, Comedian 1720–1777* (New York, 1971), p. 263.

244 'THE PREVAILING DISSIPATIONS OF THE TIME': William Cooke, *Memoirs of Samuel Foote Esq.* (London, 1805), vol. I, pp. 35–6.

245 'HANGED SOME MONTHS AGO IN FRANCE': David Garrick, *Prologue*, in *The Dramatic Works of Samuel Foote* (London, 1799), vol. I, p. lxxxvi.

245 'POSSESS HIM MERELY': *The Dramatic Works of Samuel Foote,* pp. 263–4.

245 'A STAVE TO YOUR REQUIEM': Elizabeth Chudleigh, Letter, in *Evening Post*, 13 August 1775, cited in Trefman, *Sam. Foote, Comedian*, pp. 241–2.

246 'AN EQUAL MIXTURE OF DISGUST AND INDIGNATION': William Shakespeare, *The Sonnets,* A New Variorum Edition of Shakespeare, vol. 25, ed. Hyder Rollins (Philadelphia, 1944), vol. I, p. 55.

246 'AN INFIDEL WOULD BE IT IF HE INCLINED': 10 May 1776 entry in the Boswell Papers, quoted in Trefman, *Sam. Foote, Comedian*, p. 266.

246 'VERY LITTLE REGRETTED EVEN BY HIS NEAREST ACQUAINTANCE': David Garrick, *Letters of David Garrick and Georgiana Countess Spencer* (Cambridge, 1960), p. 39, cited in Trefman, *Sam. Foote, Comedian*, p. 263.

247 'RUBBING HIS NAKED BODY FROM THE PERSPIRATION': Giles Playfair, *The Prodigy: A Study of the Strange Life of Master Betty* (London, 1967), p. 86. My play *Master Betty* (1990), explored some of the curiosities in William Betty's biography, imagining a private performance by him at the height of his career, for Lord Byron at William Beckford's home.

248 'HAVE ONLY MISCARRIED': Playfair, *The Prodigy*, p. 86–7, quoting *The Times*, 4 December 1804.

248 'AN ATTACHMENT OF THIS KIND AT SCHOOL': Percy Bysshe Shelley, *An Essay on Friendship*, in *Complete Works* (London, 1930), vol. VII, p. 143.

250 'THE ORIGINAL THEATRE OF THEIR CRIMES': Hester Lynch Thrale, 27 June 1786, *Thraliana* (Oxford, 1951).

252 'THAT ART CANNOT EXTRACT, NOR PENANCE CLEANSE?': Horace Walpole, *The Mysterious Mother* (London, 1768), vol. I, p. iii.

254 'SO I TURNED MUCH OF IT INTO MANFRED': Xavier Mayne (Edward Stevenson), *The Intersexes: A History of Similisexualism as a Problem in Social Life* (New York, 1975), pp. 359–60. This book, originally privately published c. 1908, reports a conversation between Byron and a correspondent's grandfather, in which this is supposed to have been said. Quoted by Louis Crompton, *Byron and Greek Love: Homophobia in 19th-Century England* (Berkeley, 1985), pp. 370–1, who is dubious about its authenticity.

Index